Religion and Science:
An Introduction

Religion and Science: An Introduction

Brendan Sweetman

continuum

The Continuum International Publishing Group Inc
80 Maiden Lane, New York, NY 10038

The Continuum International Publishing Group Ltd
The Tower Building, 11 York Road, London SE1 7NX

www.continuumbooks.com

Copyright © 2010 by Brendan Sweetman

All rights reserved. No part of this book may be reproduced, stored in a retrieval system, or transmitted, in any form or by any means, electronic, mechanical, photocopying, recording, or otherwise, without the permission of the publishers.

Library of Congress Cataloging-in-Publication Data
A catalog record for this book is available from the Library of Congress.

ISBN: 978-1-8470-6014-3 (hardcover)
       978-1-8470-6015-0 (paperback)

Typeset by Newgen Imaging Systems Pvt Ltd, Chennai, India
Printed in the United States of America

For Brendan, John and Ciaran

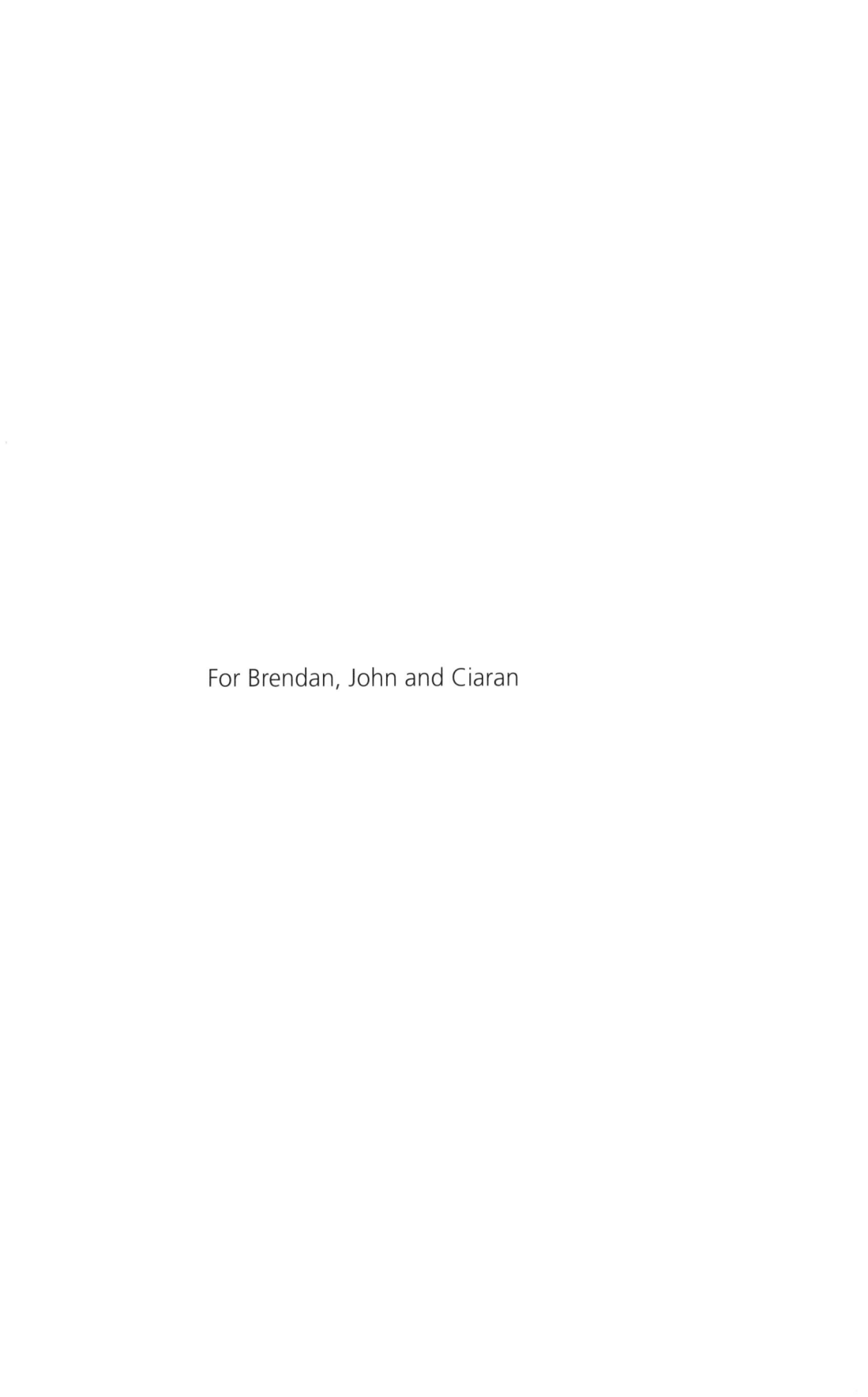

Contents

1 Introduction — 1
- Why are we interested in religion and science? — 3
- Religion, science and secularism — 5
- Some models for relating religion and science — 11
- A philosophical approach to religion and science — 20

2 Religion and Science in History — 25
- The ancient world: Aristotle — 26
- The medieval world: St. Augustine and St. Thomas — 33
- The Protestant Reformation — 40
- The Galileo controversy of the seventeenth century — 44
- Galileo and Newton, and the development of science — 46
- Eighteenth-century developments — 49
- The nineteenth century: Darwin and Freud — 53

3 Science and Naturalism in the Twentieth Century — 59
- The success of science — 60
- The scientific method and objective knowledge — 63
- Realism versus anti-realism — 66
- The undermining of truth in the history of science — 71
- The modern face of science: naturalism — 74

4 God and Evolution — 82
- Evolution and modern culture — 82
- Brief history of evolution — 85
- The theory of evolution — 89
- The evidence for evolution: questions and answers — 93
- Religious, philosophical, and moral implications of evolution — 104

5 Science and the Human Person — 118
A challenge to the traditional understanding of the human person — 120
The nature of consciousness — 121
Human free will — 128
Immortality — 134
Artificial intelligence — 136
The search for extraterrestrial intelligence — 142

6 Design in the Universe — 146
William Paley's argument — 147
The "laws of physics" argument from design — 152
Design at the beginning: the anthropic argument — 158
Intelligent design arguments — 163

7 God and the Universe — 171
The universe and the big bang theory — 172
God as first cause — 174
The significance of relativity and quantum mechanics — 180
How does God act in the world? — 185

8 Science, Religion and Ethics — 192
Mapping the human genome — 194
Stem cells and cloning — 201
Conclusion: some lessons for scientists and religious believers — 207

Notes — 210
Guide to Further Reading — 220
Index — 227

Introduction 1

Chapter Outline
Why are we interested in religion and science? 3
Religion, science and secularism 5
Some models for relating religion and science 11
A philosophical approach to religion and science 20

The relationship between religion and science has always aroused curiosity in anyone who has even a remote interest in the major beliefs of their religious worldview, in what their religion says is true about God, about salvation, about the type of universe we live in, about the kind of beings human beings are, and about moral and political values. Yet this is not only a topic of concern for the religious believer because *any* worldview, religious or secularist, should be interested in the ways in which the discipline of science, its theories and distinctive method of inquiry, might be relevant for understanding and assessing the claims the worldview makes about reality, about the universe, and our lives in it. Although there has been great interest in this topic throughout history, and many famous thinkers—philosophers, theologians, and scientists— were greatly exercised by the relationship between religion and science, it is in the present age that the dialogue and debate between them is at its most keen, and has taken on a new urgency. Indeed, it is not an exaggeration to say that the relationship between religion and science has become one of the most interesting and significant topics of our times. In terms of increasing our understanding of ourselves and of the universe we live in, as well as in thinking about the meaning of life, and about our moral behavior and our ultimate destiny, it ranks right up there alongside other important twenty-first century topics, such as debates about climate change, the spread of democracy, the influence of capitalism, geopolitical issues, and how to deal with the threat of terrorism.

One of the reasons religion and science is such an important topic today is because both subjects make crucial contributions in so many areas of our lives. In addition, much recent work in various scientific disciplines has raised a variety of philosophical, religious, and moral questions with which science as a discipline is generally not equipped to deal. Recent work in such areas as evolution, genetics, astronomy, astrophysics (the study of the physical composition of celestial bodies), stem cell research, and neurology, much of it made possible by impressive technological advances, has brought to the forefront in a dramatic way what philosophers often call "ultimate questions." These are questions about the underlying nature of reality, the cause of the universe, the meaning of life, and even about morality. The theory of evolution, for example, raises questions about the origin and nature of our own species, *Homo sapiens* (the "wise" species), such as: was the appearance of human life on earth due to chance or due to design; do human beings have a soul; do human beings differ in kind, or only in degree, from other species; might there be evolutionary explanations for the phenomena of consciousness, reason, and morality? The disciplines of astronomy and astrophysics are telling us everyday more about this immensely complex universe we live in. As well as raising the question of the cause of the universe, research in these areas cannot fail to raise fascinating if not complex questions in our minds about the ultimate purpose, or design, of the universe, about whether there is an intelligent mind behind reality. The sheer size of the universe also makes us wonder if there might not be other civilizations out there somewhere, and what they might be like. This latter topic is intriguing, especially if it is allied with some interpretations of the theory of evolution, which suggest that evolution is a process that could occur on any planet where the basic ingredients thought to be necessary for the emergence of life are present.

There are yet other areas of science that raise equally interesting questions, though questions that are also challenging, even sometimes troubling. The human genome project, which involves the mapping of 20,000–25,000 genes in human DNA, as well as determining the sequencing of the base pairs that make up DNA, has taken work in genetics into hitherto unthought-of territory. This work also raises all sorts of troubling moral questions about the legitimacy of the genetic manipulation of the natural biological structure of human beings, as well as giving rise to related moral issues concerning cloning and stem cell research. The discipline of science can discover how to clone a human being, and how to extract stem cells from human embryos for the purposes of medical research, but it cannot tell us whether these are moral things to do. We have to go outside science—to philosophy and religion—for further thinking on these crucial matters. In addition, those scientists working in the area of neurology, who study the structure and workings of the human brain, are raising questions, not just about how to cure various brain-based diseases, but about the very nature of consciousness itself. Is consciousness physical or nonphysical? What causal role does the unconscious mind play in our conscious life? This kind of research has relevance for our thinking about the existence of the soul (which many philosophers have argued must at least include the conscious mind), and also about human free will. Do human beings really have free will, or are we only sophisticated causally determined machines, part of a universe that must be understood completely in terms of causes and their effects? All of these fascinating topics are inevitably and prominently raised by the interaction of religion and science, and anyone who wants to be an informed thinker today about the deepest questions of life cannot afford to ignore them and their contribution to our understanding of our universe and ourselves as we move into the twenty-first century. These and many other related questions, themes, and developments will be the subject of this book.

Why are we interested in religion and science?

Why should we be so interested in the relationship between religion and science? There are, in fact, a number of very good reasons that draw our attention to the relationship between these two areas. The one mentioned in the previous paragraphs is obviously one of the main reasons: it is simply a fact that work in a variety of scientific disciplines raises further questions that have relevance for religion, especially as we try to understand important facts about the universe, human beings, morality, and so forth. If we ignore this scientific work, and make no effort to think through its implications, there is a risk that our own individual religious beliefs may be scientifically illiterate or uninformed, may clash with some of the findings of recent scientific research, and may become out of touch with modern developments. As a result, our religious worldview may perhaps be compromised to some degree in its aims of providing structure, meaning, and inspiration in our changing and challenging times.

A second motivation for examining the relationship between religion and science is that science is a legitimate and much respected way of knowing about reality; if we are to be responsible thinkers with regard to the truth and consistency of our religious beliefs, we must be prepared to deal with the findings of science. Indeed, we should be very interested in the results of scientific inquiry, and welcome them so that we may examine their implications for religion. There is really no need for us to be suspicious of, or intimidated by, science, an unfortunate attitude that has been cultivated by some on all sides of the spectrum. To appreciate this point, it is often necessary to look beyond the views of individual scientists today, to look past the personal beliefs of some scientists in order to focus on what the *science* actually shows. The results of scientific inquiry should not always be automatically regarded as creating a problem or a challenge for religious beliefs, but may just as easily be welcomed in general as providing more information and insight in our attempts to understand God's creation. This is how many famous scientists of the past regarded their work, such as Galileo, Kepler, Boyle, Newton, and many others.

A third reason for why we are interested in the relationship is that science raises some difficult but important *moral* questions in a variety of areas, such as in stem cell research involving human embryos, genetic engineering, human cloning, cosmetic surgery, and the like. As noted above, discussion of these moral questions is outside science as a discipline, and requires contributions from philosophy and theology. Scientists can propose empirical explanations, can show us how to achieve an effect, can offer facts and data, but they cannot *as scientists* make value judgments based on this work, about whether their results are morally good or bad, or about what the moral implications of their work might be for the human race. Focus on the topic of morality also prompts us to consider whether science in the twenty-first century should be more concerned with morality than it actually is; such is the competition and lure of fame and fortune involved in scientific work overall that morality is often forced to take a back seat to the search for ever new discoveries, even in sensitive areas such as those involving genetics and experimentation on human embryos. We also need to take into account how any proposed moral guidelines for science as a whole can have any real impact in an age under the sway of moral pluralism and moral relativism.

An important fourth reason for why religion cannot ignore science today is that many thinkers now appeal to science to justify an atheistic, secularist view of the world. A number of significant thinkers, in a variety of disciplines, whose work we will refer to throughout this book, believe that various scientific theories, such as those concerned with evolution and genetics, are actually evidence for the claim that everything that exists is physical in nature, consisting of some complex configuration of matter and energy. These theories also show, it is claimed by some, that there is likely no overall design or purpose behind the universe, and nothing particularly special in an overall metaphysical sense about man. It would follow from this, they argue, that God and the supernatural realm do not exist, that there is no soul, and that the vast majority of religious beliefs are false. Some version of secularism, therefore, must be the true account of reality, although the exact details on the various topics that a secularist worldview would have to deal with (the nature of reality and the human person, and accounts of morality and politics, and the meaning of life) still have to be worked out. Although still a minority view in the debate between worldviews today, this thesis is gaining in popularity and influence. It is therefore incumbent upon the informed religious believer to be aware of the issues raised by this approach, and of how religion in general will respond to them. Many who hold this secularist view come close to saying that modern science is atheistic in nature, and that modern scientific research shows that there is no God, and that religion is false. It is incumbent upon the religious view of the world, whatever form it takes, and in the teachings and work of whatever teacher, prophet, or thinker we might pick as our guide, to engage with this view. It is also incumbent upon those who advocate this view to carefully distinguish in their arguments between the scientific data, and their personal, philosophical, and moral views based on this data, as well as to engage with the arguments of those thinkers who offer religious critiques of this secularist approach.

Religion, science and secularism

Before we go any further, we need to introduce some key concepts and terminology so that we all know what we are talking about. In particular, we must first consider what we mean by religion, or the religious view of reality. Obviously, there are many different definitions of religion that one could adopt, depending on which features one wishes to emphasize, or is especially interested in. While typically religion includes beliefs and doctrines, moral values, and forms of worship, for the purposes of our discussion in this book we need only a general overview of the religious view of the world. We are not so much interested in thinking about the different religious denominations, or different theologies, or different sets of doctrinal beliefs (except where relevant), as we are interested in thinking about the general religious view of the world, and whether it is reasonable or not, and how it will fare in the dialogue and debate with various scientific disciplines, theories, and claims, and in the debate with a secularist worldview. Given this, *religion* may be understood for our purposes as a (usually) complex system of beliefs, which constitute a philosophy of life, or a worldview, or a way of living. The subject matter of these beliefs concerns the nature of reality (beliefs about what exists, and about the nature of the universe), the human person (beliefs about the essence or nature of human beings), and morality and politics (beliefs about the good life, and the best way to arrange our society; how we should balance the common good and individual freedom, etc.). Many of these beliefs can be described as life regulating (meaning that they influence how we live), they are expressed in certain types of rituals and practices, and are based in significant part on a belief in a sacred, transcendent (unseen) reality. In the religious worldview, there is usually a belief in God, or at least in a Supreme Being of some kind, who is the creator of all life, and also a belief in an afterlife that is significantly better than this life, and that is often our ultimate destiny. Indeed, beliefs concerning the supernatural or transcendent realm are what make the religious worldview distinctive and different from secularist views of the world. Most religions also accept that one can communicate with God through prayer. This is what we will mean by religion, or the religious worldview, in this book.

Although we will focus primarily on the religious worldview, understood in this general way, and its dialogue and debate with the secularist view of the world (which we will explain in a moment), nevertheless the religion on which we will concentrate primarily will be Christianity. Christianity is the religion we are most familiar with in the west, and it is also usually Christianity that is primarily involved in debates with science. We must also keep in mind that there are different denominations of Christianity, which have different doctrinal beliefs, different theological approaches, and different understandings of the relationship between faith and reason, and therefore different approaches to the general subject of religion and science. Different denominations within Christianity, for example, may have different approaches to the nature of revelation, and to the role of faith and reason (including science) in interpreting the Bible. There are liberal and conservative denominations, as well as liberal and conservative strands on various issues even within the same denomination. Although there will obviously be large overlap among all of the main Christian denominations on many matters, the various differences among them will also turn out to be very significant for many questions that arise in the debate between religion and science. Where it is important and relevant for our discussion, we shall refer in what follows in this book to specific interpretations, specific denominational beliefs, and also to specific thinkers who have offered interesting ideas, some from a particular denominational point of view, for how the relationship between religion and science might be best understood. But, our focus will be on the classical tradition of Christian faith in general that is derived from the Bible, and that includes Catholicism, the various forms of Protestantism, the Eastern Orthodox faith, and even some aspects of Judaism.

Turning now to the definition of *science*, we must be careful to note straight away that science is not a worldview or a philosophy of life in itself. It is rather a distinctive method or a set of techniques for studying the physical realm. The physical realm refers to anything that is physical in nature, consisting of matter and energy (all made up of atoms); so this would include the physical universe, and everything in it that is physical in nature. The scientific method for studying the physical realm is an empirical method. This means that it involves making observations, gathering facts and data, and performing experiments, all using the very latest technology available. The scientific method also involves forming hypotheses, theories, and explanations in order to explain various phenomena, and then testing them. For example, scientists might be seeking an explanation for what makes plants grow well, and they might set up a series of experiments, which involve feeding similar plants different types of food in various conditions, and observing the rates of plant growth over time. In this way, they would build up a store of knowledge about how plants grow, and would be able to explain in the future why various plants grew well or did not grow at all in specific environments, and so forth.

We must also mention that studying the physical realm is now such a large endeavor that science has increasingly split into specific disciplines that study certain areas or features of the physical. For example, biology studies living organisms, including their origin, structure, growth, and development. Chemistry studies the composition and properties of substances, and the reactions and relations between substances. Physics deals with the properties and causal relationships between matter and energy in various domains, including electricity, optics, mechanics, and at the atomic and subatomic levels. But, even within these disciplines, there are subdisciplines, for example, microbiology, which focuses on microorganisms, and their effects on nature in general; and particle physics, which studies the structure and causal interactions of subatomic particles. In addition, there are often overlapping branches within science such as biochemistry, which combines biology and chemistry in the study of the chemical makeup of living organisms, and so on. And, let us not forget mathematics ("the door to the sciences," according to Roger Bacon), which raises all sorts of interesting philosophical questions in itself, and which, no matter how abstract it may appear, still studies at some basic level the mathematical properties and relationships that are present in the universe itself (e.g., Pythagoras' theorem proves an objectively true relationship that really exists between the lines of a right angle triangle anywhere in the universe, all other things being equal). We will come back to the various scientific disciplines, and their practitioners, throughout this book as we meet the questions they individually raise about the nature of reality and our religious response to it.

The reader will have noticed from our definitions of religion and science that at first glance we seem to be talking about apples and oranges. After all, the religious worldview is a worldview, a philosophy of life, that we live our lives by or according to, that we raise our children to believe and practice, that regulates how people live and act in the world. However, the scientific enterprise does not have nearly that kind of scope; it is not a worldview at all, but a method for studying one aspect of reality, namely the physical realm. It is hard to imagine anyone living according to the scientific method, or looking to science for guidance on how to teach morality to one's children. Yet the physical realm is clearly at the heart of the real, and the scientific method has proved to be a very powerful tool for understanding the physical realm—its makeup, operation in accordance with scientific laws, how complex processes work, etc. There is no question that science has been extremely successful, and has been very beneficial for mankind. The important perspective for our purpose in this book is that the results of scientific research, as we have noted above, occasionally (but not always) have significance for larger questions having to do with worldviews. And that is why science and religion naturally come into contact with each other. In fact, in the modern world, it is no longer possible for a religious believer to ignore the work of scientists, and I think it is fair to say that the opposite is true as well. If scientists wish to think through the full implications of their scientific research, they must honestly acknowledge the significance of their work for religious understandings of the world. This means that scientists working in various fields must recognize that their work has implications for larger questions that are outside the domain of science (e.g., scientific work on the big bang inevitably raises the question of why it occurred, a question outside of science). Even if some scientists are proponents of secularism, they must still acknowledge the necessity of debate and dialogue with the religious outlook on reality, including on human experience.

Science comes into contact with all worldviews, religious or secularist. This means that it is not only the religious worldview that needs to take account of the conclusions of scientific research and theories, but also that all worldviews must take scientific claims, and the latest scientific discoveries, into account. This is a very significant point because some religious thinkers argue that the results of scientific research lend further support to the general rationality of the religious worldview, while some secularists urge that the same thing is true for *their* worldview! It is therefore important for us in this introduction to take a moment to introduce the worldview of secularism, and to bring out its connection with modern science. This is an important theme that often undergirds debates concerning religion and modern science, in much the same way it is frequently suggested that religious concerns often undergird the approach of many religious believers to the discipline of science. While the connection between secularism and science is becoming more obvious today, and is beginning to find its way into popular culture (especially popular TV documentaries and books dealing with science), it is still often overlooked in some areas of the religious/science debate, and its significance is often not fully appreciated.

Before we provide an overview of the secularist worldview, and its beliefs, thinkers and connection to science, let us first say a brief word in general about the history of atheism because atheism is the forerunner of secularism. Although there have been pockets of positive atheism in history (i.e., forms of atheism that focus on what one believes is true, rather than on what one rejects), especially after the Enlightenment period (approx. 1660–1800), it is fair to say that it was not really until the twentieth century that atheists began to think of their view of reality in positive terms. Up until that time, atheism was generally regarded as a negative view of reality, and atheists understood themselves largely in a negative way as well. Atheism was negative in three ways. First, the atheist defined his view in terms of what it was not, rather than in terms of what it was. This means that an atheist tended to think of his beliefs and values more in terms of what he did not believe, than in terms of what he did believe! Atheism was understood primarily, even by the atheist himself, as a view which *denies* that God exists, and that rejects religious teachings, and certain features of religious morality. It was because of this negative approach that, second, the atheist often regarded himself negatively from a psychological point of view. He was usually in the minority, and couldn't really help regarding himself as someone who did not believe what most other people believed (indeed some pre-twentieth-century writers often referred to the "village atheist," the guy who stood out in the village for rejecting religion!). Third—and this is the most important—the atheist also *defended* his view negatively, by attacking religion and arguments for religious belief, a kind of negative strategy. He did this rather than presenting positive arguments in favor of atheism.

However, in the twentieth century, all of this changed, and this marks in general the transition from negative atheism to positive atheism (or secularism). Atheists began to realize that one cannot (and does not) live according to a negative worldview; eventually there comes a point when one must think about what one does believe, not about what one does not believe, and also about the rationality and consistency of one's worldview, and indeed about its relationship to other worldviews (namely, religious ones). Another way to put this point is to say that one must try to lay out in positive terms the understanding of the world—the beliefs, values, and view of life—that one is already living according to and practicing in one's daily life, since one has to believe in something in order to live and act, and in order to raise one's children. Atheist thinkers have worked hard, over the course of the twentieth century especially, at developing and presenting their views in positive terms, and this has given rise to the view which is now known as *secularism* (or sometimes as *naturalism*; these terms are used interchangeably in this book). Secularists believe that human life is the outcome of a purely random, naturalistic process (evolution interpreted as operating without design), and that all of reality is physical. They hold that the universe is a random occurrence, and that its nature and structure are due to chance. In addition, the existence of human life is also due to chance, as are its physical characteristics and makeup, and biological and chemical structure. All facets of human beings such as intelligence, emotion, love, fear, even morality and free will, must be understood in physical terms, operating according to the laws of cause and effect, at least to a very significant degree. Secularists hold that we need secular accounts of morality and politics, and they generally also believe that the secularist worldview should be the main influence on society as we move into the twenty-first century.

Moreover, the defense of these claims by secularists does not consist simply of attacking the arguments for religious belief. Positive arguments are now required to support these positive claims, and it is at this point that many secularists do what many thinkers throughout history did when struggling to articulate a position—they turn to whatever ideas and approaches are available in the culture at the time to help them support their arguments. Modern science fills this gap for the twenty-first-century secularist, just as Plato's ideas on the body/soul relationship filled the gap for some of the early Church fathers who were trying to explain this relationship. Many contemporary secularists have turned to modern science, especially to prevailing current theories in such areas as cosmology, evolution, genetics, and neurology. However, this reliance upon modern science as a way of buttressing one's secularist worldview has the unfortunate effect of creating the impression in much of popular culture that modern science is really on the side of atheism. And while this is not true, it is the case that many secularists do turn to various scientific theories in an attempt to harness positive arguments and evidence to support their views. Needless to say, most religious believers do not agree with much of this. As a result, the discipline of science is often caught in the middle, making it all the more urgent not only to keep the secularist worldview and the discipline of science clearly distinct from each other, but to examine carefully the actual implications of scientific work for the debate between religion and secularism. It will be especially important throughout this book to highlight the distinction between science and secularism, while at the same time appreciating their contemporary connection. This will help us understand better the motivations and aims of many people on all sides of various hot button issues (such as evolution) that have been the subject of recent controversy.

Some models for relating religion and science

It will be helpful to briefly overview some of the ways that science and religion have traditionally been related to each other, as a way of whetting our appetite for the issues that arise in any discussion of their relationship. Let us look briefly at three well-established models for understanding the relationship.[1] The first model is sometimes referred to as the "conflict" model, and is probably the model that many readers will think of first when they think of science and religion. This model reflects the view that religion and science have had an uneasy relationship in history, and that they are basically in conflict with each other. Looking at religion and science in this way is partly due to well known and much-hyped historical and contemporary controversies, especially the Galileo affair involving the Catholic Church in the seventeenth century, and in more recent times, the controversy concerning evolution and creationism that is especially prominent in the United States. Another recent position, known as Intelligent Design theory, has also served to fuel this latter debate, and much of the reaction to this new theory falls clearly within the conflict model!

The conflict model has had some influence on how scientists have approached their work historically, and also on how religious thinkers have reacted to various scientific theories, but it is probably true to say that this model is more influential today than it ever was historically in shaping people's attitudes to religion-science questions.[2] Proponents of the conflict model hold that religion and science are basically incompatible, and this incompatibility is reflected in two ways. The first is that religious beliefs, doctrines, and various theological views cannot be reconciled with scientific claims, claims which are supported by the work of scientific research; it would seem to follow from this that we have to choose between scientific truth or religious truth. Since their truth claims are often in conflict, advocates of the "conflict" model hold, then both positions cannot be true. Since we have good reasons to hold that the scientific views are true, then the religious positions will have to be revised. This is the standard answer to this problem, but we must also point out that those who advocate a literalist reading of the Bible also promote the conflict model by claiming that scientific theories that are incompatible with the Bible should be revised. The second way religion and science often seem to be incompatible is in the contrast between the scientific method and the methods of argument that are employed to support the beliefs of the various world religions. Many who favor the conflict model hold that most religious beliefs are subjective in nature, personal, based on unreliable and untrustworthy arguments and sources (such as ancient texts or questionable authorities), and often relative to the culture, time, and place in which the religion in question is practiced. Science, on the other hand, is rational and objective, and based on universal standards of reason and evidence that are accepted everywhere. This particular view—that religion is subjective, and that science is objective—is now widely held by a variety of prominent thinkers today,[3] and has consequently seeped down into popular culture. It is a view we shall consider in detail throughout this book (see especially Chapter 3).

Yet we must be careful to clarify three important points about the conflict model at the outset that give us some much needed perspective on it as a way of understanding religion and science, and that lessen its status as a shaper of the current debate for many people. First, it is often motivated by a secularist worldview, in the manner described above. This means that those who are often most keen to promote the conflict model are themselves secularists, and are often in the position of defending their view by appealing to various scientific theories, so they have a vested interest in science being in conflict with religion. We must be careful to distinguish between thinking about the conflict model as arising naturally out of the interaction of the religious worldview and the results of scientific research, and the conflict model been promoted by those who are already committed secularists who are attempting the task of defending their views in positive terms by appealing to science. Some may claim that it is the results of science that have made them secularists, and while this may be true in some cases, it is likely not the norm. The modern secularist is usually in the position of being a secularist first, of adopting secularism as the default position in a certain type of intellectual culture, and then of seeking some more direct positive evidence and argument in order to give further justification to this view. As we noted, he often appeals to science to help in this regard. In this book, we are more interested in the claim that the results of scientific research can sometimes seem to challenge religious beliefs, a more difficult position to establish, than we are interested in the view that science can be appealed to as a resource to support secularism, a much more contentious (and ultimately secondary) thesis.

The second point is that the conflict model is selective in its account of both the history of the religion-science relationship, and even in its reading of current work in science and religion. Proponents of this view simply downplay or ignore the many times in history that religion and science were able to work together to their mutual benefit, as honest thinkers of good will working in different disciplines attempted to add to our store of knowledge and understanding. We will come back to this way of understanding science and religion in a moment, but it is a key point that, although the conflicts often get the most attention, they are not necessarily the main part of the story. Thirdly, we need to draw attention to the way our media driven twenty-first-century culture feeds on conflicts of all sorts, including on conflicts between religion and science. It is simply a fact that conflict generates news stories, and that the media around the world, especially in the United States, have been keen to play up the current controversies between religion and science because they are good press, and boost ratings. This is not to deny that there are controversies to report, since there clearly are (the controversy surrounding evolution in the United States is a fascinating, but complicated story, that is frequently mishandled by the press), but my point is that the press fuels the controversies, thereby cementing in people's minds the conflict model as the main way to think about religion and science. It is also unfortunate that those who contribute to the debate—including important authors, scientists, theologians, and other thinkers—know that promoting conflict is the best way of receiving publicity (and also the best way to raise money for their organizations or causes!).

The second significant model for understanding the relationship between religion and science is called the Independence model. This model holds that religion and science constitute two completely different realms, that they have little to say to each other, and that in general they should be kept distinct. They each deal with different areas of inquiry, and the approach and subject matter of each area is not appropriate in the other area. Religious believers should be mindful of their religious beliefs, and practice their religion, but they should not be especially worried or concerned about what the implications might be of various scientific theories for their religious beliefs. Similarly, scientists should confine themselves to their specific research areas, but should not be looking beyond their work toward its implications for areas outside of science. This is because they know little about these areas, and have no special expertise or authority to contribute to our understanding in areas like philosophy, theology, morality, and the general area of worldviews. Many of these scientists will be religious believers themselves, of course, but they should just get on with their work in science, and keep their religious worldview distinct from this work.

Although the influence of this view in the history of religion and science is debatable, especially when compared with other models, the independence model does reflect the way some significant thinkers have dealt with science in relation to religious belief. It also probably reflects more than we realize the way many religious believers deal with the relationship in their own religious life and practice. Though even here we have to be careful because I suspect that one of the reasons many religious believers have often acted as if they keep their religious beliefs and their thinking about, and attitude to, science in separate compartments is because of their general ignorance of the vast territory of science and its theories, rather than because they wish to avoid contact between the two areas. The same point can be made from the side of the scientists because they too may have little knowledge or expertise in dealing with subjects in the domains of philosophy of religion or theology, and so adopt an independent stance as the most appropriate one.

There have been a variety of different justifications offered for the independence model, and we will briefly mention a few here. One is that offered by the Protestant theologian, Karl Barth, who proposed a view that has found some favor within Protestantism as a whole. Barth advanced the view that we must start with God's revelation of himself through Christ in scripture.[4] We should not act as if revelation is in doubt, or provisional, or even, somewhat controversially, subject to reason. He used this approach to critique the attempt to know God by means of reason, or to work out our answers to various religious and theological matters by means of philosophy. For Barth, reason can be compromised by sin to such an extent that we end up with a rather subjective view of God rather than the true view, which is revealed in Christ. The problem with a rational approach to God is that it implies that there is another way to know God independently of God's grace. The rational approach would place much of the emphasis for our knowledge of God on us, and also seems to suggest that revelation is secondary. There is a fideistic strand in Barth's thinking, which stresses believing and accepting revelation as the primary starting point for our religious insights; consequently, there is a desire to divorce revelation from reason, and theology from philosophy, somewhat reminiscent of Martin Luther's attack on philosophy and science. Barth therefore holds that we should look upon any human effort to answer definitively any of our questions about the nature of God and God's relationship to his creation with suspicion. He goes as far as to say that we do not find knowledge of God from studying the natural world, but from revelation, which for Barth, comes primarily through the Bible. Science therefore cannot contradict theology because it is dealing with a different subject matter and a different approach to reality. So Barth's basic justification for the independence of science and religion is based on giving priority to divine revelation and a corresponding downplaying of the ability of reason to know reality on its own. This position, as we shall see, in not without problems.

Stephen J. Gould has argued, second, that science and religion are two "non-overlapping magisteria," and that they should stay independent of each other. The magisterium of science covers the empirical realm, and the magisterium of religion extends over questions of ultimate meaning and moral value.[5] Although Gould insists that this view is not offered merely as a diplomatic solution to the often contentious debate between religion and science, he gives little by way of positive argument in defense of it. He holds that scientists cannot address questions of morality, and that religion cannot address questions of science, yet his main reason for the "non-overlapping magisteria" thesis seems to be that by following this model both areas can pursue their goals and their work generally without interference from the other, and that from a practical point of view this model will therefore work well. Scientists would not need to worry about religion trying to interfere with their theoretical research and findings, and religious believers would not need to worry about challenges from science. Although this view might be attractive to many as a practical way around the "conflict" model, the main problem facing it is obvious, and one that we have already mentioned. This is the fact that scientific research sometimes raises questions that seem to have philosophical, theological, and moral significance, and it seems irresponsible from a logical, rational point of view to ignore these implications. It might give people comfort to ignore them, or be less troublesome for people overall (scientists in particular, which may be Gould's main motivation in suggesting this view), but the significance of certain scientific theories is still there, and surely still has to be faced, rather than our just ignoring these conclusions, or pretending that they don't exist. I am not necessarily saying that science and religion will end up in conflict; only that when science raises questions that have relevance for religion, reason requires that we look at these questions. Gould seems to suggest that, although it is true that science sometimes raises questions that may conflict with some religious beliefs (e.g., evolution vs. creationism), most of the time in most areas it does not, and most scientists and religious believers acknowledge that this is the case.

A variety of thinkers have tried to separate religion and science based on the type of questions they ask. These thinkers include Thomas Torrance and Langdon Gilkey.[6] Gilkey, for instance, argues that religion asks "why" questions and science asks "how" questions. For example, religion will ask, "why do human beings exist?", and "why is there something rather than nothing?" (why does the universe exist?), whereas science will ask, "how does the human heart work?", or "how did the species of chimpanzee come to evolve?" or "what was the composition of the big bang?" It is not within the expertise of religion to address questions about the composition of the big bang, neither is it within the expertise of science to tell us why the big bang occurred, nor what the purpose of life should be, nor what the correct moral values are. Religion, it is said, deals with the ultimate origin of the universe, and with the ultimate origin and the purpose of human life, which is the most important question of all; whereas science deals with how things work, with how to understand the physical workings of a complicated universe, with the search for discoveries in order to improve our physical comfort in terms of curing diseases, reducing poverty, easing our day-to-day lives, and so forth. "How" questions are extremely important, and indeed fascinating in their own way, and progress on them can have a huge effect on human life as we know it (even if most people know little or nothing about science), yet they are ultimately secondary questions when compared to the "why" questions. Our answers to the "why" questions, of course, have had a decisive impact on the development of civilization.

This is an interesting line of argument, yet it would not require or justify the independence model notwithstanding the general accuracy of the distinction between "how" and "why" questions. This is because some answers to "how" questions turn out to have great significance for the "why" questions, and therefore when one is thinking about a "why" question, one cannot ignore any relevant scientific research on "how" questions. Let us illustrate with two examples. If one is studying the question of the purpose of human life, one must take into account what the theory of evolution says about the origin of the species, including the species of *Homo sapiens*. The theory of evolution does not, of course, address the question of the purpose of human life in itself; it simply describes the processes and mechanisms by which it is thought human life on earth originated. Nevertheless, the way that human life originated may have some significance for thinking about the "why" question; in particular, if evolution suggests that there is some design present in nature this would obviously be important; similarly, if it suggested that there is likely no design in nature, this too would be relevant for the "why" question (this is one of the important topics of this book). Another example relates to the question of the origin of the universe. When we are thinking about why the universe exists at all, the big bang theory seems clearly to be relevant for this question. This is because it suggests that the universe began with a first event—the big bang—a finite time ago, and this forces us to confront the amazing fact that anything exists at all, as well as the nature of various types of causes, local and ultimate, and what all of this might mean for the "why" question. Of course, it might be that various scientific theories, including the ones mentioned, could be inconclusive on some of these matters, or perhaps subject to various interpretations, but this is not the same thing as saying that they are irrelevant. In general, one needs to consider all we know at any given time about a subject, including the universe and the makeup of human beings, if one is to make an honest, rational attempt to understand these phenomena. This seems to be a requirement of reason, and is an argument against allowing the independence model to guide our thinking about the relationship between religion and science.

This critical point would also apply to Barth's view, for he seems to be saying that as Christians we can commit to faith in Christ without asking questions about the prior rationality of making such a commitment. While it is true that if God exists, it would not matter much from God's point of view whether we as believers reason about his existence as long as we believe; from our point of view as human beings, however, it is important, from within our more limited perspective, to bring both philosophy and science to bear on the question of whether God exists, and the question of the reasonableness of religious belief. We must also remember to look at this matter from the point of view of science. Scientific research will raise questions that prompt us to look *beyond* science, to religion and philosophy, in search of an answer; for example, the incredible complexity of the genome raises the question of possible design and purpose behind it, and the nature of the big bang raises the question of why the big bang happened at all.

The third, and I believe the best, model, for understanding the relationship between religion and science is often called the dialogue model, or perhaps we might call it the integrationist model.[7] This model proposes that science and religion can work together in a way that is historically informed, rigorous, fair to both sides, and open to the ways in which science and religion can support each other in the quest to understand reality. This is the working model that we will adopt in this book, although the other models will obviously be relevant for several of the topics under discussion. In saying that they can work together, one can either adopt a stronger view of how this should be understood, or one may adopt a more modest perspective. The modest approach says that science can contribute to our understanding of things, that religion has nothing to fear from the results of scientific research, that we are in no danger of science solving all our problems, answering all our questions, or somehow showing that the religious view of the world is not true. Proponents of the stronger perspective hold that science and religion can be integrated to support the religious view of the world over the secularist view of the world (recall that the secularist holds the exact opposite thesis). A variety of thinkers have held either one or both of these positions, as well as some positions in between.

The dialogue model can take several different forms. One form is to attempt a reconciliation between science and religion by showing how the nature of

God and various theological views can be somewhat reinterpreted or re-understood in the light of modern science. We see this approach in the work of Ian Barbour and John Haught. Another approach to dialogue is to critique and reject the increasingly influential view that modern science is necessarily hostile to religion, to deny that current scientific theories lead to secularism (or naturalism). For example, to deny the view advanced by Richard Dawkins that evolution is evidence of the *absence* of design in the universe. Many thinkers, including Alister McGrath and Keith Ward, have adopted this approach. An extension of this view is to argue that modern scientific theories actually present further good evidence for the religious worldview. We see this approach developed in the work of Richard Swinburne, William Lane Craig, Francis Collins, Paul Davies, and recently in the thought of lifelong atheist philosopher Anthony Flew, who converted to theism because of the evidence from current scientific theories.[8] We will come back to many of these views in later chapters.

There are several reasons supporting the dialogue model. The first is that it adopts an optimistic posture toward the general debate between religion and science. It operates from the starting point that science and religion can help each other, that discussion between them is mutually beneficial, and that they are not inherently in conflict (despite the fact that there have been occasional conflicts between them). Second, this view is supported by a point we made above in our discussion of the independence model—that the dialogue approach is the most rational approach to the relationship because when we are thinking about some of the interesting questions of life in a variety of areas we should take into account all the information we have available on a topic, no matter where it comes from, and this, of course, would include scientific information. This view is based on the traditional logical principle that "all truth is one," that if something is true in one discipline, it must be true in all disciplines, and so the dialogue approach is the most rational option. Third, those who adopt the dialogue approach generally believe that the religious worldview, in particular, does not have anything to fear from scientific research, and so should welcome it as a rich resource to help us think about some of the mysteries of existence. The dialogue model is not necessarily committed in principle to the view that scientific research can never be a problem for religion, but it is committed to the view that current scientific research is not a threat to religion, despite what some secularists and naturalists might claim, or despite the way they might employ various scientific theories in the defense of atheism.

A fourth, and very important, reason in support of the dialogue model is that science has opened up new areas in recent times that naturally raise difficult moral questions, such as in the area of stem cell research, cloning, genetic engineering, artificial intelligence, etc. These dilemmas are probably going to get more acute in the future, but science as a discipline will be unable to help us with the answers. Indeed, science really offers us nothing on some of the most challenging moral questions facing human beings: is it moral to allow the creation and destruction of embryos to try to arrive at cures for various diseases; how should we raise our children; how should we organize society politically; does the modern conception of work allow enough time for leisure; is capital punishment a legitimate form of punishment for the crime of murder; are affluent societies becoming too materialistic and self-centered, and so forth? The disciplines of religion, philosophy, and theology help us think through these questions. Or to look at the matter from another angle, these are worldview questions, and will have to be answered from within one's worldview, and this will include religious worldviews, especially given that these have been the most influential worldviews in history, and still are today.

Fifth, there is a historical reason as well for supporting the dialogue model. It is simply a fact that religion and science got on fairly well throughout history, despite occasional well-publicized conflicts. As we shall see in our next chapter, many ancient and medieval thinkers adopted a blend of philosophy, theology, and science in their attempt to understand the universe and the meaning of life. Many well-known scientists throughout history also favored this approach, as we will see throughout the book, because they regarded themselves as trying to come to a better understanding of God's universe. (Isaac Newton, for example, wrote as much about religious topics as he did about scientific topics, and agreed with Galileo that God wrote two books: the Bible and the book of nature.)

A philosophical approach to religion and science

Our approach in this book will be philosophical, since I am a philosopher, and since the topic of religion and science fits nicely as a branch of philosophy of religion. *Philosophy* is a discipline that is concerned with some of the ultimate questions of human life such as the following, among many others: What is true knowledge? Is there a God? What are the correct moral values? Do human beings differ in kind, or merely in degree, from other species? What is the correct political theory? Do human beings have free will? Is religion compatible with science? The approach of the philosopher involves thinking through these questions by considering the views of pivotal thinkers, presenting and critically analyzing the reasons offered for various views, considering objections, and subjecting one's overall position to rigorous critical analysis. Philosophers focus on logical argument, and in identifying important distinctions, in order to bring clarity to complex issues. But philosophers do not overlook empirical evidence if it is relevant to the questions in which they are interested; as we have noted, the big bang theory is relevant to the question of the cause of the universe; the theory of evolution is relevant to the question of the nature of human beings; research into the structure of the brain may be related to the question of human free will. In addition, philosophers try not to assume anything that is too controversial in their arguments; they try to defend their premises as much as possible. This is one way in which philosophy differs from theology. *Theology* is a discipline that generally *assumes* the reasonability of a particular religious tradition, and the reliability perhaps of certain religious texts. It is sometimes said that theologians can get away with things that philosophers can't get away with! For example, theologians can assume that God exists, and so focus solely on the nature of God, or they can assume that religion and science are compatible, and so need only focus on explaining in what ways they are compatible. But philosophers like to look at more foundational questions, and are required to defend their various answers to these questions by appeal to reason, human experience, and philosophical arguments. This is a very valuable perspective from which to approach a study of religion and science. While the topic has got quite a bit of attention in recent years, most of the current work is carried out from a theological perspective, with some from a scientific perspective, and some from a secularist perspective, but very little from a purely philosophical perspective. This book is intended to fill this gap in the literature on religion and science.

The expository discussion in this book will therefore be philosophical, rather than theological, meaning that I will consider the main topics from the point of view of the fundamental philosophical questions raised, and my approach will involve a critical analysis of the different positions and views on various sides of the debate, and the rational arguments and evidence offered for them. Although we will occasionally refer to theological views, we will not assume the truth or reliability of any religious text, or religious authority, and will not be examining the topics from any particular denominational point of view (except where relevant). As noted earlier in this chapter, the emphasis in the book will be on western religion, especially Christianity, the religion I am most familiar with, and also likely to be the religion of most readers. Christianity has also occupied center stage, both today and in history, in the debate and dialogue with science. (I will also occasionally use the term *theist*, a term many philosophers of religion use to describe someone who believes in God.)

In our next chapter, we will examine the history of the relationship between religion and science by focusing on the dominant religious understandings at different times in history, and on the development and influence of science along the way, both in terms of its subject matter, and in terms of the scientific method. From this perspective, the chapter will examine seven broad time periods: (1) the ancient world, especially the work of Aristotle; (2) the medieval understanding of reality, especially the ideas of St. Augustine and St. Thomas Aquinas; (3) the Reformation period; (4) the Galileo affair of the seventeenth century; (5) Galileo and Newton's influence on the growth of science as a distinct discipline, and the surpassing of Aristotle's approach; (6) eighteenth-century ideas (including deism, and the materialist views of such thinkers as D'Holbach and LaMettrie); and (7) crucial theories of the nineteenth century, especially those of Charles Darwin and Sigmund Freud.

Chapter 3 turns to a discussion of science and naturalism in the twentieth century. After a brief overview of the success of the scientific enterprise in modern culture, we then look at the question of whether the scientific approach to knowledge really gives us objective truth, in a consideration of realist and anti-realist views. We also reflect on the relationship today between science and naturalism (secularism), illustrating this theme in the work of some leading contemporary naturalists, Richard Dawkins, Carl Sagan, and Francis Crick.

The theory of evolution is one of the most significant scientific theories of all time, and no educated person today can really afford to be ignorant of the theory. The theory and its significance for religion are examined thoroughly in Chapter 4. After a brief overview of the role of evolution in modern culture, and of the history of the theory, the chapter examines evolution from the point of view of three central questions. The first question asks: what *factual claims* does the theory make about the origin of the species, including *Homo sapiens*? The second question asks: what *evidence* is offered to support the factual claims, and how reliable is this evidence? Here we consider such matters as:

why is the fossil evidence important, and what does it show; why are there few transitional species; does natural selection explain how evolution works; and what should we make of the fact that many intelligent people of integrity and goodwill have doubts about evolution? The third major question turns to the *implications* of the factual claims of the theory for important topics in religion, ethics, and philosophy. We consider such matters as the status of the Bible (does evolution undermine the authority of the Bible?); the status of human beings (is the existence of the human species necessary or accidental; does evolution really occur by chance?); and the status of the universe (is evolution an argument against design in the universe?).

In Chapter 5, we focus more specifically on the possible consequences of various scientific advances and speculations for our understanding of, and reflection upon, the nature of the human person. The chapter probes further matters raised by the theory of evolution including the question of the uniqueness or specialness of *Homo sapiens* (do we differ in kind or only in degree from other species?), the appearance of consciousness in evolutionary history, the nature of consciousness, free will and moral agency, the existence of the soul, artificial intelligence, and the possibility of life on other planets.

When one is thinking about matters of science and religion, the subject of design is never very far away, and this is the focus of Chapter 6. Here we examine four of the main versions of the design argument, and their relevance and implications for the religion-science relationship: (1) William Paley's argument based on the subtle complexities of nature, an argument that introduces the famous watch analogy; (2) the modern "laws of physics" argument from design, which makes a significant appeal to the evidence of recent science; (3) the anthropic, or fine-tuning, argument, which is based on the nature of the big bang; (4) the contemporary argument from intelligent design, which again appeals to empirical evidence, particularly from microbiology, and which at the same time is a critique of natural selection, one of the key concepts of the theory of evolution.

Chapter 7 examines those questions that naturally arise when one thinks about the origin of our universe, and its nature and structure, particularly the "cosmological question": the question of how the universe got here in the first place. The big bang theory of the origin of the universe has brought renewed force to the cosmological argument (or first cause argument) for the existence of God, and both are the focus of the first part of the chapter. We then consider how the strange, even mind-boggling, scientific theories, of relativity and quantum mechanics might affect our understanding of, and religious response to, reality, before concluding with an overview of some of the ways that God might interact with his creation.

The intersection of religion and science is very evident today in the number of very challenging ethical issues raised by recent work in genetics, and related areas of research. Our final chapter will provide an overview of both the science and ethics of a number of these complex topics, including the mapping of the human genome, stem cell research, cloning, genetic engineering, and the apparent moral indifference of science as a discipline.

The overall aim of this book is to introduce readers to the varied topics that arise in any consideration of religion and science, to provide an informed, well reasoned, balanced and clear overview of the ideas surrounding the main topics, and to introduce along the way the main thinkers and positions associated with each topic (both historical and contemporary). In this way, I hope the book will serve as a reliable and wide-ranging resource on the topic of religion and science. The book is primarily intended to be an expository, readable overview and guide to the main issues, arguments and thinkers in what is a quite complicated subject area. My hope is that it will be a useful resource for those many readers today, including students, faculty and general readers, who are fascinated by the topic of religion and science, and who are seeking an introductory guide to the subject from mainly a philosophical perspective.

I owe my thanks to several people who helped me while working on this book. I am very grateful to the excellent staff at Continuum Press, led by Haaris Naqvi, for their support, their professional approach, and their hard work. I also wish to thank Bill Stancil for his invaluable comments on the manuscript, and for his theological expertise and insight. I am grateful for the advice of Edward Furton, Curtis Hancock, John Morris, and the late George O'Connor. Rockhurst University provided me with released time, and with grant support, for the project, for which I am also grateful. I have sometimes used a phrase or two, or a few paragraphs, from material I have published previously. I wish to thank the editors of *Ethics and Medics*, Continuum Books, and *International Philosophical Quarterly* for granting permission. Lastly, I owe a huge debt of gratitude to my wife, Margaret, for her always unfailing support, and to my sons, Brendan, John, and Ciaran, who were steadfastly patient (well, up to a point) when I could not always drag myself away from my work to play soccer!

Religion and Science in History

Chapter Outline

The ancient world: Aristotle	26
The medieval world: St. Augustine and St. Thomas	33
The Protestant Reformation	40
The Galileo controversy of the seventeenth century	44
Galileo and Newton, and the development of science	46
Eighteenth-century developments	49
The nineteenth century: Darwin and Freud	53

The history of the interaction between religion and science is fascinating in its own right, but also important to examine in order to understand their current relationship. This is not only because the history of the subject can throw much light on how we got into our present state with regard to religion-science questions, but because it can also give us a perspective which may help us see current issues and controversies in a fresh way. Indeed, this broader perspective may help us reach a more informed view of the appropriate relationship between religion and science. It is not possible to appreciate the various dynamics at play in the interaction between the two areas today if we have no knowledge of the scope and development of religious and philosophical questions, of the way in which these questions need to be distinguished from scientific questions, of the origin of the scientific method, and of how various influential scientists understood their overall task as scientists. We need an appreciation too of not only the various conflicts that arose in what was sometimes an uneasy relationship, but also of the cooperation and mutual support that existed between religion and science throughout history.

We should note immediately that the history of the religion-science story is vast, and impossible to cover fully even in a book-length study, let alone a chapter. In addition, there are so many different approaches to the same subject matter, as well as a vast array of thinkers, ideas, and important works, all playing formative roles in different disciplines, not to mention the various religious, social, and political influences of each age that always play some role in the development of intellectual history, that there is no neat story to be told about their relationship.[1] Intellectual history is a complicated subject, and rarely fits into neatly defined categories. With this proviso in mind, my approach to the subject matter of this chapter will be to focus on the question of how various ideas, approaches, and developments in science affected the religious worldview, how various religious thinkers responded to these developments, and how some scientific discoveries led to revolutions in our understanding of the world. As already noted, we will be looking at these matters primarily from a Western perspective, and will operate with the understandings of religion and science already explained in Chapter 1. Although there are different ways one can approach telling the story of religion and science, we will focus on the dominant religious understandings at different times in history, and on the development and influence of science along the way, both in terms of its subject matter, and in terms of the scientific method. From this perspective, we will examine seven broad time periods: (1) the ancient world, especially the work of Aristotle; (2) the medieval understanding of reality, especially the ideas of St. Augustine and St. Thomas Aquinas; (3) the influence of the Reformation; (4) the Galileo affair of the seventeenth century; (5) Galileo and Newton, and the growth of science as a distinct discipline; (6) Eighteenth-century developments; and (7) revolutionary theories of the nineteenth century, especially those of Darwin and Freud. This will take us up to the twentieth century, which will be the focus of the next chapter.

The ancient world: Aristotle

The ancient Greek philosopher, Aristotle (384–322 B.C.), one of the most influential minds in history, is an enormously significant thinker on the nature of science, the scientific method, and on the role of science in our overall understanding of reality. Aristotle developed a view of the world that was to dominate Western thinking until the time of Francis Bacon and Galileo in the seventeenth century. He was influenced by an earlier group of thinkers, often called "the first philosophers," or the pre-Socratics (seventh–fourth century B.C.), who had approached their study of reality from both a religious and a scientific perspective. These philosophers were interested in explaining such things as the composition of matter, the apparent order and stability in the universe, and (one of their major concerns) the basis of change. Thinkers such as Anixamander, Pythagaoras, Heraclitus, Parmenides, and Democritus approached these topics not only by means of philosophical distinctions and categories, but also by application of the scientific method, insofar as this was possible in their time.

Although the discoveries and informed speculations of the pre-Socratic philosophers were often accurate and profound, it is important to realize that there was no discipline of science as such in their day; in fact, science did not emerge as a distinct discipline until after Galileo. Ancient philosophers, including Aristotle, often pursued what came to be called "natural philosophy," a study of nature and the larger universe that was close to what we would now identify as the scientific point of view. There was significant disagreement later on among various thinkers about what should come under the heading of natural philosophy, just as there is today about what counts as science, and for this reason a precise definition of natural philosophy is hard to arrive at.[2] Aristotle himself distinguished natural philosophy from both mathematics and metaphysics. The aim of natural philosophy is to arrive at objective knowledge. This knowledge is to be obtained by means of inductive logical arguments rooted in human experience and observation of nature. Aristotle's approach to the study of reality, therefore, involved a combination of philosophy, religion, and science (natural philosophy), and he saw himself as completing in a more systematic and detailed manner a process of understanding that the pre-Socratics had started.

One of the most important concepts in Aristotle's approach is the concept of teleology (from the Greek word, *telos*, meaning "end" or "purpose"). As we will see presently, one of Aristotle's fundamental questions about reality is, "what is being?" or, in other words, what does it mean for something to exist? Is it possible to give an explanation of the concept of existence itself? He argued that this question is the same question as the question, "what is substance?" In his book, *Metaphysics*, he proceeds to give a detailed answer to the question of being, which then enables him to address one of his major concerns about how things change, as well as several related topics including the nature of causation, and the inbuilt purposes we discover in the objects of our experience.[3] The defining feature of (primary) substance, Aristotle suggests, is that it describes the individual thing that exists, such as *this* man, *this* horse, *this* dog. In addition, we can say that a substance, or the *individual* thing, is that which has properties (what Aristotle called accidents), but which is not itself a property (or a characteristic). For example, a dog has various properties—legs, fur, a tail—but we cannot say of the dog that, *as a dog*, it can be a property of something else. We could not say that one of the properties of a dog is that it is a cat, or has a cat for a property! We could say that a dog is a property of a dog show, but in this case *the show* is the substance we are focusing on, and whose properties we are examining. These reflections led Aristotle to suggest that there are various categories of substances, and one of our jobs is to describe and classify them.

After explaining how the definition and understanding of substance captures what it is for an individual thing to exist, Aristotle next gives a more detailed account of the nature of a (primary) substance. He is interested in common sense questions about the nature of substances and their properties, how substances come into and go out of existence, how they change, and what their purpose is. (This latter question takes him into the area of teleology.) He argues that individual substances are made up of matter and form. The matter is the material the substance is made out of, and the form is the "arrangement" of the matter (i.e., the essence or nature of the object); for example, the table is made out of wood (matter), which is arranged in the form (shape) of a table. (This gave rise to the question of whether these forms, which came to be called "universals," have an identity independent of the matter in which they are exemplified. Does the form exist only in the mind of the artisan who makes the table, or does it exist really in the object too as long as the matter exists, or does it have an existence independent of the matter and of the artisan? Plato held to the latter view, Aristotle to the middle view [he called the forms "secondary substances"], and many contemporary philosophers hold to the first view, a view known as nominalism.) Aristotle held that objects change when their properties change; for example, we can paint a table a different color. This type of change is called an accidental change, because the original substance, the table, does not change, a painted table is still a table. But there is another type of change, a substantial change, in which the substance itself is changed, as in when we dismantle a table and use the same wood to build a chair. In this case, the table (the substance) no longer exists. Aristotle held that all change could be explained in this way as either accidental change or substantial change.

He elaborates the nature of change in terms of the principles of potency and act (or actuality). He held that individual substances have actuality (or are in existence), but they also have potentialities that can either be fulfilled or frustrated. Change is the process of bringing a potentiality in a substance to fulfillment. For example, an acorn has the potentiality to become an oak tree. In this sense, Aristotle argued that actuality is therefore metaphysically prior to potency because one must have an actually existing thing with potentialities before these potentialities can be realized. Change acts on bits of matter; for example, the wood (the matter) becomes a table, and is organized or arranged as a table. But the same wood can be reconfigured into a chair. Indeed, *the wood itself* is an object made out of matter as well, and the matter is arranged as wood; this would also be true of the component parts of the wood. This means that there is a kind of underlying pure matter (somehow without form, at least in principle) behind all objects in the world. This matter is ultimate in the sense that it lies behind everything, and is prior to the matter and form coming together in ordinary objects. This type of matter is often called prime matter, and the ordinary matter, as in the wood, is intermediate or proximate matter. The process of bringing potentialities to actualization inspired Aristotle to think about the nature of causality in more detail, and so led him to the concept of teleology.[4]

Aristotle was a keen student of nature, especially of various species and their habitats, and he is often referred to as the first biologist because he provided detailed accounts of the behavior and life cycles of several hundred species, including land animals, fish, crustaceans, and many others.[5] He noticed that things in nature had limited potentialities: that is, they had the potential to develop along certain lines, and only those lines; moreover, these lines of development could be discovered by means of empirical observation of the natural object or living thing. For instance, a caterpillar has the potential to become a butterfly, but not to become a rabbit. An acorn can become an oak tree, but not a fir tree. These empirical observations led him to the conclusion that nature overall is *teleological*, that everything in nature has inbuilt goals and purposes, including human beings (a conclusion that became the basis of his influential ethical theory). This point gives us an insight into the why of nature: why does an acorn grow—to become an oak tree. To become an oak tree is the *telos* of the acorn, its highest possible good.

Aristotle developed his famous account of the four causes as a way of bringing all of these ideas about the natures of things together. He identified the material, formal, efficient, and final causes. The material cause of an object refers to the matter out of which it is made. The formal cause then would be the shape or arrangement of the matter, the pattern of the matter, which is the "essence" of the object. The efficient cause is that which brings the object into existence, or brings about change in the object, and the final cause is the purpose of the object, what it is for.[6] Aristotle thought that if you could identify the four causes of an object you would know almost everything about it. For example, the material cause of a vase is the clay, the efficient cause is the potter, the formal cause is the arrangement of the clay, and the final cause is a container for liquid. This was one of the first significant accounts of causation in the history of ideas, and it was a very thorough one, which enabled us, when combined with the rest of Aristotle's metaphysical categories, to get an excellent grasp of the nature of the world around us.

It was the notion of final cause that was particularly interesting in Aristotle's overall approach. He held that it was important to ask not just what an object was made of, how it was made, or who made it, but also *why* it was made, what purpose it served to fulfill. Of course, it might not fulfill its purpose—might not realize its potentiality for various reasons—but it still has a purpose. All objects have a purpose, natural objects (a man, an acorn) as well as artificial objects (a house, a musical instrument, since these are made of real natural substances). Sometimes their final purpose is simply to exemplify as perfectly as possible the specific form of object they are—for example, the final cause of a horse is to be the best possible exemplification of a horse (in which case the formal cause and the final cause are much the same thing). We can find out the purpose by examining objects empirically. The purpose is also a vital part of our knowledge about objects, something we can know about them, and need to know in order to have a fuller understanding of them. Aristotle is saying that most objects have a *telos* or an end, and that this is a vitally significant point about understanding the natural world. It might be the case that sometimes we will disagree about the *telos*, or we might find it hard to discover the *telos* of a particular object, but there is a *telos*, and this is a key truth about nature.

Aristotle introduced the notion of teleology into philosophy and science, and in one way or another many of our subsequent debates have revolved around this idea. The concept of teleology has very important implications for our understanding of ourselves as human beings and for our understanding of the universe. First, teleology shows that we should be interested not just in how nature works, but also in why it works the way it does. In addition to the mechanisms of nature, we also must think about the ways in which nature exhibits teleological goals, and this will eventually lead to the question of why nature seems to have inbuilt purposes (the question of design). For 1,500 years after Aristotle, it was not only philosophers who were interested in teleological questions, but also scientists, because their approach to their work was heavily influenced by his account of the nature of objects, especially his view of the four causes. It is important to keep in mind that there was no distinct discipline of physical science until the sixteenth century, so that when thinkers worked on these questions, their approach was often a mix of philosophy, theology, and science (as in Aristotle himself). This meant that it was much easier for a view like Aristotle's to be influential across a wide range of areas of inquiry than it might be if the disciplines are generally kept separate (as they are now).

Second, the question of everything having a nature naturally prompts us to ask if human beings themselves have a nature or a purpose in the universe, and what it might be. Aristotle himself approached this question purely from a philosophical point of view, rather than from a religious one. He argued that by studying human beings using a combination of reason, experience, and observation of the natural world, we could discover that there is such a thing as human nature, a nature common to all human beings. For Aristotle, our human nature consists of traits and characteristics that although part of our essence are not merely biological. These traits do not just develop naturally, but must be brought to fruition by instruction, training, and the wisdom that comes with experience. Such traits and characteristics include reason, free will, the moral virtues (which are human excellences), and the development of moral character through habitual virtuous activity. As he puts it, "any action is well performed when it is performed in accordance with the appropriate excellence ... [so] human good turns out to be activity of soul in accordance with virtue."[7] He developed this approach in detail to serve as the basis of his ethical theory; he argued that the goal of human life is happiness, which is achieved by living a moral life, which leads to the fulfillment of our nature as human beings. Aristotle therefore defined happiness as an activity of the soul in accordance with reason and virtue. His account of happiness is based on the idea that there is a right way and a wrong way to develop human beings morally so that they can fulfill their purpose, just as there is a right and wrong way to treat a musical instrument so as to bring out "the best" in it. This account of the nature of human beings, and of the moral life, naturally prompted later thinkers to ask questions about the origin of human nature, about how human beings got this nature. Is it something essential to human beings or might they not have had it? Is it relative to time and place? Could it change in the future? Again, the ultimate questions are raised by Aristotle's view, though he himself did not offer conventional religious answers to these questions.

This brings us to Aristotle's views on God, which, along with the ideas just surveyed, were extremely influential in the whole Western tradition. It is important to remember that Aristotle was not a religious believer in our sense; he lived before the age of Christianity, and was also skeptical of the Greek religion of his day. He does not appear to have reflected much on the idea of a personal God, and did not think that God was a creator of the universe, since the Greeks held that the universe was eternal. Nevertheless, his thinking about the question of change led him to suggest that we need a cause to account for the eternity of motion in the world, and this is God. This argument is the basis of the later medieval view that the universe needs an ultimate sustaining cause because, even though it might be eternal, it is still made up of beings, objects, and events that do not cause themselves. The universe consists of what St. Thomas Aquinas would later call a contingent series of events, a series of particular individual events, each one of which cannot cause itself. So, Aristotle laid the groundwork for the argument that this kind of universe cannot be the cause of itself, nor can its ultimate explanation come from within itself. It therefore needs an outside sustaining cause, which is responsible for its existence, which keeps it in existence, and this is God. Aristotle referred to God as the Prime Mover or the Unmoved Mover: "for there is something which always moves the things that are in motion, and the first mover is itself unmoved."[8] He argued that God must be a nonphysical or incorporeal being because if God were made of matter, he would be in potency and would need a cause. This point also leads him to suggest that God is pure actuality (or pure act), meaning that because he has no matter, he has no potential to change in various ways, and so he is a perfect being. In terms of his doctrine of four causes, Aristotle argued that God is the final cause of the universe, a cause that attracts the universe by desire. God can't be the efficient cause because this presupposes that "the moved" would also act on "the Mover," which means that God could change, but because God is pure act this is not possible.

Even though Aristotle did not develop this idea of God in any detail, it became the foundation of the medieval worldview, and also was of great significance in the historical development of Christianity right down to the present day, and has therefore been very influential in shaping modern culture. Aristotle's view of God can be seen as a logical consequence of his metaphysics, not a view he held in advance because of prior religious commitments, or a view that he developed his metaphysical views in order to support. As a result, Aristotle's philosophical support for this view of God made his overall system very attractive to later philosophers who were thinking through their religious beliefs philosophically (such as Aquinas). Aristotle's view shows how God must be the ultimate cause of the universe, how he is incorporeal, perfect, etc. It was an easy matter then for Christian thinkers to fit this view of God, with appropriate modifications, into the biblical account of God, and the Christian worldview. It was not until the twentieth century that this view of God was significantly challenged both within philosophy and theology (as we will see as our story unfolds throughout this book).

The medieval world: St. Augustine and St. Thomas

The influence of ancient philosophy on both St. Augustine and St. Thomas was profound. It was not just the content of ancient ideas that attracted them, but also the philosophical method that Plato and Aristotle, in particular, had practiced. This method offered Christian thinkers a way to approach their subject matter that helped them throw further light on the question of the relationship between faith and reason. These Christian thinkers, and many others, were not content simply to accept Christian truth on theological premises alone. They also wished to subject these theological premises, and the substantive theological content of their worldviews, to philosophical analysis, in so far as they could do this. As a result, there is much in the work of Augustine and Aquinas (and many other medieval thinkers) that is purely philosophical even though they are concerned with religious questions, themes, and doctrines. These thinkers were engaged in philosophical analysis within the context of the truth of Christianity in the way that many modern thinkers, some of whom we will consider in this book, engage in philosophy (or science) within the context of secularism. Indeed, religion was to medieval thought what secularism and naturalism are to contemporary thought.

However, even within the medieval context there were (sometimes sharply) different views about the proper relationship between philosophy and theology, yet there was a general consensus that philosophy was the "handmaiden to theology." This was the idea that philosophy, especially the ideas of Plato and Aristotle, should be used as a tool to understand better the truths of revealed theology, but not to interrogate them or supplant them. In this way, philosophy need not be seen as a threat to theological truth, but rather as a way of further supporting it. This approach had already been very popular with the early Church fathers such as Clement of Alexandria (c.150–c.215), Gregory of

Nazianzus (c.325–389), and John of Damascus (c.676–c.749), and was therefore an attractive model for medieval philosophers to adopt. St. Anselm (1033–1109) had expressed this point by saying that his motive in probing the rationality of religious belief was *fides quaerens intellectum*, faith seeking understanding. Christian thinkers recognized that while there is a degree of faith involved in committing to religious claims, that the reasonability of these claims is still an important question, and that the intelligent, philosophically minded believer should address this matter. These philosophers were not content to hold the view that religious beliefs are a matter of faith, and so there is no need or room for a rational discussion of them. They were, therefore, very committed to the discipline of philosophy as a way of questioning, clarifying, and supporting the main beliefs and concepts of their religious worldview.

St. Augustine was influenced by the view we mentioned in Chapter 1 that "all truth is one," the view that many areas of study (including science) can discover truths concerning various areas of life, and that religious belief, if it is to be rationally grounded, must seek to welcome and accommodate these truths. If a claim is established as true in one discipline, St. Augustine held, it must therefore be true in all disciplines. This basic principle of logic was accepted by many early and medieval thinkers (including Aquinas), and it defined the way they approached theological questions. It also counters the "conflict model" sometimes presumed to govern the relationship between religion and other disciplines (including science), and suggests a dialogue model where all disciplines should work together in an attempt to understand a little more about God's creation.

As Richard Blackwell has noted, St. Augustine was occupied for many years with the question of how the book of Genesis, especially the account of creation, should be interpreted.[9] Should it be read in a fairly literal way, or was there some room to suggest that the biblical writers had used occasional literary license in telling the story of creation? Augustine noted that both science and religion make truth claims about reality, and that sometimes these claims do not appear to agree with each other. He wondered what one is to do when this happens, using the Genesis story as an illustration. He accepted the principle that all truth is derived from God, which means that science and religion cannot be in ultimate conflict. He also accepted the view that science as a discipline can attain truth about the physical universe. Therefore, it follows that if a scientific truth conflicts with a biblical truth, one of them will have to be revised. Augustine proposed that if we are certain that the scientific claim or theory is true, then the biblical claim must have been misinterpreted and so should be reinterpreted. Although this approach has become generally accepted in many religions, it is still controversial, especially in the contemporary debate concerning creationism and evolution (see Chapter 4).

These reflections led St. Augustine to the question: what are we to do in a case where a scientific claim conflicts with a biblical claim, but where the scientific claim is less than certain? Suppose, as is often the case, that a scientific theory is proposed to explain a given phenomenon, but that the evidence for the theory is suggestive, but not conclusive? In this situation, Augustine advised that our religious beliefs should be given preference over the scientific hypothesis. But if it does become necessary to revise a biblical account, such as the biblical account of creation, for instance, Augustine believed that this does *not* mean that the biblical account is false. This is because, although the literal facts of the story might not be true, there are deeper philosophical and theological points being made which are true: that God created the universe and all of the species, according to a particular plan, and that human beings are the highest form of species. Thus the actual story of how God created the universe and life is revisable, according to St. Augustine, but the deeper point that God did create the universe and life according to a plan is *not* revisable. He thought that religious believers run the risk, if they are not flexible on biblical accounts, such as the creation story, of later been proved wrong by science. This is exactly what happened in the case of Galileo in the seventeenth century, and also what happened in the case of evolution in the nineteenth and twentieth centuries, two controversies we will come back to later in this chapter.

The proper relationship between philosophy and theology, the relationship between faith and reason, the relevance of scientific evidence for matters religious—all of these themes were prominent in the intellectual culture at the time of St. Thomas Aquinas. Plato, and the influence of neo-Platonism, especially Plotinus (204–270) and Dionysius the Areopagite (c. sixth century), was initially more influential than Aristotle, especially with regard to the notion of the hierarchy of being, which placed God at the top of the chain of being, followed by angels, humans, animals, plants, and inanimate existence, an idea embraced by many medieval thinkers. But on religion-science questions, Aristotle's work became more significant. His work had been lost for several centuries, but around the ninth century Aristotle's texts was translated into Arabic, through which they were rediscovered by Western thinkers, of whom Aquinas was the most significant. Several Arabian philosophers made an important contribution at this time to various ideas that were influential in the development of thinking about religion in the West; these included Al Kindi (c.810–873), Al Farabi (878–950), Avicenna (980–1037), Al-Ghazali (1058–1111), and Averroes (1126–1198). The latter is probably the most highly regarded of the Arabic philosophers in the West, and his work was referred to frequently by Aquinas, who called him "the Commentator" because of his influential commentaries on Aristotle

Aristotle's works spread quickly throughout European centers of learning, and generated great interest (as one can imagine) in his ideas relating to metaphysics, teleology, natural philosophy, mathematics, logic, and many others topics. These ideas were studied at new universities in Paris and Oxford. But although Aristotle's ideas were popular and influential, they were not without critics, and some looked upon them with suspicion. Not only did Aristotle's work introduce new ideas into the theological context of the time, such as matter and form, causation and teleology, final causes, etc., but they also introduced a distinctly philosophical approach to the important questions of life, including theological and moral questions. This prompted much debate over the question of the proper relationship between Greek ideas and Christianity, between philosophy and theology.[10]

St. Thomas Aquinas was a pioneering thinker in this debate.[11] It is often said of St. Thomas that he baptized Aristotle, because he produced a great synthesis of Aristotelian philosophy and Christian theology, which became known as Thomism, and which had a great influence on not only Catholicism, but on Western thinking as a whole. Although St. Thomas was primarily a theologian, he was greatly influenced by both Aristotle's use of philosophical reasoning to work out answers to some of the great questions, and also by the content of Aristotle's metaphysics and ethics. Aquinas saw in Aristotle and other thinkers a way to help him develop a sound philosophical defense of Christianity, and although the Catholic Church was initially skeptical of this approach (especially during Aquinas's life time), and somewhat wary of Greek metaphysics, they eventually came round to see the wisdom in Aquinas's approach (and eventually adopted the Thomistic approach as the official philosophy of the Church in the nineteenth century).[12] Aquinas also accepted the principle that "all truth is one," and was interested in obtaining knowledge about the universe, wherever it could be obtained, including from science. He regarded the universe as intelligible and nature as good, and it was our job to use the tools God had given us, especially reason, to figure out as much as possible about God's creation. In this way, reason in general, and philosophy, theology and science in particular, complement revelation.

Aquinas is probably best known for his five arguments for the existence of God. Although the arguments are short, they have generated countless discussions, and are at the forefront of the fascinating debate about what reason can tell us about the existence of God. He begins his great work, *Summa Theologiae,* with his claim that it is possible to show that it is reasonable to believe in God through the process of natural theology, that is, by examining the evidence in the natural world, including from causation, change, and order, and working back to the conclusion that there must be a necessary being behind the universe. St. Thomas then proceeds to develop the view of God that became known as traditional theism (or classical theism). According to this view, God created the world out of nothing (*creatio ex nihilo*), but God is also the sustainer of the world. This means that the world would not remain in existence even for a second if God withdrew his sustaining power, because contingent things do not have the power to keep themselves in existence. God is a necessary being or an eternal being, because this is what the argument for the existence of God shows—that one must invoke a necessary being to explain contingent being, otherwise one cannot explain contingent being. Our rational human minds strongly resist that latter alternative because it is not rational. (We examine this argument in detail in Chapter 7.)

The traditional view of God proposes that God in his own being is immaterial, a personal being, a being who is perfect, omnipotent, omniscient, and worthy of worship. Aquinas argued that we must speak of God analogically, and not equivocally or univocally. This means that we can compare God to human beings in some respects, like saying that God exists or that God is a personal being, but we must recognize that God does not exist and is not a personal being in the same way that you or I exist, or are personal beings. This is the best way to talk about God because it allows us to speak analogically of his attributes by comparing them to our attributes, while recognizing that they are of a fundamentally different order than the attributes of human beings.[13] Medieval theologians have also approached the question of the nature of God by means of negative theology (*via negativa*)—an attempt to describe God in terms of what he is not rather than in terms of what he is. For instance, we could say that God is not ignorant, without saying how much knowledge he possesses, or in what way he possesses it; or we can say that God exists without meaning that he exists in the same way that you or I exist.

Aquinas also argued that God is a perfect being, which means that he is immutable, and does not change, but as pure act he is also a dynamic being because he is pure spirit. God is understood to be perfect in every way, including morally perfect. Being, as St. Thomas argued, is the basis of all perfections, and since human beings have limited being, then we would only have our perfections in a limited way. But an unlimited, infinite, eternal being, a being whose essence is supposed to be his existence, would have these perfections in the highest possible way. It is also because God is perfect that we think that he is worthy of worship; if we conceive of God as any way less than perfect, it gets harder to see why we should give him our devotion.[14] This view of God was to become dominant in Western thinking in both philosophy and theology, and it was not until the eighteenth century that it was seriously challenged, a challenge that has continued on into the twenty-first century, though Aquinas's view is still the dominant view of God even today.

St. Thomas also developed the natural law theory of ethics, again heavily influenced by Aristotle's view of the moral life, which was based around the pursuit of happiness and the practice of virtue. One of the essential points of this theory for our purposes in this book is that there is a human nature which all human beings share (as noted earlier). In this sense, both St. Thomas and Aristotle developed a view of human life and morality that was based around what was natural for human beings, based around what was in accordance with human nature, around how human beings should conduct themselves. This was a very common sense view of morality, and was adopted in essential aspects by many societies (and its development, of course, was not unique to Aquinas). He argued that developing our nature in the right way would lead to human fulfillment and happiness. This can be done by living the moral life, which means practicing the virtues. For example, if we live lives of honesty and moderation, just to take two popular examples, these virtues will lead to fulfillment, whereas if we live lives of dishonesty and of excess, this will lead to lack of fulfillment, dysfunction, even misery. This is also how one figures out whether a particular practice is moral or not—by seeing whether it helps to fulfill one's function, and whether it leads to happiness and fulfillment. Aquinas expanded Aristotle's basic account to argue that man's final end is not to be sought in anything belonging to this life, but is to be found in the enjoyment of an eternal relationship with God in the next life, what he called "the beatific vision of God."

Another important consequence of this view is that human beings must be understood as differing in kind, and not just in degree, from other species, by virtue of the fact that we have reason and free will, that we are moral agents, that we are created by God for a moral purpose, and to enjoy a final relationship with him. In this sense, we are the center of creation, and are special in the eyes of God in comparison with other species. This particular teleological view of human beings and their place in nature—that God created man with a certain nature, that this nature can be properly or improperly developed, that the correct development involves morality and leads to happiness, and that human beings differ in kind from other species—all of these ideas would be challenged by the theory of evolution in the nineteenth century.

We see emerging around the time of St. Thomas Aquinas, and in the work of other medieval thinkers from a variety of backgrounds, a combination of revealed theology, philosophy, and science (natural philosophy) as a way of thinking about the big questions of human existence, and the meaning of life. In fact, St. Thomas argued that we needed a combination of reason and of revealed theology to know the truth about God and about society. The articles of faith, such as the Trinity and the Incarnation, are beyond the comprehension of the human mind, and we have to accept these mysteries in faith. But the existence of God is something we can work out through reason, as is the natural moral law. Of course, there are often tensions, problems, and questions of interpretation raised by the interaction between philosophy and theology (and science too), but medieval thinkers accepted that any difficulties could be resolved, and that the three disciplines could work together profitably to help us understand God's creation, and our place in it.

All of this was before the Protestant Reformation, and so there was only the Catholic religion in the West; so there were no denominational conflicts concerning biblical interpretation, doctrine, or Church authority, and it was much easier for the disciplines to work together. In addition, questions about the truth of Christianity as a whole were less likely to occur, as were problems of Christianity clashing with other areas, such as natural philosophy (science), or even with philosophy itself. Nevertheless, one can see that in the combination of revealed theology, philosophy, and natural philosophy (science), there was the potential for problems to occur later on. If, for instance, circumstances were to change so that we were dealing with many religious denominations, with an increased perception of science as an independent discipline, and also with a growing atheistic approach to reality. Developments like these would not only set the stage for interesting debate, but also for conflict! Of course, circumstances did change!

It is important to note before moving on that, although Christianity has often had an uneasy relationship with science, there are some thinkers who argue that it was actually the dominance of Christianity that made the rise of science possible. Stanley Jaki argues that there is a reason that science developed and flourished in the West and not in the East, and that this reason was the dominance of a Christian culture.[15] According to Jaki, a Christian culture emphasized ideas that were hospitable to science, such as the ones just discussed: human beings are rational creatures made in the image of God (*imago dei*), the universe is intelligible, the value of nature in itself (Eastern religions often had a negative view of nature), the view that all truth is one, and so forth. Jaki believes that these ideas played an important role in the development of science, especially when we take into account that for most of history the vast majority of major scientists were Christians, who saw themselves as studying God's handiwork in nature, and who frequently argued that the intricate workings of nature, which they were continually learning about, were evidence of the existence of God.

The Protestant Reformation

Before we move on to look at the work of Galileo and Newton, and its implications for our concerns in this book, we need to emphasize a few developments that emerged during the Protestant Reformation that were important for the subsequent path of the religion-science relationship. The Protestant Reformation began in 1517 when Martin Luther nailed his ninety-five Theses to the church door in Wittenberg, Germany. Luther was complaining, in particular, about the practice in the Catholic Church of selling indulgences to the faithful. The Catholic Church teaches that in some circumstances the Church can grant an indulgence to a sinner; the indulgence involves remission of the temporal punishment that is attached to a sin that has already been forgiven. The teaching surrounding indulgences was much abused in Luther's time, and there was a widespread practice of selling indulgences to the faithful as a way of raising money, in this case to rebuild St. Peter's in Rome. Luther felt that many church activities had become important for their ability to generate money, rather than for any spiritual benefit they might give, and that they were especially aimed at the poor and vulnerable. To make a long story very short, Luther's protest escalated over the next 10 years, and he ended up being excommunicated from the Catholic Church, surrounded by much social, cultural, and religious unrest; his "protest" set the events in motion that eventually led to the founding of a new version of Christianity, Protestantism.

Some of the main beliefs of Protestantism typically are: a rejection of the Apostolic succession (the foundation for the belief that the Pope is the successor of St. Peter), and therefore of papal authority; an emphasis on scripture as the only source of revealed truth (and not church tradition or the papacy); the doctrine of justification by grace through faith alone, which means that God restored human beings to a right relationship with himself, and this is brought about by the faith of the individual in the sacrifice of Christ, not by good works. The Protestant religion also supports only two sacraments, baptism and communion (against the Catholic Church's seven). The Protestant view is often summarized by appeal to the "five solas" (in Latin): *sola fide* (by faith alone); *sola scriptura* (by scripture alone); *sola gratia* (by grace alone); *sola christus* (by Christ alone); and *soli deo gloria* (glory to God alone). Luther was joined in his protest at various stages over the following years, and in different ways, by theologians like John Calvin, Thomas Cranmer, and Ulrich Zwingli, among many others, who, although united in their opposition to, and sometimes hatred of, Catholicism, nevertheless had sharp disagreements among themselves (e.g., over the meaning of the Eucharist).

So, by the year 1700, we had a rival to Catholicism, and this rival was itself split into various denominations, such as Lutheranism, Anabaptism, Presbyterianism, Calvinism, Puritanism, Congregationalism, Anglicanism, Methodism, and so forth. So, the stage was now set, as it were, for religious divisions and tensions, and eventually conflict among these denominations and Catholicism, as well as between the various new denominations themselves. The establishment of individual denominations of Protestantism in various European countries (including Germany, Holland, Switzerland, and England) did not happen easily. As we know from the history of the Reformation, it led to violent, bitter struggles in many countries and communities over the next years, and showed a very ugly side to religion, the side of violence and civil unrest. This by itself made later generations suspicious of religions and their disagreements, and this fact had crucial significance, not only in the way various thinkers thought about the relationship between religion and science, but also for the development of the modern political state.

We need to highlight several points that came out of the Reformation disputes. The first is the differences that emerged between Catholicism and Protestantism over scripture. One of the central points of contention was who had the authority to interpret scripture. The Catholic Church held the view that the Bible was the revealed word of God, but that it needed to be interpreted for the mass of believers by the Pope and the Bishops. The Church would take into account also ideas from Church tradition, and the works of key figures over the centuries, like the Church fathers, and St. Augustine and St. Thomas. Luther, and the Protestant reformers, rejected this view. They proposed that individual believers could go directly to the scriptures, read and understand them, and guide their lives and behavior in accordance with their teachings. This approach, of course, required that the Bible be available in the language of each country, but it also required that the text be read in a fairly literal way in order to ensure that there was good uniformity of interpretation among believers. And so the Protestant reformers adopted a special focus on the Bible (*sola scriptura*) that required a fairly literal reading of the text. Although all traditions accepted that the Bible also has passages that are meant to be read metaphorically and allegorically, nevertheless the Protestant traditions adopted a fairly literal approach to most of the Bible, holding that it was not especially difficult to tell which passages were meant to be metaphorical and which were meant to be literal, although, crucially, there is obviously room for some disagreement about which passages are which. For example, should we read the account of creation in Genesis literally or metaphorically? Later, this matter would become contentious, since it was accepted that not everything described in the Bible was meant in a literal way. But the Protestant reformers held that in general this was not a difficult problem to solve. This approach would have important implications when a scientific theory, such as evolution, came along which seemed to challenge a literal reading of some parts of scripture.

The notions of *sola fide* and *sola christus* were also momentous. The Protestant reformers placed a great deal of emphasis on the notion that all one needed was faith in Jesus Christ as being sent by God to insure salvation for our souls. One did not need a teaching authority, such as the Catholic Church, to explain, support, and ratify one's faith, although Protestants did not reject tradition by any means. But this emphasis on faith in Jesus as savior meant that the reformers were suspicious of the attempt by some to support their religious worldview by reason. Luther was often suspicious of both philosophy and science, seeing them as yet more worldly goods that could get in the way of true faith (he was especially critical of the scholastic philosophy of Aquinas). Later Protestant thinkers were suspicious of attempts to argue for the rationality of religion, seeing it as a sop to the Enlightenment project, rather than as a rational requirement of genuine religion. Their view was that the Bible teaches that one is justified by faith alone, and that one does not need to worry about rational arguments, or about giving a philosophical justification for one's religious beliefs. This does not mean that one can believe whatever one likes;

we have the revealed word of God already in the scriptures, and this is a sufficient guide for us. Indeed, Calvin argued not only that reason itself was compromised by sin, but also that people are born with an innate disposition to believe in God (*sensus divinitatis*), a disposition some suppress due to the effects of sin.

These thinkers held that it is appropriate to think philosophically about several difficult concepts in the Bible, such as the Incarnation or the Resurrection or the meaning of the Eucharist (as they did themselves), but this is not the same thing as putting reason above your faith, and subjecting your faith to interrogation by reason. It must be stressed that many of these points are a matter of emphasis in different religions, and that the Catholic view (outside of the political context of the Reformation) could agree with much of this too (e.g., about the proper relationship of philosophy to theology). Nevertheless, these matters became significant for the way in which religion responded to science later on, because the Protestant traditions in general downplayed reason and elevated faith, and were consequently reluctant to allow any questioning of biblical passages or teachings. This led some to look upon science with suspicion, because it was a branch of reason, and, later on, often seen as a symbol of an Enlightenment way of looking at things, a way that was usually hostile to religion.

A third point to draw attention to is that the Reformation also gave us the fact of religious pluralism. After the Reformation, we now had a diversity of religions, as we have noted, along with the still powerful and influential Catholic Church (indeed the Catholic Church had launched in response a movement that became known as "The Counter-Reformation"). These religions now had different approaches to the Bible, different doctrinal teachings, different paths to and accounts of salvation, different attitudes to philosophy. Not only did this as a practical matter set up the possibility of conflict (especially when allied with other political and social issues, which had happened in the wars of the Reformation), but it also meant that religion was more ripe in general for clashing with science as science developed over the next 200 years. And let us not forget that when the Enlightenment came along (which we shall consider later), it gave rise to various worldviews of its own, including what we would now describe as more liberal religious worldviews, as well as various atheistic and secularist approaches, all of which had the effect of increasing the potential for conflict with more established religious worldviews.

The Galileo controversy of the seventeenth century

One scientist whose genius came to fruition during all of this ferment was Italian astronomer, Galileo Galilei, and his revolutionary research eventually led him into trouble with Church authorities. By 1600, Galileo's work had convinced him that Polish astronomer, Copernicus's (1473–1543) theory of planetary motion—the heliocentric theory—was correct (presented in Copernicus's *De revolutionibus*). This theory proposed that the earth revolved around the sun, and that the sun was the center of the universe (and so the geocentric theory, proposed by Greek astronomer, Ptolemy, in the second century, was wrong). Although heliocentricism had been around a long time, and had generated debate among astronomers (German astronomer, Johannes Kepler supported it, but Danish astronomer, Tycho Brahe, did not), it had little influence in the wider world. But Galileo had obtained a telescope made in Holland around 1608, and, realizing its potential for work in astronomy, constructed a much larger instrument, which allowed him to study the heavens. The telescope enabled astronomers to look beyond the earth in a meaningful way for the first time, and in that sense it must go down as one of the most significant inventions of all time. Among the observations recorded by Galileo included the mountains and valleys of the moon, four of the moons of Jupiter, sunspots, and the phases of Venus. Over time, he came to accept Copernicus's view that the earth revolved around the sun, but he knew that he did not have conclusive proof. Indeed, looking back on it now, it is quite ironic that much of Galileo's evidence for the heliocentric theory turned out to be wrong (e.g., he claimed that the tides were caused by the earth's motion, whereas it is, in fact, the gravitational pull of the moon and the sun that causes the tides, a conclusion later suggested by Newton).

As everyone knows, Galileo's views led him into conflict with the authorities in the Catholic Church. As well as being an affront to common sense, the heliocentric theory seemed to contradict biblical passages that indicated that the earth was at rest in the center of the universe, and that the sun revolves around the earth from east to west. Passages frequently cited to criticize Galileo's views were Joshua 10.12–14, Psalm 19.4–6, which suggests that the sun is in motion, and Psalm 104.5, which says that the earth does not move. As Richard Blackwell has noted in a definitive study of the affair, the subsequent controversy was made all the more intense by the fact that it took place shortly after the Reformation, when the Catholic Church was especially sensitive, not just about questions concerning the interpretation of Scripture, but also about who has the final authority on this matter.[16] As we have seen above, this had been a contentious issue during the Reformation. At the Council of Trent in 1546, the Catholic Church declared that the Pope and the Bishops had the final say in matters of faith and morals, which included questions about biblical interpretation.

Galileo was called to the Vatican to answer charges about his views, and was put on trial by the Church in 1616 (at this time the Pope was also the civil ruler of the Papal States, in which Galileo lived). He attempted to defend the heliocentric view by appealing to the views of St. Augustine, mentioned earlier, and by appealing to the distinction between literal and metaphorical uses of language in the Bible. Unfortunately, the Copernican theory fell into the gray area that Augustine had worried about. The Vatican Cardinal dealing with the matter, Cardinal Bellermine, argued that the best scientific evidence of the day regarded the heliocentric view as far from conclusive, and he urged Galileo to present his view as a hypothesis, a proposal for discussion, but not to advocate it as fact. Eventually, the Vatican Congregation of the Holy Office officially declared that the heliocentric view was false because it was contrary to Scripture, and Pope Paul V accepted this recommendation.

All was quiet for the next few years. However, in 1631, Galileo published his famous book, *Dialogue Concerning the Two Chief World Systems*, which caused quite a stir. The book debated the merits of the heliocentric theory versus the Ptolemaic theory, with the argument clearly favoring the heliocentric position. This led to a new trial in 1633, not concerning which theory was true, according to Blackwell, but concerning whether or not Galileo had violated the earlier injunction not to promote the heliocentric theory. At this time the new Pope Urban VIII was under pressure from within the Vatican to show that he was dealing effectively with dissent. This political reality contributed to the Church taking a hard line on Galileo (an example of how political and social matters are very often intertwined with religious matters). He was found guilty, and sentenced to house arrest for the rest of his life.

It is important to remind ourselves of the details of the Galileo affair for this generation of readers interested in the discussion surrounding religion and science for a number of reasons. First, it is important to dispel the many myths about the affair, and to know what actually happened. Second, Galileo is now the poster child for the conflict model of the relationship between religion and science! The affair gave the Catholic Church in particular a bad name, at least in the eyes of secularists, naturalists, and those hostile to religion. The Galileo affair is the case most frequently cited by those who wish to show that religion and science cannot work together. Third, the case suggested to many religious believers a good principle for dealing with apparent conflicts between science and religion. It is based on St. Augustine's approach that in general we should leave scientists to do their work, while accepting the view that all truth is one, and that, although the details of how God might have created the universe and the various species could be argued about, the underlying truths were what really mattered. This would become a key way of approaching science and religion in the modern era. Fourth, the Catholic Church in particular was reluctant to provoke further arguments with scientists, and adopted a general position of giving them greater latitude in the future.

Galileo and Newton, and the development of science

It is commonly agreed that we see significant development in the discipline of science, and in the scientific method, in the work of both Galileo and Sir Isaac Newton (1643–1727), and other scientists of this time. Let us first describe this change and how it came about, and then we will discuss its implications. In 1638, Galileo published his last book, *Two New Sciences*, and it led to him being called "the father of modern physics" (the new sciences were "strength of materials" and "motions of objects"). His ideas defined a new approach to studying the physical realm. Galileo held that the book of nature was written in mathematics, by which he meant that nature, understood as small particles related in uniform ways, and changing through motion, exhibited physical and mathematical relationships that could be identified and studied. Nature was increasingly understood as consisting of small particles of matter, which operated according to the laws of physics; the developing discipline of science would progressively identify these laws, and also probe further into the mathematical laws, which seem to be present in the architecture of the universe.

This understanding of the universe contributed significantly to the development of the scientific method. The discipline of science gradually became a way of studying the physical universe on a quite practical level. This was the way Galileo himself did science—he would observe things, such as the motion and positions of various planets; he would then carry out various experiments;

these would lead him to form different hypotheses aimed at explaining the "how" of what he was working on (how the planets move in relation to each other, for instance); he would then test these hypotheses in various ways, by making predictions based upon them, by having other scientists verify them, and so forth. Although fascinating in itself, this was a quite practical, often tedious, even pedestrian, way of gathering information, and it was a method that gradually left the larger questions—the "why" questions—in the background. It was not that these questions were not important, or that the scientists were not interested in them (they were), it was simply that they seemed to be outside the domain of the new scientific method. In short, the "why" questions were beginning, within the developing discipline of science, to take a back seat to the "how" questions. It took a while for scientists like Galileo to see this, for him to appreciate that he could explain "how" the earth moved, but not why it did. (Yet, the temptation to comment on the "why" question is also very strong, one Galileo himself could not resist!) It seems that this relegation of the "why" questions to the background of scientific investigation occurred because of the way science progressed, and the way its subject matter became more clearly defined, and was not the result of a conscious decision by scientists to push "why" questions out of science. Various scientists over time began to see that their methods and subject matter did not equip them to answer "why" questions, despite the temptation, even today, to talk sometimes as if they have some special authority to address the "why" questions because of their expertise with the "how" questions.

The work of Newton was also indispensable to the progress of science. Newton developed a widely acclaimed mechanical view of the operations of nature in his *Principia Mathematica* (1687). This work described the structure of the physical universe in terms of an increasingly mechanical model, and covered the notions of the movement of bodies according to mathematical and physical laws, which Newton explained and demonstrated (his second law of motion, for instance, says that the force of a body is equal to the mass of the object multiplied by its acceleration). He offered ground-breaking views of the nature of bodies, on motion, rest and force, on the attraction of bodies in relation to each other (the law of gravity), and, as a pioneer in the development of calculus, was one of the greatest mathematicians the world has seen.[17] Newton's discoveries encouraged the view of the universe as a machine, whose parts and interrelationships could be studied using the tools of reason and mathematics. But Newton himself was careful to distinguish between the "how" questions and the "why" questions, noting that while gravity can explain the motions of the planets, it cannot explain who set the planets in motion. Newton's development of both the scientific method, and his scientific discoveries, had a profound impact on the development of the discipline over the next few centuries.

The implications of this overall approach to science were important. First, it meant that the new developments in science had the gradual effect of removing teleology from the discipline. As noted, science became more focused on how things worked, rather than on the larger "why" questions, yet Newton clearly saw the difference, and like many scientists, could not help thinking about the "why" questions in his writings on religion. In an important sense, the "why" questions are always there even if one is (as in science) almost exclusively focused on the "how" questions. But a consequence of focusing on the "how" questions meant that Aristotle's four causes no longer dominated scientific inquiry; the final cause, in particular, dealing with the purposes of things, was relegated to the background. Scientists became concerned with describing *how* something works—in what way the planets move, for example, and how to support their theories with evidence, but it did not seem as if the question *why* they moved in one way rather than another was now in their domain, because it was not a question *their particular method* could address. It is still obviously a crucial question, but it belongs in the domains of philosophy and religion, not science.

This led directly to the second implication, which is that science began to carve itself out as a separate discipline. It was no longer intermingled with philosophy and religion (or alchemy, a blend of many different disciplinary approaches common up to at least the eighteenth century, and practiced by many scientists, including Newton) but was now increasingly regarded as a distinct subject matter and method in its own right. This meant that its domain became more restricted than it had been; it also meant that scientists would have to leave the larger questions (including those involving teleology) to others. Another consequence of this was that scientists were now seeking and to some extent were gaining a certain independence to do their own work in their own way. This separation would work fine, and perhaps to the benefit of all, until science came up with the occasional theory (e.g., evolution) that seemed to have significant implications for, and to perhaps impinge on, matters *outside* of science, an issue that has come down to us today.

There is one other important implication. The beginnings of a naturalistic worldview are latent in the approach of Galileo and Newton, though it was not until later that this point was brought out, and only partially at that. But the idea that the universe is particles in motion was a forerunner to modern atomic theory, and contains the basis for a rejection of Aristotle's account of substance, matter, and form. The idea that nature is particles in motion, operating according to scientific laws, and that nature is a law-abiding machine, also suggested to later thinkers of the Enlightenment (as we will see presently) that perhaps all of reality is like this, including living things, including human beings. Newton did not think that the soul, for example, or that the human mind, consisted of particles in motion. He thought the soul was an incorporeal substance that was outside the domain of science. He rejected the view that human consciousness could be approached and studied by means of the scientific method. But it was not long before some who were rightly enamored of this powerful new method began to reexamine these questions, and to push science in a naturalistic direction.

Eighteenth-century developments

A number of intriguing developments in the eighteenth century—the age of Enlightenment—led to the further popularity of the naturalistic approach to reality and to a naturalistic interpretation of science. We must emphasize again that these developments did not happen as neatly as the historians often state them, that many of them overlapped, that some were undeveloped in certain thinkers, that they were the subject of contentious debate and critique all along the way, and that many of them did not gain a significant foothold in intellectual or political culture. Nevertheless, all were important and their influence is especially evident in the twentieth century (as we will see in the next chapter).

Before we look at some trends in the eighteenth century itself, we should briefly mention as background a few key ideas from the previous century in the work of French philosopher, René Descartes (1596–1650). Descartes is often described as the father of modern philosophy. This is because he was committed to the power of reason to understand reality, was a strong supporter of mathematics and science, and was trying to get beyond medieval philosophy, which he thought involved too much of a blend of philosophy and theology. Descartes is famous for his work in epistemology, for his attempt to show, after a methodological detour though various skeptical arguments (including the evil genius argument), that human knowledge is reliable and objective. But it is his work on the body/mind problem that is most relevant for the topic of religion and science. Philosophers had long pondered the relationship of the body (by which they mean the brain) to the mind. The "mind" refers to consciousness, thoughts, reasoning ability, logic, memories, imagination, etc. The body refers to the physical stuff of the brain such as the cortexes, neurons, cells, membranes, dendrites, etc. Descartes defended the view known as substance dualism, which holds that the mind is a nonphysical, mental, spiritual substance, the seat of our consciousness, memories, and personal identity.[18] This view is opposed to materialism, the view that the human mind is either completely physical, or else that it depends upon the physical (we will look at these views in more detail in Chapter 5). Descartes's view was sophisticated and intriguing, and generated a debate on the nature of the human person, rather than on the nature of the physical universe, the usual concern of science at this time. It raised the question of whether the human person is also a totally physical being, whose properties could, at least in principle, be explained by the scientific method. Descartes argued that human beings had a body and a mind, and that the mind was not reducible to (could not be explained in terms of) the brain, but he held that other animals were complex machines, which did not have nonphysical minds. It was only a matter of time before some thinkers would claim that he was right about other animals but wrong about human beings—because we too are just physical machines and so some version of materialism must be true.

Two people who defended this materialist view in the eighteenth century were French thinkers, Baron D'Holbach (1723–1789) and Pierre Laplace (1749–1827). Indeed, both are forerunners of the naturalistic/secularist view that we will consider in the next chapter. D'Holbach wrote books arguing for the materiality of nature. He was particularly interested in the body/mind question, and presented a theoretical argument that the mind was completely physical in nature. D'Holbach even argued that human beings do not have free will because "the faculties which are called intellectual, and those qualities which are styled moral, have been explained in a manner purely physical and natural ... [our] ideas come to [us] involuntarily ... The will is a modification of the brain, by which it is disposed to action ..."[19] Laplace adopted a similar worldview, arguing that nature could be explained in completely naturalistic terms, operating according to the laws of science, and that science was the tool for unlocking all of the mysteries of nature, including those associated with the existence of life, and the nature of the human species. He went on to propose *causal determinism* about human actions, the view that there is no free will and that all events in the universe, including human actions, are caused by prior states of the universe, operating according to the laws of science. When Napoleon asked Laplace why his book on the natural systems of the universe did not mention God, Laplace is supposed to have replied: "I have no need of that hypothesis!" Neither D'Holbach nor Laplace fully appreciated some of the difficulties facing their views, especially concerning the wider implications of the denial of free will for the arrangement of society, for our understanding of the meaning of life. Nevertheless, their views became attractive especially to those who were interested in developing some alternative account of the human person over the religious account.

Other significant French thinkers who held similar views were Denis Diderot (1713–1784) and Julien Offray de La Mettrie (1709–1751). Diderot was one of the chief editors of the French *Encyclopedie* of the eighteenth century, supposed to be the definitive word on latest matters in philosophy, arts, and science. It proved to be an extremely controversial work because of the views of its various authors on religion, politics, and morality, which challenged the established views of the day. Diderot's ideas were an early version of a thoroughgoing naturalism. He saw nature basically as matter in motion, and hypothesized a materialist theory of living things, including human beings, going so far as to agree with D'Holbach and others that the human mind was but a property of the brain. La Mettrie argued that the soul was really produced from matter, thereby giving metaphysical priority to the body in the study of human life, and to science in the study of reality (rather than to philosophy or theology). His book, *Man a Machine* (1748) expressed the view (now becoming familiar) that human beings are totally physical beings, and that science is the best way to approach the study of human behavior. This was a significant work because La Mettrie argued that human actions were ultimately determined by prior causes from both nature and the structure of the brain, albeit in a very sophisticated way that we don't yet understand. He did make an attempt at offering a theoretical account of how he thought this might work, an account which relied on emphasizing the similarities between human and animal characteristics and behavior. La Mettrie expresses his conclusion thus: "Now look, all the faculties of the soul depend so much on the proper organization of the brain and of the entire body, since these faculties are obviously just this organized brain itself, there is a well-enlightened machine!"[20]

Although these ideas were undoubtedly materialist and were advanced to support what we would now describe as a secularist account of reality, they also contributed to the development of a new way of looking at nature and the universe among those who were also religious believers, a view which became known as deism. After Newton, many thinkers began to look at the universe as a giant machine operating according to fixed laws.[21] This approach need not deny that God is the creator of the universe, but most versions of this deistic view either denied or downplayed any involvement for God in the workings of the universe after it had been created. Deism is opposed to theism, the traditional view that God continues working in the world in various ways after the creation. The deists found attractive the idea that God created the world, and then stood back as it were and let it develop and change on its own. God is regarded as the mechanic or the clock maker who set things in motion, but who then leaves them to their own devices. This view was attractive because it placed an emphasis on reason, morality, and what was sometimes called natural religion (the idea that human beings have a spiritual dimension which can find expression in different ways), while at the same time downplaying, relegating to the background, or sometimes denying outright, revealed theology and religious doctrines. Deists were therefore seen as quite radical and liberal, and their views were sometimes regarded as a kind of disguised atheism. This is because, as English philosopher, Samuel Clarke (1675–1729) argued, deism inevitably leads to the downplaying of God and God's plan because the idea of nature as a machine or as a clock conveys the view that God is not necessary for the operation of the universe. Clarke argued that this view was wrong because there is no such thing as "the course of nature"; there is only intelligence, either God's or ours, operating on the laws of nature.[22] Deism is in opposition to Clarke's view (also St. Thomas's view) that God sustains the universe in existence at all times, and is immanent in creation.

Deism was also attractive in the eighteenth-century climate because it promoted the position that reason could affirm that God was the creator of the universe (so it was not really atheism), but in placing the emphasis on reason rather than revelation, it was thought that it could transcend religious divisions by focusing on a common core of religious beliefs, and it could also be hospitable to science. It was held by a number of influential figures including Voltaire (who argued stridently that there was no need for the Church), Thomas Hobbes, Jean Jacques Rousseau, possibly even John Locke. Deist views were also to have phenomenal significance in political history, influencing the founding fathers of the United States, including Thomas Jefferson, Benjamin Franklin (who, in his autobiography, noted a list of truths one can know about God from reason alone), and possibly George Washington.[23] Although deism waned in the twentieth century, it was a significant view because it suggested a way that religion and science might be compatible, while at the same time emphasizing both rational religion and the independence of science, two themes that are still with us today.

The nineteenth century: Darwin and Freud

Charles Darwin published his book, *On the Origin of Species*, in 1859, and it quickly became one of the most significant scientific works of all time. Darwin presented in this book his theory of evolution, aimed at explaining the origin and development of the various species of plants, insects, and animals, including *Homo sapiens*, the human species. Every now and again in history a theory comes along in science that appears to have great significance outside of science. Such is the case with evolution, for it appears to have some serious implications for religion, philosophy, and ethics, implications that we are still trying to draw out and understand better. Yet it is important to keep distinct the scientific claims of the theory, and the scientific evidence to support these claims, from conclusions we might further draw in philosophical reflection upon these scientific claims (if we can conclude anything with any degree of probability). This distinction has not always been observed or recognized, of course, and the temptation (especially among prominent scientists) to speculate beyond the scientific evidence can often prove irresistible, as it did even to Darwin himself.

We will provide a full discussion of evolution in Chapter 4, but a few overview points here will be helpful in order to establish its significance in the history of the relationship between religion and science. We need to see how it set the stage, coupled with other ideas (such as materialism, secularism, and developments in psychology), for twentieth-century trends that largely shape the subject matter of the debate today. Darwin was fascinated by how species change and develop new features, and also by how they come into existence in the first place. His theory challenged the prevailing view of the origin of species—the fixity of species—that species were created just as they are by God, and that there was little variation over time in the basic types. Darwin's research led him to argue that species develop their biological structures over time by natural selection, the view that favorable traits are passed on to future generations, and eventually dominate, and unfavorable traits diminish over time. This is the idea that the process of evolution—the struggle for existence in a particular environment involving various species with their specific biological structures—favors those species best able to cope with their environmental conditions. Those who are the "fittest" in this sense survive best because their inherited traits enable them to cope best, given the environment they find themselves in, and the species with which they have to compete. The same process of "survival of the fittest" (a phrase Darwin adopted from Herbert Spencer) applies to human beings too. Just like other species, our species of *Homo sapiens* survived because our particular characteristics enabled us to survive in our particular environment.

Darwin addressed the question of how we get substantially different species in the first place, such as plants, elephants, chimps, and human beings. This led him to the thesis known as macroevolution—the view that *all* species have common ancestors, or are genetically related; the theory of evolution claims that all of the present species in the world evolved from common ancestors, right back to the very first life-forms, which some speculate were one-celled organisms that appeared between 4 and 5 billion years ago. Gradually, more complex life-forms developed over time, life-forms that are genetically related to the more simple life-forms. This is a key claim of the theory of evolution, and the one that has often generated controversy. The theory holds that all life-forms, including all plant and animal species, are *genetically related* to each other in the sense that they all share common ancestors.

Although we will look at the scientific details of the theory and the evidence for the theory in more detail in Chapter 4, the theory raised what many regarded as uncomfortable questions for religion. The first is that it represents a challenge to a fairly literal reading of the book of Genesis, which says that God created the species directly as it were, that no gradual process of development was involved. If the theory of evolution is correct about this latter point, then the biblical account cannot be literally true. Many, therefore, saw the theory of evolution as an attack on the Bible, some as a hostile attack, others as a mistaken scientific hypothesis that needed to be quickly rejected. A second implication is that Darwin appears to be suggesting that the processes of evolution occur by blind chance and randomness, that there is no design involved in the origin of the species. This meant that the existence of the human species was therefore an accident. The theory seemed to be saying that man did not have to evolve, that if things had gone a little differently in natural history we would not exist, or we could have ended up with a different biological structure than the one we have (and perhaps a different form of consciousness, different type of intelligence, etc.). The theory also suggests that man is not special in the way most religions teach, because *Homo sapiens* is now genetically related to other species, and emerged from the same random process that produced them. In short, the theory of evolution suggests that human beings differ in degree, but not in kind, from other species.

There was a mixed reaction to the theory of evolution as a result of these radical implications. Many religious believers rejected it on one or a combination of two grounds: first, that it conflicted with the Bible, and so could not be true; second, from the scientific point of view, many argued that the theory was nothing more than a series of speculations for which there was little convincing empirical evidence. Many religious thinkers struggled with how to respond to it from the point of view of their particular theologies, and even today theologians have not fully come to terms with this matter. But, mainstream Protestant, Jewish, and Catholic thinkers thought there could be some accommodation if the theory turned out to be true, along the lines suggested earlier by St. Augustine.[24]

The theory generated much discussion within science, as one might expect, and distinguished scientists, such as Lord Kelvin, criticized the theory. Others thought it left too many questions unanswered, even if there was some truth to it; for example, it had nothing to say about human consciousness, reason and free will, the key features of humanity. In addition, it was hard for many to accept that any process so complex as this could not be the result of design. Asa Gray, the leading American botanist, accepted the theory, but argued that the whole process was compatible with divine guidance. Others, such as Darwin's friend, Thomas Huxley, saw it as evidence that the religious view of the world, especially the Bible, was not true. Evolution, therefore, came into conflict with religion almost immediately, and gave fuel to the conflict model.

While all this was going on in biology, Sigmund Freud was developing some revolutionary ideas about the human mind. These ideas were to have enormous influence, even though many of them are difficult to take seriously, and have been largely discredited with the passage of time. Writing in Vienna, Freud suggested that the human mind, which had resisted explanation, could be studied scientifically. But Freud was not talking about dissecting and studying the organ of the brain; he was talking about trying to discover psychological laws based on a study of human behavior, coupled with what little was known about the brain and its pathologies. Freud was embarking on a notoriously difficult and perhaps necessarily speculative enterprise.

In *The Interpretation of Dreams* (1900), Freud proposed that the mind was divided into two parts, the conscious mind and the unconscious mind.

He argued that the unconscious mind was primarily formed during early childhood by environment and family upbringing, and it in turn had a significant influence on our conscious states and beliefs. This was a radical thesis, because it challenged the prevailing view that our conscious states and beliefs are significantly under our control. The established view was that our free will enables us to have a large degree of power over various experiences and events in our lives so that these experiences and events, and the human actions surrounding them, cannot be said to be caused in any meaningful scientific sense. But Freud was proposing that the unconscious mind was in fact causing many of our conscious states in ways that we did not realize.

This was true, in particular, in the area of mental illness, such as neuroses (mental imbalances, leading to patient distress that is often expressed in feelings of anxiety). Freud argued that neuroses (e.g., phobias) are often caused by traumas in early childhood that are repressed or buried in the unconscious mind, but that then occasionally intrude into our conscious lives. Finding a way to access these repressions might provide a means for a patient to overcome them. Freud developed a new method, called psychoanalysis, aimed at unlocking these traumas, and hopefully curing them by causing the patient to confront them (sometimes our dreams are expressions of our unconscious as well). Psychoanalytic techniques included encouraging the patient to talk about their feelings and problems, as well as transference (projecting feelings onto the analyst, who often became the new "priest"), and sometimes hypnosis. Freud then suggested that many of our normal states of consciousness, including our attitudes, beliefs, and moral customs, are formed in essentially the same way. Needless to say, all of this was extremely nebulous, lacked detailed illustrations, and did not seem to be very scientific. His views proved very controversial because, as many have argued, there are too many unknown variables present for Freud's views to be tested practically, and many critics also questioned whether his psychological techniques could actually help people.

Nevertheless, Freud's influence was significant because it gave credence to the view that the mind could be studied scientifically, and so perhaps we are closer than we realize to unlocking the mysteries of the mind, and therefore of much of human life (including the origin and influence of our most cherished beliefs and attitudes). His views also clearly supported a naturalistic account of human life; indeed Freud himself was a strong atheist, and became well known for arguing that religious belief is not rational. He did not, however, engage the arguments for the existence of God, or some of the other arguments for the rationality of religious belief, but simply assumed (in his book *The Future of an*

Illusion) that they were unsuccessful, and that religion did not hold up to the test of reason. His approach, therefore, is negative in the sense that he does not engage the question of the truth of religious beliefs, but aims to show that they are produced by human psychology; he never considers the positive side of religious beliefs, their value in human life, and the irrepressible spiritual side of our personalities. He aims instead for a reductionist approach that attempts to explain all of the facets of religion in terms of set of vague claims about the development of the human mind in early life.

Freud held that religious beliefs are based on the need for and respect for a father figure (God), and that they may also result from attempts to deal with the experiences of guilt and shame that regularly occur in our lives. He went as far as to claim that religion is a form of neurosis. Religious beliefs must have "a psychical origin," must be a product of our deepest emotional states, and, therefore, are really illusions. He defined an illusion as a belief based on wish-fulfillment that disregards its relations to reality. Religious illusions have their origin in the need for a father figure who will protect us throughout life, and who also offers us comfort, supports our moral values, and promises a future life. (Ironically, some recent thinkers have argued that atheism may also have psychological origins rooted in various neuroses associated with the absence of a good father.[25])

Although it might be hard for many to take such views seriously, especially since they are little more than assertions rather than arguments backed up by empirical research, Freud's general approach has proved attractive, particularly to those atheists seeking an alternative explanation for the origin and power of the religious worldview in the lives of human beings. It has often been suggested, after Freud, that religious beliefs have a psychological cause, yet demonstrating this point in a reasonable and convincing way is quite another matter, especially in a way that would also adequately explain the positive effect of religion in the lives of so many millions of people (i.e., that explains why what are supposed to be false beliefs can be so beneficial morally and so enormously satisfying). This perhaps explains why the influence of Freud's theory of the psychological origin of religion has waned.

Over the course of our survey of the important moments in the history of the relationship between religion and science, we have seen the surfacing of many of the important concepts and themes that are at the forefront of the debate today between the two subjects. These themes include the following: the concept of teleology, and the closely related question of design in nature, a topic of great significance for the meaning of life; the medieval conception of

God and the beliefs that there is a rational basis to religion, that nature is intelligible, and that science is to be welcomed in the quest for human knowledge; the differences between Catholics and Protestants after the Reformation, with regard to the interpretation of scripture, the relationship between faith and reason, and the role of philosophy and science in the understanding of God's creation; the emergence of science as a discipline, and the development of the scientific method, in the seventeenth century, as well as the fact that pioneering scientists believed that religion and science operate best when in dialogue; the surfacing of a more materialist view of man and the universe in a number of thinkers as an alternative to religion, a view science was pressed into service to support, a consequence of which was that the discipline was caught in the middle of the contentious arguments between religious thinkers and materialist thinkers. All of these matters are still with us today; they define the critical issues that are at the heart of many contemporary questions and controversies surrounding religion and science, as we will see in subsequent chapters. In the next chapter, we need to take a more detailed look at modern science: its successes, its claims to objective knowledge, and its relationship in the twentieth century to materialism and secularism in the work of a number of influential thinkers.

Science and Naturalism in the Twentieth Century

Chapter Outline

The success of science	60
The scientific method and objective knowledge	63
Realism versus anti-realism	66
The undermining of truth in the history of science	71
The modern face of science: naturalism	74

We have described "revolutions" in our understanding of both the theories discovered by scientists, and in the development of the scientific method, in our examination of the ideas of leading thinkers in the history of religion and science, and in our overview of how various movements, trends, and pivotal ideas inspired religious and scientific change over the centuries. All of this leads us naturally to focus in this chapter on the current state of science as we move into the twenty-first century. We are not only interested in the success of science, which is obviously an important part of the story, and which has attracted well deserved admiration for the discipline; but, we are also interested in the effects of this success, not only in our everyday lives, but, especially from the point of view of our discussion in this book, for the task of seeking objective knowledge and truth about the universe, and about the human condition.

We need to consider how the tremendous success of science influenced various important thinkers to propose that science might not just be a highly significant and crucial form of knowledge, but that it might be the *only* way to knowledge about the natural world and the universe, and also about all of the so-called ultimate questions of human existence. This view elevates science to a very high status, and over time calls religion into question in its very foundations. It suggests that the religious worldview is false, and in time will be proven so, that it has little to contribute to the quest for human understanding and advancement, to our efforts to answer the ultimate questions. Although religion has been decisively influential throughout human civilization, various thinkers who propose this elevation and extension of science into all areas of life claim that the time has come to start moving beyond religious ways of looking at reality, and to embrace what they regard as the powerful and enlightening discipline of science as an alternative.

After providing a brief overview of the success of the scientific enterprise in modern culture in the first section of this chapter, we shall go on to consider the question of whether the scientific approach to knowledge really gives us objective truth. In particular, we shall consider the anti-realist thesis about knowledge whose proponents claim that all knowledge, including scientific knowledge, is compromised in its claims to objectivity because of the modifying structures of the human mind in the act of knowing. We shall also consider the relevance of the fact that many scientific theories once thought to be objectively true have now been abandoned and replaced with other theories, and whether this will happen with our current theories. This will bring us lastly to consider the relationship today between science and naturalism (secularism). We will illustrate this relationship by a consideration of the work of some leading contemporary naturalists, Richard Dawkins, Carl Sagan and Francis Crick.

The success of science

It is important to provide a brief overview of the great successes of science in a number of different areas in order to remind ourselves of its vast subject matter, its explanatory power, and of why it often claims so much authority in our culture. The most obvious area where science has been extremely successful is in medicine, and the treatment of disease. Many diseases, which were usually fatal to most people in the past, some of which wiped out whole populations in epidemics, have now either been eradicated completely, or can be quite easily cured, such as small pox, tuberculosis, polio, measles, etc. Scientists have also made great strides in the treatment of other recalcitrant diseases, such as cancer, heart disease, lung disease, diabetes, and Parkinson's disease, as well as in the treatment of childhood diseases. Surgeries and the development of drug treatments for almost every type of illness and painful condition have improved in ways unimaginable 100 years ago. The result of all of this is that, in the developed world, which has benefited from the fruits of medical advancement more than anywhere else, the mortality rate has decreased significantly. Infant death has gone from being the norm a few centuries ago, to being quite rare, and people everywhere in the west are living longer. These advances were made possible by scientists who, through hard work, careful experimentation, and testing in their various disciplines, studied disease and its treatment over long periods of time, by means of the scientific method. This collective effort, after much trial and error, and many setbacks, progressively achieved incredible triumphs. Medicine is an area that touches everyone in one way or another, an area where we can all appreciate in our day-to-day lives the great strides of science.

Another obvious realm of scientific advancement is the field of global communications. This includes the development of radio and television, and now more recently of satellite dishes, computers, and the internet. As in medicine, here we see a clear illustration of significant scientific discoveries (e.g., how to transmit pictures and sound through the air), going hand in hand with technological developments that make scientific discoveries practical and useful. Technology often develops right alongside science, and nowadays is an essential part of it, and makes possible the practical application of many scientific discoveries. Advances in the world of global communications have transformed our daily lives as TV and the internet, and the world of the image, have come to dominate modern culture.

Global communications may also be said to include the invention of the engine, and modern forms of transportation. Transportation has changed the world in astonishing ways. Before the invention of machines that made it possible to move people and goods over large distances in short periods of time, most people grew up and raised their own families in the area where they were born. They traveled little because the distances were too large. There was no source of power other than water or wind, and many thought there never would be. But the inventions of the engine, of steam power, of electricity, of the telephone changed the world completely. These inventions, and many more, were made possible because of work in various scientific disciplines and subdisciplines, for example, physics, chemistry, engineering, electronics, computing, and aeronautics. Largely because of the success of science, the world today is truly a global village, a very small place, as different from the time of the eighteenth century as chalk is to cheese. Air travel means that we can be on the other side of the world in a day, a reality that has tremendous business implications alone. Rocketry and advanced aeronautics have enabled us to explore space, and technological breakthroughs (astonishing in their complexity and sophistication but often taken for granted by most of us), like the Hubble telescope, bring us very detailed knowledge about the structure of the galaxies. Scientific breakthroughs, and their practical application through technology, have not only made our lives vastly easier than the lives of people even 50 years ago, but they have also lengthened our lives, and greatly improved our quality of life, at least in the areas of material comfort, food production, medicine, etc. These achievements have not yet spread all over the world, but in the future they will, and it is no longer silly to talk about a time when hunger, for example, will be eliminated.

Yet, despite the undeniable and welcome success of science in so many areas of life, and the subsequent temptation to think that perhaps science can explain everything that needs to be explained—that perhaps science can solve all of our problems (a view we will consider in the next section)—it will no doubt have crossed the minds of many readers that science has given us many problems as well as many benefits. For example, science has given us the threat of nuclear war, the dangers of weapons of mass destruction, as well as from advanced weaponry of all kinds. Science and technology, working hand in hand, make murder on a large scale, like the Holocaust, possible. Some would no doubt extend this point to argue that at least some of the inventions of scientists, such as television, are actually bad for human beings; some may argue that modern culture, in which science and technology are dominant influences, makes us too materialistic, too selfish, and that morality, religion, and spirituality suffer as a result. These are all interesting points of view, but we must note right away that it is not science itself that brings about evils such as war, but it is people using science and technology in the wrong way. Yet it is not quite as simple as that since we know that once something is invented, like gunpowder, it will inevitably be used for evil as well as good. Television makes it possible to watch the news, and political and sporting events, but it also tempts some to become "couch potatoes," watching mindless and mind-numbing talk, entertainment and reality shows, made by those on the other side of the camera—who succumb to the lowest common denominator in modern culture. Cell phones are convenient, but tempt us to drive while using the phone, and to spend too much time on the phone. Eventually, cell phones will have internet access, computing services, and access to TV stations. These kind of scientific advances bring with them a new set of problems for human culture, yet science itself, despite what some thinkers might claim, cannot help us with these problems once encountered, for it is not within the domain or competence of scientists to solve moral problems for us, to make moral judgments, or to be a guide for the development of society and culture. We will come back to this question in Chapter 8, but we must now consider whether the successes of science would justify us in placing our confidence in the discipline to discover objective truth, and to throw significant light on the various mysteries of life.

The scientific method and objective knowledge

It is important to reflect on the question of what kind of knowledge science gives us. And this question is a forerunner to a question that will occupy us in the next part of the chapter: is the great success of science, and the development of the scientific method, a reason to think perhaps that science as a discipline can give us total knowledge of everything, that we should look *only* to science to answer all of our problems? The former question concerns whether or not the kind of knowledge we get in science can be described as objective knowledge, a question that often interests philosophers of science more than it does scientists themselves, but a crucial question for probing the limits of science.

Objective knowledge may be defined as knowledge that is objectively true independent of human opinions, knowledge that tells us the way the world really is in itself. It is universal knowledge, in the sense that it is true for everyone who wishes to discover it, think about it, and learn from it. It is not relative to any specific person or group, or to any time or place. It does not change to accommodate current fashions, and it is, therefore, not subject to revision. Does science give us this kind of knowledge?

First, we must distinguish between a scientific theory and a scientific claim, or what is sometimes called an observation claim.[1] The everyday business of science works with observation claims. These are claims that are based on our ordinary, everyday approach to knowledge, which involves an appeal to reason and sense experience, especially the five senses. At some level, we must be able to observe and touch the data that constitutes empirical evidence in science. Other scientists must also be able to verify our data—this is one of the criteria that is said to make science objective. We make common sense observations about the world, and reason about them in various ways, and others can do the same. Scientists nowadays also use sophisticated technology to help them make some observations; these observations must also be verifiable by other scientists, and they constitute what is described as "empirical evidence." A simple example would be Galileo's development of the telescope as an instrument to study the movement of the planets. Using his telescope, he discovered many things unknown up to that point; for example, he discovered four of the moons of Jupiter, the phases of Venus, and sunspots. These discoveries were all presented as facts that were based on observation; Galileo recorded them meticulously, and other scientists (and, in principle, anyone) could study them and verify them by means of the telescope (seeing for themselves as it were), and follow his calculations, inferences, deductions, and so forth. (It is important to keep in mind that the "facts" can sometimes be the subject of debate themselves, but that is not our concern at this point.)

Let us consider the specific case of sunspots to further illustrate the scientific method. Sunspots appear as reddish smudges that seem to be on the surface of the sun. Galileo could see them with his telescope, and sometimes they can be seen without a telescope. They are important in a number of areas of scientific research today, but in Galileo's time they were also particularly relevant to the debate about heliocentricism because they appeared to show that the sun moved, and was not standing still, thereby challenging the traditional view of Aristotle that the heavenly bodies are inalterable. Galileo became involved in a debate over their existence with Christoph Scheiner, a Jesuit astronomer, who held that the spots were probably small stars moving across the sun. Scheiner held this view because he reasoned that if the spots were on the sun, they would disappear as the sun rotated, and then reappear later. But this was not what he observed. He noted that the spots disappeared and new ones appeared in a different place. Galileo argued that this was because the spots were impermanent. He produced evidence to support this view: that the same sunspots move at different speeds, that sometimes they disappear on the way across, and that the size of a particular sunspot will sometimes change. His strongest argument was based on the foreshortening effect that was visible in the changing shape of a sunspot as it travels across the sun. These, and other arguments, supported by mathematical calculations, convinced many that Galileo was right, including later probably even Scheiner himself.[2] This debate over sunspots is a very good example of the scientific method in action. It involves observations initially made with the help of the telescope, competing theories to explain the observations, arguments to support one theory over the other, and eventually rational acceptance of one theory, which is then accepted as the true theory.

We come, second, to the theoretical part of science, the part that sometimes generates disagreement, lively debate, and often extreme controversy. On many questions, scientists will propose a theory to explain the facts they see before them. The theory should fit the facts, of course, yet it is often the case that the theory goes beyond the facts as well. This means that scientists will sometimes propose conclusions that are not fully obvious given the facts before us, or will offer conclusions that are suggested by the facts, but not proved by them. A theory may stick closely to the facts; but some theories might be more speculative, and therefore more subject to debate. A theory gains respectability if there is a general consensus among scientists that the facts upon which it is based are true, that they do support logically the theory which is proposed to explain these facts (though we must keep in mind that a consensus by itself, logically, does not guarantee that a theory is true). To come back to Galileo, he proposed the heliocentric model of planetary motion—that the earth moves around the sun—as the best explanatory theory for the facts about planetary motion that he had recorded and reported. This was not only a bold theory, but it also went against the Ptolemaic theory, and so led to controversy. Many were skeptical of Galileo's theory at first, not just theologians, but also many scientists; but eventually, as astronomers checked his observations and arguments, most accepted that the heliocentric theory was supported by the facts.

It is clear that both the observation statements and the theories they lead to are put forward by science as *objectively true*. For example, Galileo claimed that there really were spots on the sun, that the sun was really rotating, that the foreshortening effect caused by the sunspots was really happening, and so forth. German physicist Georg Ohm (1784–1854), who worked on electricity, discovered what later became known as Ohm's law relating to electrical circuits. This law says that the relationship between voltage {V}, current {I}, and resistance {R} is $V = I \times R$. Ohm is arguing that these relationships hold objectively in the real world between voltage, current, and resistance. Logically, this also means that alternative claims about the relationships between these phenomena are false; for instance, if Ohm's law is correct, then it is false that the relationship between current, resistance, and voltage is $I = V \times R$; if Galileo is right then it is false that the earth is not moving around the sun, and so forth for all scientific claims.

Of course, we must be careful to take note of the common sense logical distinction between scientists proposing that a claim is objectively true, and it actually being objectively true. Sometimes a claim is put forward as objectively true that turns out not to be; for example, in the late nineteenth-century, scientists posited that there was an luminiferous ether-like substance around the earth that light traveled through, but the existence of the ether could never be satisfactorily confirmed by experiments. After Einstein's theory of relativity came along, the ether theory was abandoned. But these erroneous claims are usually honest mistakes. The common sense, and indeed the dominant, answer to the question about the status of scientific claims and theories from the vast majority of scientists is that they are put forward as objectively true claims, as telling us about what really happened, about how things are really related or structured, about how the world really is.[3] Of course, we may discover further evidence in the future to make us doubt, revise, or abandon some of the claims of our various scientific theories (and indeed this is quite common in science), but the *new* or *revised* claims will then be presented as objectively true claims. We will simply be noting that what we thought was objectively true was not in fact true, but that our (now) revised view is objectively true (as in the ether example). So, scientific knowledge is generally advanced as objective knowledge, knowledge that tells us how the world really is.

Realism versus anti-realism

This general position about knowledge is known in philosophy as *realism*, the view that true knowledge tells us the way the world really is, that that which is known exists independently of the human mind, and is not significantly modified or altered in the act of knowing (by, e.g., our conceptual schemes, cultural perspectives, various biases, etc.). Apart from being firmly rooted in common sense, this view seems to be the most rational approach to knowledge. Realism is a position one adopts with regard to every kind of knowledge, not just scientific knowledge. Psychologists, historians, medical researchers, archeologists, astronomers, and so forth all adopt the realist view, in the sense that they believe the claims they are making in their disciplines are objectively true claims, for example, that the human mind has various mechanisms for dealing with fear, that Hitler invaded Austria and Czechoslovakia leading to World War II, that stone age man used various tools, etc. Indeed, the analysis of realist theories of knowledge is a fascinating and ongoing topic in philosophy; it is not a task we need get into here except to note again that it is the dominant view in science that scientific statements and theories are telling us the way the world really is. The general understanding is that a scientific statement makes a claim about how some part of the world really is, and is backed up by empirical or observational evidence, or which is demonstrable in some other way. This position clearly fits in well with a realist approach to science.

However, realism as an approach to knowledge has often been challenged by various thinkers, who have advocated anti-realism as an alternative. Anti-realism represents a general approach to the question of the status of knowledge claims in philosophy that is then applied in the various knowledge disciplines, including science. Anti-realism is the view that the mind *in the process or act of knowing* somehow modifies the content of what is known. This modifying affects all aspects of knowledge, not just specific domains. Therefore, the anti-realist claims that when I come to know that the tables and chairs in front of me exist, and have certain properties (are brown, made of mahogany, etc.), this knowing is compromised or modified *in the act* of knowing itself. So, there is a *difference* between the chairs and tables as they are in themselves, and as they appear to me in human knowing. In addition, all I know is how they *appear to me* in human knowing. I cannot get outside of my knowing structures to see what they are like *in themselves*.

Think of the knower as someone who has put on what we might call "knowledge glasses" in order to see the world; the anti-realist holds that the glasses cause you to see everything in a certain specific way; let us say they make you see everything in green. Now suppose you did not know that you had the glasses on. You might think that everything really was green; whereas in reality the objects themselves are not green at all, but are modified in the act of knowing (represented by the glasses). Well, the anti-realist claims, it is the same with human knowing in a more general sense. A question prompted by the anti-realist view, and one which many readers will no doubt raise is: *how does the mind modify the contents of knowing (or acts of consciousness)?* Different philosophers in history have given very different accounts of this modifying, for example, Immanuel Kant, Martin Heidegger, Jacques Derrida.[4] It is beyond the scope of this book to examine these views, but the specific account of anti-realism one holds will depend on which philosopher one thinks has given the best general explanation of how anti-realism works.

An extension of the anti-realist critique of the problems with finding objective knowledge is the claim that the knower always brings ideological biases to the subject under study, no matter how hard one tries to avoid this. These biases can influence one's interpretations of the facts when the facts are suggestive but not conclusive on a topic. And because the facts by themselves are seldom decisive—there are always facts that need to be interpreted—then our biases play a much larger role in what we think is objectively true than we realize. So, for example, according to this view, Scheiner was perhaps reluctant to embrace Galileo's view at first because of his belief in Aristotle, and not entirely because he found Galileo's evidence unconvincing. But this is not all there is to be said, of course, because Galileo himself would have had biases that influenced *his* interpretation of the facts. This would also be true of *any* conclusion put forward as a result of a scientific investigation, including those of *the anti-realist himself*, a relativism about knowledge that many will not find credible, notwithstanding the point that one thing we can learn from the anti-realist position is that we should be mindful of the biases we might bring to an issue, and try not to let them influence our conclusions.

This is indeed a major problem for anti-realism: that it leads to both epistemological and moral relativism about knowledge. This is because it seems to be a short step from the claim that the human mind modifies the acts of consciousness in human knowing to the view that this happens in *different* ways for different cultures, groups, historical epochs, even genders. And so what we often end up with if we travel down the path of anti-realism is the view that knowledge claims are modified *relative to each group*, and so there are no objective truths across all groups, no ahistorical, or transcultural truths. A further important consequence of this view is that one cannot therefore criticize the values of another group or society. Cultural relativists in morality, for example, will claim that one cannot criticize the moral values of another society because all moral values are *defined* by the specific beliefs, traditions, and biases of one's own culture. Religious relativists will claim that this point is also true in religious matters, that no religion can claim to be the truth, or that no religion can consistently criticize another religion, and so all religions have a certain legitimacy, and so forth.

Readers will surely recognize this view, and will likely have come across many references to various forms of it in different places. It is a very popular and enormously influential view, especially in university and media circles. Many people find it attractive because, irrespective of the great difficulties in defending it, it gives one a mechanism to criticize, and therefore to undermine (usually traditional) views of religion, morality, and politics one dislikes, and just about anything else (such as society and cultural norms, the correct approach to the study of literature, the traditional university curriculum, etc.). At the same time, it gives one an opportunity to promote alternative views one finds more congenial.

This book is not the place to get into a detailed discussion of this fascinating and challenging view of knowledge, and its radical implications, but we are interested in how it would apply to science. A major consequence of anti-realism is that it must apply to all knowledge claims; one can't just apply it to some knowledge claims, such as religious and moral ones, but then exempt other knowledge claims from its effects, such as scientific ones. Anti-realism has sounded plausible to some when it is invoked in the areas of religion, morality, literature, and culture, but when it is invoked in the disciplines of science, history, psychology, and other areas it sounds quite less plausible. For the anti-realist is forced to say that, just like religious or moral claims, scientific claims are also the product of the modifying structures of the knowing mind, and are similarly influenced by language, culture, and conceptual scheme, perhaps even race and gender.[5] This would mean that science as a discipline cannot make any claims to objective truth. When applied to scientific claims, this view seems very implausible and inevitably runs into problems of contradiction. We cannot say that heliocentrism is more correct than geocentrism on this view, but only that we have exchanged one theory for another because of our particular historical circumstances. On its face, anti-realism seems to be an absurd approach to science, and it is no wonder that those who are drawn to various forms of epistemological anti-realism and relativism have often tried to exempt science from this radical view (as, e.g., in the work of American philosopher, Willard V. O. Quine).[6]

Anti-realism is not a popular view in science, though different versions of if have been defended by Thomas Kuhn, Larry Laudan, and Quine, among others.[7] Others have offered theories to explain the kind of knowledge we get in science that are not as radical as anti-realism, but that still fall short of realism. Although we cannot consider these in any detail, and refer the reader to the interesting literature on this topic,[8] let us conclude this section by mentioning one general approach. This is the approach known as constructive empiricism, a quite popular view philosophers of science often appeal to when they are confronted by challenges to the status of scientific knowledge, especially the challenge of the popular argument (which we will consider in the next section) that science has abandoned many theories it once accepted as true. The constructive empiricist claims that we should hold only those observational statements on which theories are based to be true because these are directly verifiable, but that, although we do hold that the entities and theories extrapolated to from the observational statements are true as well, we must accept that, because we can't directly verify these entities and theories, truths concerning them must be held in some more provisional way.

This does not mean that we should act as if these theories are not true, or as if some entities do not exist, or indeed as if we could never commit to their truth; we can commit to their truth if they have been around for a long time, and have led to repeatedly successful predictions and success in scientific research. But we recognize that they could nevertheless, in principle, be falsified by some future data. The observation statements would not be falsified, of course, but the theory based on them could either be falsified or significantly revised, however unlikely we may think this will happen with various current popular theories. So, for example, we know that objects will behave differently on the moon than on earth, because we have directly observed this; we know many things about the size and structure of our universe because we can see them with our telescopes (including the amazing Hubble telescope). But on more theoretical matters, such as the theory that electrons (subatomic particles with negative charge) exist, we must be somewhat more provisional, simply because we cannot directly observe them, but reason to their existence through their effects. The phenomenal success of electricity allows us to be very sure of our commitment to and reliance upon the existence of electrons.

Constructive empiricism may not satisfy everyone, because it falls somewhat short of realism, which is the common sense view, the view most scientists practice, but it does claim at least that the empirical evidence upon which scientific theories are based is true, that we do think the unobservable entities really exist, but it ends by saying that *empirical adequacy* rather than truth is really the aim of science. For those who advocate this view, "empirical adequacy" seems to play much the same role as truth does for the realist, and is frequently accepted as if it has all of the advantages of truth, at least in practice, even though in principle it is not supposed to have. For instance, empirical adequacy is enough to accept theories with apparent certainty (e.g., evolution), and enough to refute various others theories, a further example of it being difficult to follow anything other than a realist approach in practice (despite what one might claim to believe in theory). This serves to underscore the point again that a general realist view is the most rational position to adopt in both science and religion (and secularism). In this way, their major claims are understood as being objectively true, and so can then be subjected to rational scrutiny.

The undermining of truth in the history of science

Despite the general commitment of science to realism and objective knowledge, the enterprise of science is also somewhat undermined not just by anti-realism and constructive empiricism, but by a much more familiar and less philosophical-type argument. This is the argument that is founded on the claim, not that scientific statements should not be interpreted in a realist way, but that even if this is the most rational, common sense way to approach science, we are still not in a position to claim that scientific theories give us the truth. This argument might be called the "inductive argument from the failure of past scientific theories." It is a logical argument based on inductive reasoning concerning scientific theories that were accepted in the past as true but which have now been abandoned. It is a fact that many scientific theories and beliefs once accepted as true are now rejected. Examples often cited include: the humors of medieval medicine; the effluvia of early theories of static electricity; the view that electricity and magnetism were distinct (Michael Faraday was frequently ridiculed for holding that they were linked[9]); the existence of phlogiston; the vital force in physiology; the electromagnetic ether (referred to earlier); circular inertia; the theory of spontaneous generation, etc.[10] It follows from this, by inductive reasoning, according to proponents of this argument, that we will eventually discover that our *current* scientific theories are wrong in significant respects, and so some of these will be abandoned at a future time. The general conclusion, therefore, is that this is how science works overall; we must conclude that all scientific theories are provisional, and although they usually tell us something about the natural world, we must stop short of claiming that they give us the truth. We know from studying the history of science that no matter how certain we are that a theory is true today, tomorrow the theory will be significantly revised, even abandoned. And so, given this point, it would be wrong to claim, for instance, that the theory of evolution is true, because we will discover at some point in the future that it actually misses the mark.

This approach to science does not claim that the observation statements, and other obvious empirical evidence cited in support of a theory, are false, but only that the theory which is proposed to explain the facts will turn out to be wrong. To come back to evolution, this view would agree that the facts upon which the theory of evolution is based are true: for example, that we have adequate fossils of various species of finches to conclude that they are likely related, that these species did live in various parts of the Galapagos Islands, that the species can be dated in relation to each other, and so forth. But it would claim that the more theoretical parts of the theory, such as the processes of natural selection—the processes by which the various parts of species are supposed to have come about—which we do not directly observe—along with the other theoretical claims of the theory, may well (and probably will) turn out to be false. The more of a "gap" there is between the observation statements, the direct empirical evidence, and the theory extrapolated to from this evidence, the more likely it is that the theory in question will turn out to be wrong. The closer the theory is to the evidence the less chance that it will be significantly revised.

Sometimes this phenomenon is explained by noting that many scientific theories are *underdetermined* by the scientific evidence—the empirical evidence, the facts, observations, and experiments used to support them. Some hold that modern science works like this: that although there is a fruitful interplay between fact and theory, that science works by proposing hypotheses, models, theories, to account for facts and data, but that many of these theories are speculative, removed, underdetermined. Many of the latest scientific theories seem to follow this pattern; often there is not enough evidence to fully support a theory, or to put it the other way around, the available evidence might be used to support more than one theory. This tends to be true with regard to some of the modern, dramatic theories such as those relating to quantum mechanics, chaos theory, string theory, cosmology, the origin of life, etc. In addition, scientists today are not above offering extremely speculative theories, for which there is currently no firm evidence, such as some aspects of Alan Guth's theory of the inflationary universe, or the theory that there may be multiple universes, of which ours is just one, a view that has been taken seriously by more than a few scientists and philosophers.[11] Scientists often present these speculative theories in popular books aimed, not at other scientists, but at the general public. These theories then make their way into popular culture, with the ordinary person not knowing how seriously to take them. In addition, determining whether a theory is close to or far from the evidence is itself controversial, and often the subject of fierce debate, both within and outside of science.

Some scientists, including Pierre Duhem, have responded to the above problems and doubts about science by proposing the view known as *instrumentalism*.[12] In a way, instrumentalism tries to sidestep the question as to whether scientific theories tell us the way the world really is in favor of a more modest claim, that a scientific theory is better understood as an instrument for our practical use, rather than as a true description of a part of reality. This means that we should regard scientific theories as instruments to help us understand observable phenomena, and to make predictions about observable phenomena. In doing this, we are sticking as close as possible to the actual empirical evidence, and so can avoid claiming that theories tell us the way things really are. Instrumentalists claim that even though the theory may be, and probably will be, abandoned in the future, it does allow us to make useful predictions now, and this is a point in its favor. This view is more realist than anti-realist because its proponents do claim that the observation statements are true, and do tell us the way the world really is. They are more influenced by the arguments that the present theories will be abandoned or revised in the future, and by the general point that most theories are underdetermined by the evidence, than by any anti-realist sympathies.

This discussion prompts the question of how does one judge whether a scientific theory is a good theory or not, which is often related to the question of how do we tell the difference between science and nonscience, or pseudoscience? Several thinkers, including Karl Popper, have given their attention to this fundamental matter. Popper and others have proposed that some of the following criteria are necessary for a good scientific theory. (1) Falsifiability: this concept refers to the fact that one must be able to say what evidence, if discovered, would falsify a scientific theory. Popper thought that this was a logical requirement, a requirement of reason as it were, because if a scientific theory says certain things are true of the world, then logically this meant that certain other things are false, and so one should be able to state what these things are. For example, if the theory of general relativity says that the laws of physics hold everywhere in the universe, we could then say that if we visited Mars and discovered that the laws did not hold there, this would falsify the theory. Popper argued that this requirement ruled out Sigmund Freud's theory of psychoanalysis as a scientific theory, because Popper held that any evidence one considers, even apparently disconfirming evidence, can be turned into evidence that supports psychoanalysis because we are mostly dealing with hidden psychological states which all people, to some degree, are supposed to have. It has often been claimed that Marxist theories, as well as the theory of evolution, also do not satisfy this criterion.[13]

(2) Another criterion is our ability to make successful predictions based on the theory, as we noted above: for example, Newton's laws of gravity predicted that an object "thrown" at the right speed would "fall" around the earth at a

constant distance and rate because of gravity. This principle has been used to place satellites in orbit, as well as the space shuttle, and to explain why the moon stays in orbit around the earth. (3) Testability is also thought to be a criterion: the idea that one should be able to test the claims of a (good) theory. Sometimes this will involve predictions. Of course, a theory (logically) could be true, but not testable; yet unless we can test it, we would not be able to say whether it is true or not. (4) Simplicity: This criterion refers to the principle that, if two hypotheses explain something equally well, then, all other things being equal, it is more logical to opt for the simplest explanation of the two. "Simplest" describes that explanation that has the least amount of explanatory content required to explain the effects. There are other criteria too that one might list such as coherence (a good theory must be consistent with current scientific knowledge), but at some time or another all proposed criteria have been disputed as being the mark of a good theory.

Indeed, a moment's refection on any of these criteria shows that they are not as clear cut as might at first sight appear, yet another indication of the provisional nature of much that goes on in science, despite our tendency to treat it as a source of certainty. Our discussion in this section has shown us that while we strive for objective knowledge in science, and agree that science at least attempts to describe the way the world really is, we should always remain cautious about claiming too much for our theories, and should be careful about the biases that we bring to research—financial, moral, and political—as well as those that stem from our individual worldviews. If nothing else, the history of science should chasten us against total confidence in our theories.

The modern face of science: naturalism

As pointed out above, despite these various misgivings about whether science can actually give us the truth, and despite the amazing prevalence of anti-realism, allied with epistemological relativism, throughout modern academic disciplines, most scientists, as distinct from philosophers of science, adopt the common sense view of realism, as do most people. But some well-known scientists and other thinkers in a variety of disciplines go further than arguing that realism is true, and that science gives us objective truth. They argue that science is the *only* way to knowledge, and that science may be able to answer all of our questions about human life and the universe (a view which used to be known as "scientism"). They are so taken with the success of science that they have an incredible trust, almost a faith, in its potential to offer the best hope of answering all of our questions. These thinkers, who would include Richard Dawkins, Carl Sagan, Francis Crick, John Searle, Steven Weinberg, Daniel Dennett, and others, further argue that the religious worldview, in whatever form it takes, is false.[14] We need to examine this view, and its specific connection with science, in more detail.

In Chapter 1, we made a distinction between positive and negative atheism, recognizing that atheists in the twentieth century—now called naturalists (or secularists)—became more sophisticated, realizing that they need to state their views in positive terms, to state what they believe about the important questions of life, and not just what they disapprove of. In short, they need to develop a naturalistic worldview, with its own account of reality, the human person and the nature of moral and political values, and with developed positions on various other matters. One of the problems facing this view in general, especially in terms of the debate between this worldview and other (religious) worldviews, is that, although naturalists have done quite well in the task of stating their beliefs and values in positive terms, they have been less successful in adopting a positive temperament toward alternative views. Proponents of naturalism, at least in its contemporary forms, very often regard themselves as "enlightened," and this attitude tempts them to give short shift to other views, without a proper debate. This attitude is especially obvious in the work of two scientists whose work we will briefly consider in this section, Richard Dawkins and Carl Sagan.

These two scientists, and many of their fellow travelers (such as Stephen J. Gould, Steven Weinberg, and E. O. Wilson) are widely recognized public intellectuals, and so they have significant cultural influence, obviously more than the average scientist. Some, like Dawkins in particular, with his recent best selling book, *The God Delusion*, have helped shape public debate on matters relating to religion and atheism, the nature of science, and the meaning of life. It is therefore incumbent upon us to consider the significance of their ideas for our understanding of the relationship between religion and science. Dawkins has actively promoted a naturalistic worldview as an alternative to that of religious belief. In *The God Delusion*, he appeals to atheists worldwide, especially in the United States and Britain, to come out of the closet so to speak, in order to promote their beliefs in politics. A very significant part of Dawkins' approach to secularism is that he appeals to science to justify his secularist, naturalistic worldview, and therefore in the minds of many people he forges a clear link between science and atheism.

Dawkins holds the view that everything that exists is physical in nature, and consists of some sophisticated combination of matter and energy, acting according to the laws of science. Various scientific theories, such as evolution, genetics, and other biochemical advances, progressively enable us to discover the processes and mechanisms that govern physical reality (especially nature), and while this approach may not be able to answer all of our questions, he argues that naturalism is an immensely more satisfying view than any religious alternative. This is in part because it is a more rational worldview than the religious worldview. Dawkins defends his thesis with a number of positive and negative arguments. Let us look at them in turn.

The first positive argument, and indeed his main argument overall, is the appeal to evolution. We must first note that it is important to distinguish between evolution and secularism (or naturalism), to recognize that evolution officially is a scientific theory that makes no claims to be able to explain everything, such as the origin of life, the origin of the universe, or the design in the universe. It is a theory which Dawkins, being an evolutionary biologist, has co-opted to explain more than it was intended to explain. Dawkins holds that evolution shows that all of our species are genetically related to each other in the way Darwin argued for, and that the origin of the various species is due to random accident. Genetic research shows that mutations in DNA lead over long periods of time to the origin of new species, and that these mutations are accidental, and have many (random) causes stemming from the environment of the organism as well as from its original DNA structure. This evidence shows, he claims, that human beings occupy no special place in the universe, that they were not created by a supreme being for any particular purpose. Dawkins has gone so far as to argue that the design we see in the universe in the form of the laws of physics is itself the product of chance (a view we will return to in Chapter 6). This evolutionary naturalistic account is also a direct challenge to the authority of the Bible because it shows that the creation story in Genesis is false, and is another reason to recognize that these stories are myths, that the Bible is a bunch of fairy stories, as Dawkins often derogatorily puts it.

How did life originate in the first place according to this view? At this point naturalists (or secularists) like Dawkins further extend the theory of evolution to the question of the origin of life itself, and even to the nature of the universe. He endorses a view developed by Sagan, Crick, Lynn Margulis, and others.[15]

These thinkers argue that the first life-form most likely originated from nonliving materials in a process of chemical evolution. This may have occurred when the right building blocks were present in the right environment at the right time in history, all of which would have happened by chance, of course. Naturalists often appeal to the experiments conducted by Harold Urey and Stanley Miller at the University of Chicago in the 1950s to support this view. Their research involved a process where they started out in lab experiments with only nonliving (inorganic) materials, and attempted to produce from this material *living* (organic) organisms, all in an attempt to mimic how life might have originated on earth by means of a similar process (a process sometimes called abiogenesis).

Urey and Miller used only those ingredients they thought would have been available on earth around about the time life is believed to have started (water, methane, hydrogen, ammonia). Their experiments succeeded in producing amino acids, part of the building blocks for life as we know it, but only a small part, and not actually living cells themselves (see Chapter 8 for more on amino acids, proteins, and DNA). Some thought it would only be a matter of time before experiments like this one led to the production of proteins and more complex organic material, but this has not happened. Fifty years later, there is little further progress, and Simon Conway Morris has described abiogenesis as "a story of abject scientific failure."[16] Of course the Urey-Miller results are still the product of design, and from a statistical point of view the probability of DNA randomly emerging in this way on the earth is too small to be taken seriously, yet supporters still point to these experiments as likely evidence that this is how life began; many atheists appeal to this work as an ongoing research project still in its infancy. Francis Crick has advocated a variation of this view which claims that life on earth might have originated from life on some other planet, either by some simple life-forms such as microorganisms somehow getting to earth (perhaps in meteorites), and then replicating (and here we all are!), or by some intelligence on a distant galaxy creating life on earth.[17] Neither of these alternatives though would answer the ultimate question of how life began in the first place, so some theory of life originating from nonlife is still required by Crick's view.

While Dawkins's positive strategy revolves around evolution, his negative strategy involves an attack on religion. He never loses an opportunity in his writings to attack religious beliefs and religious believers, and in his book, *The God Delusion,* he shows nothing but contempt for religion. His view is that religion is irrational nonsense, silly superstition, and he champions the "conflict model" of the relationship between science and religion as the best way to think about them. He holds that science will provide a fairly satisfactory explanation for the whole of reality, and so we don't need religion. Dawkins also attacks religion by pointing to all the wrongs and excesses of religion in history, arguing that these problems show that the religious worldview is false. This is an important part of his overall argument in *The God Delusion*. However, it is an elementary logical point that it does not follow that because some wrongs have been done in the name of religion, that this shows that all religious beliefs are false, or that the religious worldview is false. Moreover, as many have pointed out, secularism in the twentieth century has not been reassuring in this respect. What about all of the evil that has been carried out in an attempt to advance secularist, atheist ideologies, for example, Hitler in Nazi Germany, Mao in China, Pol Pot in Cambodia, and Stalin in the Soviet Union? An estimated total of sixty million people were killed under these regimes, a staggering moral failure. Dawkins wants to give atheism a pass in the face of this criticism by claiming that these were evil people who just happened to be atheists![18] But this seems to be a case of specious reasoning; why not give religion a similar pass and recognize that religion too can be used to carry out evil in the wrong hands, just as all worldviews can be? Unfortunately, these kinds of arguments are quite typical of contemporary atheists as they try to argue that religious belief is dangerous and irrational, and that naturalism, supported by an appeal to science, is a better alternative.

Another well-known public scientist associated with an explicitly secularist worldview, especially in the United States, is the astronomer Carl Sagan. Before his death in 1996, Sagan worked on many projects aimed at promoting a purely naturalistic view of the cosmos and of the human person.[19] He is best known in popular culture for a series of best selling books on science, and for his 1980 TV series *Cosmos*, which was watched by millions of people. Nobody can watch this influential series, and fail to notice that Sagan is not just explaining current scientific facts and theories from the field of astronomy, but that he is also promoting through this 13 part series his own naturalistic and secularist worldview. The series (and the book) open with the famous line "the cosmos is all that is or was or ever will be."[20] But this is not a scientific claim, a claim based on empirical evidence. It is what philosophers would call a metaphysical claim about what exists, about the nature of reality; it is also a claim that has a religious ring to it. The TV series is also full of moral pronouncements, especially concerning Sagan's pet topics: the state of the environment, global warming, and the production of nuclear weapons. For instance, he devotes an episode in the series to the perils and foolishness of nuclear arms build up.

Like Dawkins, Sagan does not hide his contempt for religion, and never misses an opportunity to show it in its worst light.

Sagan and others have attempted to apply the concept of evolution to the universe as a whole, by appeal to the concept of "cosmic evolution."[21] He argues that we can describe the universe itself as evolving from the time of the big bang onwards in the sense that each present state of the universe is casually produced by the preceding states. This is an interesting idea, and it might help us in some way to think about successive states of the universe, but clearly it is not going to help us explain the *origin* of the universe. In order for one state of the universe to evolve into another state, the matter and energy involved in the first state has to exist in certain environmental conditions; likewise, this prior state itself would have evolved out of an even prior state, and so on back to the big bang. So, this view still would not provide us with an explanation of the first state of the universe that led to all of subsequent states. This theory of "cosmic evolution" is another example of naturalists attempting to use current scientific theories in order to try to explain those ultimate matters that we would normally turn to religion to explain, yet the naturalistic theories do not address the ultimate question.

Let us mention very briefly one other example of the naturalistic worldview, which employs science as its main defense. This is the view of a scientist we have already mentioned, Francis Crick, who did pioneering work in the study of the makeup of DNA. Crick tells us that: "I went into science because of [a distaste for religion], there's no doubt about that. I asked myself what were the two things that appear inexplicable and are used to support religious beliefs: the difference between living and nonliving things, and the phenomenon of consciousness."[22] This remark shows clearly that Crick understands his work as promoting a naturalistic worldview at the expense of the religious worldview. In his book, *The Astonishing Hypothesis*, he defends what we referred to in Chapter 2 as a materialist view of the mind. We saw that Descartes had argued that the mind is a nonphysical entity that is related to, but not reducible to, the brain, and that has independent causal power in its own right; the mind may also be able to survive the death of the body. This was how many thinkers explained immortality; they held that consciousness, which is part of the mind, could survive death, because the mind could survive death. In addition, since the mind is nonphysical, it follows therefore that not everything is physical, and that naturalism is false. Crick rejects all of this and attempts to sketch out in his book how all aspects of mental life might have a physical explanation, including awareness, attention, memory, the vision process, and consciousness. He recognizes that this thesis is difficult to accept, but nevertheless believes it is true: "The Astonishing Hypothesis is that 'You', your joys and your sorrows, your memories and your ambitions, your sense of personal identity and free will, are in fact no more than the behavior of a vast assembly of nerve cells and their associated molecules."[23] While recognizing that there are different approaches to the scientific study of consciousness, none of which can operate without controversial assumptions, Crick's approach starts from the assumption that all of the different aspects of consciousness employ a basic common mechanism, and that if we can find the key to one, such as visual awareness, we may find the key to others. He then offers an anti-realist account of the vision process as a way into what is essentially a research project on the nature of consciousness, arguing that various processes in the brain, involving sets of neurons firing, produce the objects of awareness and knowledge, which are filtered through the physical processing that occurs in the brain. As Crick puts it, "It is essential to think in terms of neurons, both their internal components, and the intricate and unexpected ways they interact together. Eventually, when we truly understand how the brain works, we may be able to give approximate high-level accounts of our perceptions, our thinking, and our behavior."[24]

Crick believes that something like this approach, if not his own explanation, will eventually succeed in explaining the nature of consciousness. One is struck in reading the work of Crick by how many controversial assumptions he makes, by how he is satisfied with theories that can't be supported by physical data, by how he seems to accept materialism about the mind as a matter of faith (indeed he acknowledges that much of his view is speculative). We will come back to the problem of consciousness in more detail in a later chapter, because it is a problem that has vexed naturalistic-minded philosophers in the twentieth century. The human mind has proved remarkable resistant to all attempts to explain its nature and operations scientifically. There seems to be too many intractable problems involved, such as the nature of ideas, subjectivity, rationality and logic, meaning, free will, and personal identity, that for many it is difficult to see how these mental phenomena could either be just another part of the brain, or how they could be explained fully in terms of brain activity, or could have evolved through purely physical processes.

The naturalistic view is now the modern face of science, despite the attempts by some scientists to provide an alternative view, such as Owen Gingerich, Paul Davies, Francis Collins, Simon Conway Morris, and others (whose work we will come back to in later chapters).[25] Like these scientists, it is important for us to recognize that science should not to be identified with naturalism, and that it is naïve and somewhat dogmatic, as well as being very unrealistic, to regard it as being the only way to truth. It is true that science does adopt a stance toward the study of the physical realm called *methodological naturalism*, which means that only physical, testable explanations will be considered and pursued. This is a proper stance for scientists to adopt working within their discipline. But it does not follow from this that the only possible explanations for any aspect of reality are physical ones (this would be *metaphysical naturalism*). Unfortunately, some prominent scientists fail to maintain the distinction; they approach some of the important questions of life from the position of a prior *commitment* to metaphysical naturalism, which then often creates a bias in their reading of what the scientific evidence actually shows. Richard Lewontin has been refreshingly forthcoming about this commitment of naturalists:

> Our willingness to accept scientific claims that are against common sense is the key to an understanding of the real struggle between science and the supernatural. We take the side of science *in spite* of the patent absurdity of some of its constructs, *in spite* of its failure to fulfill many of its extravagant promises of health and life, *in spite* of the tolerance of the scientific community for unsubstantiated just-so stories, because we have a prior commitment, a commitment to materialism. It is not that the methods and institutions of science somehow compel us to accept a material explanation of the phenomenal world, but, on the contrary, that we are forced by our *a priori* adherence to material causes to create an apparatus of investigation and a set of concepts that produce material explanations, no matter how counterintuitive, no matter how mystifying to the uninitiated. Moreover, that materialism is absolute, for we cannot allow a Divine Foot in the door.[26]

Unfortunately, views like those of Lewontin, Dawkins, Crick, and Sagan only promote the "conflict model" of the relationship between science and religion, and succeed only in politicizing science to a significant extent, and to making enemies out of many who would otherwise be enthusiastic supporters. We are far better served if we do not allow ourselves to be guided by the "conflict model" because of its many shortcomings. Indeed, the interests of everyone will be better served if we all recognize the distinction between science and naturalism, between methodological naturalism and metaphysical naturalism, and if we carefully avoid allowing the scientific evidence to be corrupted by prior metaphysical biases. This way both science and religion can engage in a fruitful and intriguing dialogue.

4 God and Evolution

Chapter Outline

Evolution and modern culture	82
Brief history of evolution	85
The theory of evolution	89
The evidence for evolution: questions and answers	93
Religious, philosophical, and moral implications of evolution	104

Evolution and modern culture

The theory of evolution is one of the most thought provoking and influential scientific theories of all time. It is such an important theory that nobody today who is interested in the relationship between religion and science, or who is engaged by the question of whether there is an ultimate purpose to human life, or in pondering the place of human beings in the overall scheme of things, can afford to be ignorant of the theory. In this chapter, our aim shall be to explore the theory fully, concentrating mainly on three important questions: (1) what *factual claims* does the theory make about the origin of the species, about the human species, and about the structure and development of species; (2) what is the *evidence* offered to support the factual, scientific claims of the theory, and how reliable is this evidence; (3) what are the *implications* of the factual claims of the theory for other important issues in religion, ethics, and philosophy (e.g., what is the significance of evolution for our understanding of the nature of human beings?)? These questions are a good way to organize the complex topic of evolution and religion because they allow us to see as clearly as possible where numerous related matters fit in the discussion, as well as to keep questions that belong to the domain of science separate from those that belong to the domains of philosophy and religion.

It is important to emphasize that the first two questions are logically distinct from the third question. While it is the job of evolutionary biologists to try to answer the first two questions, it is the job of philosophers and theologians to think about the third question. Unfortunately, this line often becomes blurred in the cultural debate concerning evolution, especially in the United States, with the result that there is a great deal of confusion in the minds of many about what the theory of evolution actually says, about which aspects properly belong to science, and about which matters are outside of science. It is important not to underestimate the significance of this confusion in today's cultural debate over evolution. It has led to theologians and philosophers sometimes attempting to do science (or at least appearing as if they are doing science), to enter into areas of science where they have little expertise; but it has also led scientists to pronounce on matters in religion, philosophy, and ethics, areas where they have no expertise. This cultural confusion has also contributed to a reluctance on the part of scientists to debate and discuss the evidence for the theory in a way that would help clarify the first two questions above in the minds of the general public; because of the cultural climate surrounding evolution, scientists have sometimes understandably adopted a defensive posture toward the theory. Scientists are in a difficult position here because they are trying to promote a theory to an often suspicious (and sometimes hostile) audience, yet this reluctance to discuss the evidence for evolution has the practical consequence of adding further fuel to the doubts of an already skeptical general public. On the other side, we have some religious believers who are too defensive about their own views, who will not give a hearing to evolution, and who are unwilling to explore the ways that religion and evolution may be compatible.

So it is important to avoid these pitfalls by keeping the first two questions distinct from the third question. We need to appreciate at the outset that the way a scientific theory originates and is developed applies to evolution just as much as it does to any other theory. Scientists, in this case biologists, discover various bits of empirical evidence from nature, much of it based on observation of living things, fossils, skeletons, habitats, environmental influences, time scales, etc., record it meticulously, and analyze, discuss, and confirm their findings with other scientists working on the same subject matter. Then they appeal to a theory—the theory of evolution—to explain the evidence they have before them. Like all scientific theories, the theory is subject to debate, revision, and critique; in the case of evolution the theory came to be accepted by a majority of scientists. From a logical point of view, this is all evolutionary biologists can do: gather and present the evidence, and then formulate, test, and defend the theory based on the evidence. Critical analysis of the theory will involve examining the empirical evidence to see if it is as the biologists say it is (e.g., what does the comparison of two whale fossils show?), and then looking at the theory proposed to see if it does indeed explain the evidence pretty well. It is not the job of scientists working in the area of evolution to say what the philosophical, religious, or moral implications of the theory are. These are all important, indeed crucial, issues, but they need to be addressed by philosophers and theologians and other experts on these topics, not by scientists. Of course, a particular scientist will have a view on these matters, but when he/she advances his/her view he/she is not doing science, but is operating in the area of philosophy, religion, and the general area of worldviews. What this means is that the skills one has as a scientist—discovering and recording the evidence, and proposing a theory to explain the evidence, and many other skills in between—are not skills that one can appeal to when thinking about one's philosophical, religious, and moral views. The scientist's job is to say that these are the facts as we see them; what the facts mean, or what their implications are, is not for him to say *as a scientist,* just as Galileo reported *how* the earth moves, but it is not for him to say *why* it moves one way rather than another (meaning that the evidence he has to show how it moves does not tell him why it moves). This latter question is not a scientific question (though Galileo could not resist the temptation to say why it moved; one can see that there may be a strong temptation to say more than one's expertise can justify!).

    The matter is further complicated in the case of evolution simply because the theory makes radical claims that are not only difficult to believe on their face, but that also appear to have profound implications for philosophical, theological, and moral questions. Most scientific theories remain in the restricted domain of science. They have no significant implications for other issues outside of science, for example, the theory of photosynthesis, or the theory of electromagnetism, and so most people seldom give them a second thought. They do not bother about whether a particular theory is true or not, are not interested in examining and debating the evidence for the theory, could care less about these topics. A second significant point is that for many theories (though not for all) we can see them confirmed in our own experience; for instance, we use electricity everyday, and while we have no desire to debate the evidence supporting the theory of electricity (the laws of electricity), the fact that we can see electricity in action is strong confirming evidence that electrical theory is true. Of course, the fact that electrical theory has no philosophical or moral implications also means that the theory is of no pressing concern to us. But these points do not apply to the theory of evolution. This is because, as we have noted, the theory makes radical claims, and this means that people are going to look at the evidence more closely and more critically than they would for other theories. Because of its radical claims, evolution is going to attract attention automatically, and in fact, as we noted in Chapter 1, evolution was a controversial theory from the very beginning.

The third point to consider is that we cannot see evolution in action in the way that we can see electricity in action; this can be a cause of further worry for many—it is a theory that is hard to verify and confirm. To many, there seems to be an elusiveness about the evidence in support of the theory that generates controversy. It is important to note this fact because it is a key point that is relevant in the cultural discussion about evolution. It is not just scientifically illiterate people, or people who have a strong religious motivation against evolution, who have difficulty assessing the evidence; many fair-minded and very intelligent people look at the evidence, and are not quite convinced by it, or can't quite see how it supports the theoretical claims of the theory. This is an interesting point in the debate about the theory, one that can further complicate the relationship between religion and evolution. It is important, therefore, to approach the topic by means of the three questions we have mentioned above. Our aim in what follows will be to identify the main points under each question, to raise the important issues that people have raised as a way of navigating through this complicated topic, so that we can make up our own minds on each question, and can arrive at an informed view. The theory of evolution is a fascinating and radical theory, and so an informed, logically careful, and dispassionate discussion of it is essential; too much hysteria on all sides surrounds the theory, and unfortunately only has the effect of adding to the confusion.

Brief history of evolution

The theory was first proposed by Charles Darwin (1809–1882), an English naturalist, in his book *The Origin of Species* (first published in 1859).[1]

(In Darwin's time, students of nature were often called "naturalists," not to be confused with the contemporary meaning of the term employed in the previous chapter.) The initial research, which led to the book, was gathered on a voyage Darwin made to South America over a five year period on the British ship, *HMS Beagle*, including a visit to the Galapagos Islands in 1835 (islands 600 miles off the coast of Ecuador). The book is concerned with providing an account of how all of the various species we see in nature, including not just human beings, but also animals, insects, even plants, came to be. Darwin was not so much interested in what we have called the ultimate question of how they came to be, but in the more localized question of how they came to exist in nature when they did, how they came to have the physical makeup and structure they have. Before Darwin, there was no accepted theory answering this question, and many scientists believed in "the fixity of the species," the view that the species always existed in their present form. Many held that the species were created just as they are by God, a view that was consistent with the Bible and also with Aristotle's physics.

It is rare for a scientist to discover a theory completely on his own, with no help from previous work by other dedicated scholars, and Darwin's theory is no exception to this rule. Many of the main points that Darwin brought together in proposing his theory had been individually developed before him, but their full significance had not yet dawned on earlier scientists. It is also true that much of the fossil research he relied upon to build his case for evolution was completed by other scientists. Among the influential forerunners and contemporaries of Darwin were James Hutton (1726–1797), George Cuvier (1769–1862), Charles Lyell (1797–1875), Carl Linnaeus (1707–1778), and Jean Baptiste Lamarck (1744–1829).[2]

Cuvier, a French naturalist, is often credited with developing the fields of comparative anatomy and paleontology (the study of life in prehistoric times) because he carried out a systematic study and classification of fossils. Fossils are the skeletal or trace remains of species, including plants and animals that have been preserved in sand and mud, and other strata, sometimes for millions of years, eventually becoming sedimentary rock. Locating, studying, and classifying them is a key part of evidence gathering for paleontologists. By studying and classifying fossils, Cuvier started the process of focusing on various species, trying to relate them to other species, studying their biological structures, and learning something about how they lived. He believed that many species had in fact become extinct due, most likely, to their environmental conditions (a radical view at the time because many thinkers held to the view that no species had ever become extinct because this would be a challenge to God's perfection). He also proposed the theory of catastrophism, the view that the earth had been hit over time by a series of catastrophes (most likely floods) which were responsible for wiping out various species, and which also significantly affected the environments of surviving species. The theory of catastrophism would also account for the significant gaps in the fossil record. After each catastrophe, a particular region would be repopulated by new species immigrating from surrounding areas. Among Cuvier's discoveries were the classification of various species of elephants; the proposal (later confirmed) that there was a time when reptiles had been dominant; his principle of correlation of parts—he suggested that by examining a single bone of a species found in a fossil, one could determine the species, and sometimes the genus, to which it belonged, a good insight into how comparative anatomy works. Cuvier rejected evolution, however, because his research showed that there were no significant changes over time in the fossil record, and that species bred true to type, with only small variations.

Jean Baptiste Lamarck, a French naturalist, was among the first to present a more developed model of evolution, and his views had a significant influence on Darwin. Lamarck argued that organisms developed their characteristics by adapting to their environments; the environment plays a large role in the development of the biological structure of an organism. Examples he gave to illustrate were the way repeated hammering by the blacksmith leads to the development of bigger biceps over time, and giraffes having to constantly stretch to reach tall trees for food leads to the development of long necks little by little. The idea is that this repeated behavior gradually leads to the development of the various characteristics in species along certain lines that are advantageous to the species, and that help the species to survive. Lamarck then argued for the "inheritance of acquired characteristics," the view that these characteristics would then be passed on to the offspring of the species in question, so that, to return to our giraffe example, eventually most giraffes would have long necks. One can see how perhaps in the case of the long necks of giraffes this view might be plausible (and even here it is a stretch!), but Lamarckism was controversial. Nevertheless, many were inclined to accept this theory to explain how species had the particular characteristics they had (including Darwin for a time). Lamarck also held that evolution was gradual, that the species were not fixed, but could change over time. Cuvier rejected some of Lamarck's conclusions because he held that the fossil record had too many breaks to support gradual evolution, and the inheritance of acquired characteristics was rendered suspect by the fact that these characteristics were often not passed on in future generations.

The work of Charles Lyell, especially in his *Principles of Geology* (1833), also had far-reaching significance not just in biology, but also in all of science, and its implications are still being debated. Lyell was influenced by geologist James Hutton's gradualist view that the current state of the earth could be understood by studying past causal activities, and that great change was brought about by small successive changes over a very long period of time. Lyell thought it reasonable to assume that the scientific laws which he observed operating in his own work had always operated, and so he came to the conclusion that the state of the earth in various fields, including geology and biology, was shaped by the laws of science operating on prior causal states over very long periods of time to produce present states and events. This view was known as uniformitarianism, and was presented in opposition to catastrophism, though the ideas are not necessarily incompatible once one remembers that catastrophes would be produced by the laws of science like any other event, and their effects would also occur according to the laws of science with the catastrophe as the prior cause. But, Lyell's idea that we could understand current biology by looking at past biological and geological states, along with the fact that the fossil record was being filled out in more detail, had a strong influence on Darwin. These conclusions, and various others, pointed to the fact that the earth must be very old, and that small changes over a long period of time could add up to profound change overall from one era to another.

So what we see is a series of key ideas emerging from different sources in order to explain significant phenomena in both biology and geology. These include: (1) the study of fossils, which not only helps us study and date many species, organisms, and life forms, but also helps us to think about how they might be related, and the role of comparative anatomy in thinking about these matters; (2) scientists started to focus especially on the task of classifying species, of noting the differences between species, of thinking scientifically about how species came into existence and went out of existence, of how species got their various characteristics, and of how these characteristics change from one species to another (e.g., in the elephant); (3) they began to look at the operation of scientific laws throughout nature, and at links between events in biology and their prior causes. We see that these scientists are not only doing fascinating work, but that they are dealing with a vast subject matter (think of the amount of species that have to be classified, along with the fact that they are spread all over the world, often in very remote locations, in addition to the time frame over which they stretch), and also a subject matter that is enormously complex, and open to different interpretations. In addition, because we are dealing with vast time scales (which we will survey as we go through Darwin's theory), much of the direct evidence is not even available, except for what we can find in the discovery, excavation, and study of fossils, a painstakingly slow enterprise. Not to mention the fact that this subject matter has a bearing on topics that inevitably have religious and philosophical significance, because we are talking about how species come into and go out of existence, how they develop their individual natures, whether these natures can change, the mechanisms by which nature in general operates, and how all of this would apply to our own species. Into this fascinating and somewhat perilous debate stepped Charles Darwin.

The theory of evolution

Darwin relied heavily on the research done by others, as well as his own work, to develop a more comprehensive theory of evolution, one that went beyond then current views, and also offered a radical set of claims about the origin and development of species. After Darwin returned to London from his voyages on the *HMS Beagle* in 1836, the main ideas of the theory of evolution were already beginning to form in his mind, but he spent the next 20 years gathering further data, refining his ideas, and sharing them with a select few (including Thomas Huxley), before he was willing to publish the theory. His book, *The Origin of Species*, basically brought a wide array of facts and research in biology and geology together arranged around a single organizing principle: evolution. This was one of the features that made his theory attractive, even though ultimately it would have to be judged on the evidence that Darwin put forward to support it.

One of the most helpful ways to think about what the theory of evolution actually claims about the origin of species is to work with an example, as a way of illustrating the main, general theoretical concepts of the theory. We must note before we begin that the concept of species refers to life-forms of a certain general kind or type. A species is usually defined as a group that interbreeds among themselves and produces fertile offspring, but that does not breed with any outside group; this is sometimes described in biology by saying that a species is a group that is "reproductively isolated" from another group (e.g., bobcat, cheetah, and cougar are different species of cat).[3] A genus groups together species of the same type (e.g., all the various species of cats). There are also varieties within a species; these would have slight variations in their characteristics, for example, the different varieties of finch Darwin saw on the Galapagos Islands. On his trip, Darwin had noticed that in general South American fauna and flora were quite different from those in Europe. He also found that most of the species on the Galapagos are unique to those islands, but that they resemble species on the mainland of South America. These findings suggested certain conclusions: that the species on the Galapagos were descendants from those on the mainland (e.g., there were three distinct species of mocking bird on the Galapagos that were closely related to, but different from, one on the mainland).[4] The differences were slight, which suggested that descent with modification (as Darwin called it) was gradual, not sudden, as some had suggested. It seemed also to imply that change occurs when populations are isolated from each other. The big question was: how did the evolution in the species take place?

After his return, Darwin began to see that we could account for the origin and nature of species by employing the concepts of descent with modification, natural selection, species adaptation, survival of the fittest, the main ideas eventually outlined in his path-breaking book. The idea of natural selection was suggested to him by a study of artificial selection widely used by farmers in England to produce desirable herds of cattle and dogs. If artificial selection could be used to produce small changes in animals in a relatively short time, then natural selection could produce significant changes operating over a very long time. Darwin got the idea of survival of the fittest after he read (in 1838) a pamphlet by English economist, Thomas Malthus, in which Malthus argued that since there are limited resources, there would inevitably be a struggle for existence among human beings. Let us further illustrate these ideas that became the basis for the theory of evolution with the example of the finch.

Darwin had noticed different species of finch on the Galapagos Islands. He speculated that millions of years earlier mainland finches had flown out to the Galapagos, and that these present finches were the descendants of the mainland ones. The mainland finches were of a different species than the present Galapagos species. They may have had different colors, different body sizes, different wing spans, and, in particular, different beak sizes. Darwin was not sure how they got these various characteristics originally, though he believed this was not a crucial matter for his theory; the important fact is that they have these various features, and that they are passed on to the offspring by the parents. He proposed that over very long periods of time, using the finches on the Galapagos as an example, there was a struggle for existence going on in nature between the various species, and that those who survive this struggle do so because they have some kind of advantage over other species. So those finches, for instance, that survive do so because they are the "fittest," meaning not the strongest or healthiest, but that they are best able to cope—apparently because of chance—with the particular environment they find themselves in.

He argued that the beaks of finches (to take a specific biological characteristic) evolved in various ways due to environmental factors that influenced the source and supply of food. Those finches that had long beaks may have survived because the food was in inaccessible places requiring long beaks to hunt it out, and so those with short beaks often died. At other times, those finches with beaks most suitable for digging out insects survived best in climates when insects were more plentiful, and those with beaks not suitable for hunting out insects gradually died. Eventually, those finches with beaks suitable to find the available food came to predominate in a certain area, and interbreed, and passed on their characteristics to their offspring, and so only finches with beaks suitable for eating the type of food available in that area survived. And so he rejected Lamarck's view that the repeated beak-activity of a finch would lead to the development of a longer beak; what happens, he argued, is that some have long beaks and some have short beaks, and those with long beaks survive better, and pass on their characteristics (including the long beak) to their offspring, so that eventually long-beaked finches dominate. This appeal to evolutionary principles, he believed, could explain all of an organism's features. For example, it could explain why certain birds have a certain type of body size, wing span, eye structure, hearing arrangement, and so on. This story about the evolution of the finches illustrates the two main points of Darwinism: first, that species are genetically related to each other (common descent); and second, that natural selection is the process or mechanism that drives evolutionary change.

This leads to the concepts of microevolution and macroevolution. Microevolution is often defined as evolution within a species, or within and between closed related species, such as within the class of finches, or elephants, or whales. (Recall that a group of species that are closely related to each other is called a genus [plural genera].) Microevolution refers to the fact that Darwin's account of how a species survives, and of how it gets its individual characteristics, also entails that many of the species within a genus, for example, within the genus of finches, *are related to each other genetically*. This means that today's finches on the Galapagos Islands are descendants of past species of finches who lived nearby on the mainland. But this then raises the question as to whether *all* species of finch are genetically related to each other as well?

Might they all have the same common ancestor? Might they all be descendents from the same parents (or same species?). This then suggests the question of macroevolution: might it be the case that widely different species (in different genera), such as human beings and chimpanzees, might be genetically related? Could it be that human beings and chimps have a common ancestor? Might human beings, chimps, fish, and birds have a common ancestor? Might it be that all the species that have ever lived are genetically related to each other, going back to a single life-form that lived billions of years ago?

Darwin's theory of evolution proposed the radical claim that all species that live now or that have ever lived are genetically connected to each other, including not just human beings and lower animals, but also insects, plants, bacteria, and other simpler organisms. This genetic connectedness of all the species is nowadays known as macroevolution. Darwin came to the view that all of the present species in the world evolved from common ancestors, right back to the very first life-forms, which some speculate were one-celled organisms that appeared between 4 and 5 billion years ago (in the sea). He argued that more complex life-forms emerge over time from simple life-forms, by means of the mechanism of natural selection—the struggle for survival in nature in which only the fittest survive, and which also determines the physical makeup of the various species. A diagram of the history of this whole process (which can be found in many biology textbooks) is referred to as the tree of life. In most books, it begins with one single-celled organism, which reflects the view of many evolutionary biologists (but some say it could have begun in different places with several different initial life-forms). For the first 2 billion years, life existed only in microbial, single-celled organisms, yet, gradually over the next billion years, more complex species began to evolve, and in the last half a billion years many of our most complex species began to appear, of which the present species are descendents, including *Homo sapiens*, human beings. (In *The Origin of Species*, Darwin was reluctant to get into a discussion of man, but did do so in his later book, *The Descent of Man* [1871].)

Around about 520 million years ago we had the Cambrian period, in which we find the "Cambrian explosion," the rapid appearance of many major species ancestral to several modern species (such as shellfish and corals). The best-known source of fossils in this period is the Burgess Shale, discovered in the Canadian Rockies in 1909. By the end of the Cambrian period, there is evidence for nearly all major animal groups.[5] After this point, new organisms appear in a pattern of historical succession that is very well documented. The first fish appear in the Ordovician period (480 million years), the first amphibians appeared 380 million years ago, the first reptiles 40 million years later, and the first dinosaurs appear 80 million years after that in the Triassic period (250–200 million years ago). The first birds appear in the Jurassic period (155 million years ago). All of this is based on a study of, and interpretation of, the fossil record.[6] Only in the last 3 or 4 million years did the ancestors of human beings and the higher primates begin to appear.

According to the theory of evolution then human beings and chimpanzees had a common ancestor (3–5 million years ago). Gradually two distinct lines of new genera split off from this common ancestor, evolving over a few million years so that eventually we have new species of chimp on one line, and of *Homo sapiens* on the other line, with many related species in between. For example, on the line that led to *Homo sapiens*, we also had earlier species, such as *A. africanus* (3.5 million years ago, of which the female skeleton, Lucy, is the most famous fossil); *H. habilis* (2 million years ago); *H. neanderthalensis* (Neanderthal man) and *H. erectus*, our closest ancestors (1–2 million years ago), and then *Homo sapiens*, the only surviving species from this lineage (200,000 years ago).

The tree of life hypothesis, therefore, says that you and the chimps in the zoo and the plants in your garden and the bacteria in your trash can have, if we go back far enough, a common ancestor; we are genetically related to all of them, and indeed to every other species or life-form, simple or complex, that has ever existed (or that ever will exist in the future).

The evidence for evolution: questions and answers

One can see that the theory of evolution is very radical, especially the macroevolution part of the theory. And this brings us to the question of the evidence for the theory. Initially, many people (including many scientists) either rejected the theory, or were very suspicious of it. This was not only because they found its conclusions unsettling (which many did), but also because they thought it would be quite a hard theory to establish, that much of the evidence offered was suggestive, speculative, and circumstantial, but hardly decisive or compelling. Darwin himself thought that the mechanism of natural selection occurred too slowly to be observable. And, outside of science, that is where many people still are today who look at the evidence for themselves (and not counting those who are convinced because scientists are convinced).

The examples referred to above to illustrate evolution concerning the finches, and other species, are mostly made-up stories to illustrate the main claims of the theory. What this means is that these illustrations are not based on actual, detailed known case examples of natural selection in action that have been fully discovered and reported by evolutionary biologists. The theory Darwin proposed to explain the evolutionary development of the finches was speculative; once he had the main concepts of the theory in place, he used the finches' story to illustrate how it might have happened, but the story is not based on actual empirical evidence about how the finches did evolve. How could it be, since most of the fossils, and other essential evidence we would need to know how the finches lived, survived, developed, and reproduced is long gone, including evidence relating to the environmental habitats, climate patterns, food types, competitors of the finches, not to mention detailed evidence about the biological structure of the finches' ancestors. Even if this evidence were available, it would still be difficult (indeed impossible) to reconstruct exactly the path of development of the finches. The story about the finches is based on what lawyers would call circumstantial evidence: we have fossils of finches with different size beaks, we know something about the climate in which they lived, about the food available to them (both now and in the past), about their ancestors, about their competitors, but we still have to reconstruct much of what we think might have happened in their evolutionary development not only to explain what the theory of evolution is saying, but also to show that the theory is true.

In considering the theory, the same common sense questions about the evidence for evolution, and related matters, always come up, especially among students and members of the general public. These questions are likely to be on the mind of readers of this chapter. I think one of the best ways to explore the topic further is by considering a number of these common sense questions and responses to them. Our objective in considering these questions is to cover the main concerns that arise in relation to the subject so that we can have an informed view as we make up our own minds about the significant claims made by the theory of evolution.

1. Why is fossil evidence important, and what does it show?

The fossil evidence is one of the main planks of evidence for the theory of evolution. By studying and classifying fossils, which is obviously an ongoing process, paleontologists believe that we can discover the nature of various species, and learn something about how they lived. We can also discover species that are thought to be closely related that lived nearby at the same time. That way we can document the various species of elephant, for example, and also the similarities and differences between them. The close proximity of the fossils, paleontologists argue, both in terms of time and in terms of location, make it reasonable to conclude that the species are *genetically* related to each other. Examples often cited in this regard include the species of whales, elephants, and gorillas, whose lineages have been well documented. Since Darwin's time, thousands of fossils have been found and classified showing evidence of a host of species.

Evolutionary biologists argue that the evidence from the fossil record makes it reasonable to conclude that various species are genetically related to each other. This is because, if you have the fossils of various species of elephants, for instance, as Kenneth Miller has pointed out,[7] and you place them all in a row according to their age, with the oldest placed first, down to the youngest, which is last, and you also note that they lived in the same geographical area, and that they have very similar anatomical structures (modern elephants, 10,000 years old, and extinct elephants, 34 million years old, have very similar skull and trunk structures), then it is reasonable to conclude that the younger ones are descendents of the older ones, even though direct links are very difficult to establish. The same is true for human beings. At the time of Darwin, there were no fossils linking human beings with apes, but since then, many fossils have been found (as described above), and the closer these fossils are to the present time, the more similar they are to modern humans, so the inference is made that they are recent ancestors of human beings.

Other circumstantial evidence includes the fact that common descent would account for why we find similar species mostly in the same place (e.g., similar species of both finches and armadillos on and near the Galapagos), for the similarity between the anatomies of different species (e.g., between the forelimbs of whales, birds, dogs, and human beings), for the overall basic similarities between species (e.g., in their digestive, circulatory, and nervous systems), for the fact that the embryos of different species have many similarities in their early stages (e.g., human and dog embryos), for the fact that the fossils over time become gradually more complex, and it also may account for the presence of vestigial (or redundant) organs in some species (the appendix in man, or the wings of ostriches). Evolutionary biologists also argue that the view that the species are not genetically related, but were either directly created just as they are by God, or that they came about just as they are by some natural process other than evolution, is not reasonable.

2. Why are there few transitional species?

Critics of evolution often claim that in order to support macroevolution many transitional species (or intermediary forms) should exist in the fossil record, and that not many have been found. Evolutionary theorists, such as Stephen J. Gould, have also recognized this problem.[8] A transitional species is a species that would be somewhere between two very different species (possessing traits together that are later separated out in distinct lineages), such as the common ancestor of apes and human beings, or the common ancestor of fish and birds, and so forth. The common ancestor of fish and birds, for instance, might have feet and wings, meaning that it could live on land and fly, as well as survive in the water. Then, as this species evolved, two new distinct species separated off from it, one of which lived on the land, could fly, but could not live in water, and one of which lived only in the sea, and could not survive on land, or fly. So, in addition to having fossils of the one that later lived in the sea and the one that later lived on the land, we should also have fossils of the ancestor who has significant traits of both of the younger species.

It is a fact about evolution that although there are some transitional species, there are not as many as one would expect to find. Darwin himself noted that this was one of the main objections to his theory. Biologists reply to this objection by insisting that they have discovered hundreds of transitional species. Two of the best known are *Archaeopteryx* and *Ambulocetus*. *Archaeopteryx* is a fossil of the earliest bird, which lived around 150 million years ago (in Germany), and is evidence of a transition between dinosaurs and birds. *Ambulocetus* (50 million years ago in Pakistan), is a whalelike crocodile, which seems to have been amphibious, and is thought to be a common ancestor of modern whales and land mammals. Biologists also argue that despite the gaps in the record, the record does move from simple life-forms to more complex ones. (This means that evolution could perhaps be falsified if fossils of complex species were discovered that predate the simple life-forms; so far, none have been found.)

There are larger questions about the evidence for macroevolution that transitional species may not help us with. For example, if the tree of life as it is presented in most biology textbooks is true, this would mean that life started as a single-celled organism, which then divided and reproduced, and eventually we ended up with all of the species we now have (including us), as well as the millions that became extinct along the way (90 percent of all species, according to some estimates). This is a very speculative claim that would require many detailed transitional fossils in order to lay it out clearly, and indisputably. This evidence would also have to show how the two sexes originated, and how they became perfectly reproductively compatible. Biologists argue that the fossil record will eventually establish these claims as it becomes more complete, and critics argue that until we do have this evidence before us, macroevolution remains little more than a speculative hypothesis.

3. Does natural selection explain how evolution works?

The genetic relatedness, or common ancestry, of all the species is one of the main parts of the theory of evolution, but the second main part is that it is the mechanism or process of natural selection that drives evolutionary change, as we explained above. Most evolutionary biologists argue that natural selection is now well documented, even though in Darwin's time most scientists thought the evidence for selection was weak, and that some other theory of the process of change would replace it in due course. It is possible to accept the common descent of all species without accepting that natural selection is the process of change; there are also many biologists who accept natural selection but who do not think it can explain everything about the nature of species. The finches example, mentioned above, is the example most often cited in biology textbooks to illustrate the process of natural selection. Darwin agreed that there were obstacles to accepting this second facet of his theory. As he put it: "To suppose that the eye, with all its inimitable contrivances for adjusting the focus to different distances, for admitting different amounts of light, and for the correction of spherical and chromatic aberration, could have been formed by natural selection, seems, I freely confess, absurd in the highest possible degree." However, he thought these difficulties could be overcome: "If it could be demonstrated that any complex organ existed, which could not possibly have been formed by numerous successive, slight modifications, my theory would absolutely break down. But I can find no such case.... Numerous cases could be given amongst the lower animals of the same organ performing... wholly distinct functions." He cited several examples, including the swim bladder in fishes that was originally used for flotation, but then later for respiration (and so he thought natural selection could further convert it into a lung in higher animals).[9]

The thesis of natural selection proposes that the different parts of the eye evolved over time, for example, the optic nerve, giving the species a distinct advantage that enabled it to survive better than a similar species that did not have an optic nerve. However, the advantage was not sight, because in order for sight to occur, one would have to have most of the eye in place already, as well as the optic nerve, and the connections to the eye and brain. The same is true for the separate parts of the eye as it was forming, for example, the retina, cornea, lens, pupil, iris, etc. The cornea, for instance, evolved and gave the species an advantage but again the advantage was not sight. The problem arises because we do not know in most cases what advantage each evolutionary development conferred on a species, and are forced to speculate about this matter. As one can see, there are an awful lot of gaps, ifs and speculations about this process, a lot of what some call "just so" stories to explain how natural selection works in various species. But it looks impossible to ever reconstruct the actual process of natural selection in any particular species. Many people look at the explanation of the process of natural selection, and conclude that it is not reasonable to think that the process gave rise to not just enormously complex organs like the eye, but to all of the anatomical and biological features of all species. If natural selection is true, it would be the case that, to take human beings as an illustration, the eye, ear, mouth, heart, lungs, etc. all originated through this process, *each* distinctive feature of *each* organ selected out (e.g., the heart, with its various parts such as the ventricles, atriums, valves, arteries) because of the struggle for survival in nature, and then eventually all organs ended up working together (individually *and* collectively) as the organism became ever more complex.

It is not unreasonable for people to look at this explanation and to ask for more direct evidence before accepting it, so critics argue. Supporters of evolution argue that because we can document reasonably well how finches ended up with long beaks in some circumstances, it follows that this is how other features of the finch (and of all other species) evolved. Evolutionary biologists also point to examples of microevolution as models for how macroevolution might have occurred, such as development of resistance to antibiotics in bacteria (this occurs because bacteria exist in huge numbers and multiply rapidly, so that a mutation that enables a species to become resistant to a drug is likely to occur eventually) and the case of flowers adapting in different ways to their insect pollinators. Critics reply that there is still a huge gap between microevolution and macroevolution; that the finches story also has many gaps in it, and is still quite circumstantial, that it is a stretch to move from this essentially speculative account to affirm with apparent certainty that this is how all features of species, and how all new species, originate.

Some have also raised questions about how natural selection can account for the advanced form of consciousness we find in human beings, including our capacity for reason, free will, and morality (which we will discuss in the next chapter).[10] Darwin discussed this question in *The Descent of Man*, where he argued that human beings and animals differ in degree and not in kind. To make this argument, he engaged in a device still common today: he exaggerated the capabilities of animals, especially in the areas of intelligence and communication, and downplayed the uniqueness and complexity of human qualities. He speculated (like Richard Dawkins has done today) that many human qualities, such as love, the desire for knowledge, and religious beliefs, might have survival value. His ideas are clearly moving in this book toward a materialistic account of man, but they proved extremely controversial and were rejected by many scientists who accepted much of the rest of his theory, including Lyell, Alfred Russell Wallace, and Asa Gray. These scientists argued that it was too much of a stretch to reach such a conclusion based on such sparse evidence, and that Darwin had ignored or downplayed the enormous complexity of human beings when he suggested in *The Descent of Man* that our moral values amount to no more than rationalizations of social instincts which we inherited from apes who developed them because they lived in groups.

4. What about the evidence from genetics and DNA?

The work of one of the pioneers of genetics research, Gregor Mendel (1822–1884), became very significant for the theory of evolution. Mendel was an Austrian monk who documented a law-like process (in 1865) that could produce new species of pea plants from hybrids of existing species. The significance of this achievement was not appreciated for another 30 years until biologists realized that Mendel's laws offered an insight into how evolution worked. (One of Mendel's laws states that each inherited characteristic is determined by two heredity genes, one coming from each parent, which are responsible for determining whether a gene will be dominant or recessive.) Influenced by Mendel's discoveries, scientists then posited the existence of genes in various species to explain the passing on by parents to offspring of traits that later turned out to be advantageous for survival. Alterations in the genes of an individual—called random or chance mutations—would affect the trait being passed on, and its survival value. These mutations are caused by problems inherent in the DNA itself, as well as by environmental factors, including diet. So, the existence of genes that are subject to chance mutation, and the process of natural selection, would work together to produce new species.

In recent times, scientists have begun to focus on the makeup of the gene through an analysis of its DNA, which is seen as offering further evidential support for evolution. Recent work in genetics shows that there is a 95 percent similarity between the DNA of human beings and the DNA of chimps, and 60–70 percent similarity between the DNA of human beings and mice (indeed some researchers have recently argued that DNA evidence shows that chimps are closer to *Homo sapiens* than they are to gorillas, and so should be in the genus *Homo*, which contains only humans). This suggests, therefore, that such species are genetically related, based on the same principle that enables us to tell that two men are brothers, or that one man is the father of another, the basic idea being that the closer the genetic similarities the more closely related the species are. We can now document by an analysis of DNA that part of the tree of life that illustrates the linkage of human beings, chimpanzees, gorillas, and orangutans, all the way back to the common apelike ancestor of all these species. Combining the fossil evidence, the evidence from comparative anatomy, along with DNA evidence for evolution, is called "the modern synthesis."[11]

One might wonder if the DNA evidence actually shows what it seems to show. Critics argue that an intelligent designer could have designed all life with a similar DNA structure, and so it would not follow logically that species with similar DNA are genetically related to each other. Even without knowing the DNA evidence, it is sometimes argued, we always knew that chimpanzees and human beings were similar in structure, but we did not think they had a common ancestor. The DNA evidence only shows that the various biological structures are even more similar than we thought. As an analogy, we observe great similarities between new models of the same make of car each year (usually moving from the simple to the complex), but we don't infer that they are genetically related; we know that the reason they are similar is because they have been designed that way! Might it not be the same with nature?

Francis Collins, former head of the Human Genome Project, has raised this point, but he argues that the similarity in DNA is so striking that it inevitably points in the direction of common descent. Collins compares the mouse genome with the human genome, both of which have been determined to a high degree of accuracy. Several features point to common ancestry, Collins argues, including the similar size of the genomes, the remarkable similarity of the inventory of protein-coding genes, and the ordering of the genes in both which is substantially the same over long stretches of DNA (e.g., all of the genes on human chromosome 17 are found on mouse chromosome 11). There are also similar sequences of "junk DNA" in both mouse and human, and the clincher for Collins is that sometimes this DNA is damaged (and as a result cannot function), and "in many instances, one can identify a decapitated and utterly defunct section of DNA in parallel positions in the human and the mouse genomes."[12] Collins recognizes that some will object that "junk DNA" may not really be junk at all, and that the ordering of genes in the chromosomes is crucial for development and so the different ordering in different species should not be taken as a similarity but as a difference. Nevertheless, he thinks that "unless one is willing to take the position that God has placed [this DNA] in these precise positions to confuse and mislead us, the conclusion of a common ancestor for humans and mice is virtually inescapable."[13] (For more on DNA, see Chapter 8.)

5. What are we to make of the fact that many intelligent people of goodwill have doubts about evolution?

It is a fact that, unlike many other scientific theories, evolution has a lot of doubters, even among the intellectual classes.[14] We are not referring to doubts and criticisms from within the movement of creationism, which we will discuss later. But it is true of the theory of evolution that while the majority of people accept the overall outline of the theory, there are a very significant number of people who have doubts about some of its features. In this respect, it is similar to theories about global warming. Like global warming, many of those who accept evolution (including most scientists who do not work in the area of evolution) do so "on authority," which means that they accept it because the major evolutionary scientists are convinced that it is true, and not because they have studied the theory for themselves and have examined the evidence. Few could probably give an overview of the main claims of the theory and the main lines of evidence for these claims if called upon to do so. There is nothing wrong with accepting a scientific theory on authority in normal circumstances; indeed, most of us believe most scientific theories on the say so of the scientists who work on them (especially those that we cannot confirm in our own experience). Yet if a theory is controversial, and there are many reasonable people of goodwill who doubt it, it is perhaps no longer satisfactory to accept the theory on authority, but necessary to examine the theory more closely for oneself.

It may be tempting to dismiss the views of those who question evolution by saying that people are afraid of its consequences for religion because it challenges the notion of design in nature, and the special status of man in the great scheme of things (and we have seen in earlier chapters how some have used the theory as a support for atheism, an approach I suggested is misguided). It is true that some people reject the theory primarily out of fear or because they don't like the religious or philosophical implications of the theory. However, I think this is only one of several reasons for why people have doubts about evolution. The fact that the consequences of evolution are very significant only makes people more cautious about accepting it, and more inclined to look hard at the evidence for the theory. It is reasonable to look carefully at the evidence for any theory that makes such momentous claims as the theory of evolution does. This is why people are interested in, and concerned about, evolution in a way that they are not interested in other scientific theories, such as theories about relativity or the laws of mechanics. The theory of evolution makes such radical claims that it is natural for people to insist that it satisfy the highest standards of evidence, that those who defend it present the evidence for it clearly, and examine it responsibly.

This is why it is accurate to say that there is another answer to the question as to why so many intelligent people have doubts about evolution. It is because the evidence for the theory appears to many to be suggestive, but not conclusive. Many people look at the claims of the theory of evolution, and then look at the evidence for these claims, and judge that the evidence has too many gaps in it, too many unknowables, too many "just so" stories, too many shots in the dark, as it were. The theory contains enough statements that are "unscientific" to make people wary (assuming the definition of a scientific statement as one for which there is reasonably good evidence). To confirm this point we only have to look closely at the story told about the finches above which is supposed to illustrate natural selection. The comparison of the fossils of the finches would be a source of good scientific evidence, but the story told for how the beaks of the finches evolved over time is mostly speculation, as is, for instance, the story told to explain the evolution of other bodily organs, such as the eye.

The theory of evolution appears to rely upon more unscientific statements and "stories" like these than many other scientific theories, and this is a constant worry not only for those who doubt the theory, but also for those who support it. Books on evolution by well-known experts such as Stephen J. Gould, Richard Dawkins, and Christian de Duve are chock-full of these stories, chock-full of "unscientific" claims.[15] When making an informed judgment about the evidence for evolution, one has to make up one's own mind as to whether the scientific statements that are backed up with evidence support the theory fairly well over those unscientific statements that are not backed up with evidence.

We have not been helped in trying to grasp the evidence by the political nature of the debate about evolution that goes on in many countries around the world, including the United States. It may be that cultural reasons play a significant role in the fact that many people are not familiar with the evidence for evolution. The political and social issues raised by the theory have made many scientists reluctant even to discuss the theory in public; indeed, one can seldom have a discussion of the theory on a purely scientific level without getting into the political issues as well. This situation has made many scientists very defensive about the theory in general; understandably, as they attempt to argue for the theory, they see their main critics, not as other scientists, but as creationists, and various religious denominations. This has prevented us from having a substantive, honest, and open debate about the evidence. This kind of debate might help people to see the evidence that is available more clearly, and to better understand the theory overall; it would also discourage scientists from taking the attitude that there are no problems with the evidence, and from impugning the motives of those who question the theory. Richard Dawkins, for instance, does not want to allow any noteworthy critical discussion of evolution. He thinks there is no controversy about the theory, and even though others may disagree, Dawkins has argued that *his* view that we should not "teach the controversy" surrounding evolution should prevail in our institutions of higher education.[16] But Dawkins' position is shortsighted. For it is a cultural fact about evolution that many have doubts about aspects of the theory, especially natural selection, and this debate is one that the scientific community, particularly evolutionary biologists, has yet to come to terms with; indeed, it is a debate which should have more influence than it does now on how evolution is taught in educational institutions.

Religious, philosophical, and moral implications of evolution

We must now move on to look at the implications of the theory of evolution, which have proved just as controversial as the debate over the evidence. Evolution raises a host of questions about three main areas: (1) the status of the Bible, and other revealed texts; (2) the status of human beings in the universe; and (3) the question of design in the universe. Let us examine each of these areas in turn by again asking some interesting questions.

1. The status of the Bible: does evolution undermine the authority of the Bible?

It is often argued that evolution undermines the authority of the Bible. (Since we are mainly dealing with western religion in this book, we will concentrate on evolution and the Bible, but our analysis will apply to all claims about revelation in any religion insofar as they address the subject matter of creation, and the origin and development of life.) This is because if the theory of evolution is true, it seems to contradict the book of Genesis. This book says that: "God made the wild animals of the earth of every kind, and the cattle of every kind, and everything that creeps upon the ground of every kind. And God saw that it was good. Then God said, 'Let us make humankind in our image, according to our likeness; and let them have dominion over the fish of the sea, and over the birds of the air, and over the cattle, and over all the wild animals of the earth, and over every creeping thing that creeps upon the earth'" (Gen. 1.25–26). This means that God created the species intact and complete, as it were, and in a relatively short time, and not by means of an evolutionary process that took place over a much longer period. It also seems to mean that there was no struggle for survival, no extinctions, no natural selection, and so forth. The book of Genesis conveys the point that human beings are special, that they differ in kind and not just in degree from other species (a point we will return to in the next section). There are conflicting views over whether the biblical passages suggest that life (and also the universe) came into existence quite recently, a view that would contradict many scientific theories (not just evolution), whose data show that the universe has been around a very long time (such as the big bang theory in cosmology). It is estimated that the process of evolution from the beginning of the tree of life up to our present time took about 5 billion years; in addition, the big bang is thought to have occurred between 10–15 billion years ago. For most of that time there was no life on earth, so various passages seem to put the Bible on a collision course with evolution, as well as with other scientific theories.

Biblical literalists, also called creationists (especially in the context of this discussion), are particularly opposed to evolution because they hold that in general the Bible should be read literally, though they are not committed to the view that it does not contain any metaphor, symbolism, allegory, parable, or allusion. But creationists argue that a literal reading of the Bible is the most reasonable approach to biblical interpretation. Their view is that for Christians who regard the Bible as reliable, as the word of God, it is more reasonable to think that, in general, it should be read in a literal way because God would not reveal key features of his actions and his message in metaphors or stories because of the danger of them being misunderstood. Therefore, just as we should not think that the resurrection or the incarnation in the New Testament are metaphors, we should not think that the Old Testament account of creation is a metaphor. Creationists do not expect this argument to convince the secularist, but they do think it is a good argument to offer to other religious believers who accept the Bible, but who favor a more metaphorical approach to the creation story. Creationists also sometimes adopt another strategy when dealing with evolution. This involves leaving all issues of theological interpretation aside, and considering the theory of evolution simply as a scientific theory, and offering an appraisal and critique of the evidence on its own merits. They sometimes mix both approaches in their public discussions of this matter. In addition, some creationists are "young earth creationists" and some (perhaps the majority) are "old earth creationists" (who accept the big bang theory).[17] (Creationism should not be confused with Intelligent Design theory, which we will hold off discussing until Chapter 6.)

So creationists in general propose the view that if a scientific theory like evolution comes along that contradicts a literal reading of the Bible, then the scientific theory must be wrong in significant respects, and should be revised. Otherwise, the authority of the Bible is undermined. They further argue that if we are to accept that significant parts of the Bible are metaphor and symbolism (e.g., the creation story), why not accept that most of it is? This would have the effect of undermining the reliability of the Bible under the influence of what they regard as dubious science. They point out that evolution has in fact had this very effect on the Bible, because many religious believers today, often under the influence of science, have come to the view that the Bible is mostly metaphor, including accounts of the incarnation and resurrection of Christ. Modern theologians such as Rudolf Bultmann have asked how we can believe in the Bible in the age of electric light, as if we should allow contemporary science to dictate what can be true in all areas of life, including the areas of biblical interpretation and religion.[18] In addition, biblical literalists point out, atheists too have joined this bandwagon, such as Thomas Huxley in Darwin's time, and Richard Dawkins today, in claiming that evolution does in fact undermine the Bible, shows that the Bible is unreliable, is just a series of stories and not the revealed word of God.

But many theologians and religious believers are not nearly as vexed about the implications of evolution for the status of the Bible as creationists are. These theologians argue that evolution does not undermine the Bible in any serious way, and so we need not worry about the theory being antireligious. It is true that evolution would show that the biblical story of Genesis is not literally true, but many accepted this point long before the theory of evolution came along, including St. Augustine (as we noted in Chapter 2). Many find St. Augustine's general way of handling this point very persuasive (including thinkers in both theology and science, such as Howard Van Till, John Polkinghorne, John Haught, and Kenneth Miller).[19] Augustine argued that if a scientific theory is supported by good evidence, but conflicts with the Bible, then we should revise our understanding of the biblical account. But the deeper philosophical and theological points being made in the Bible by means of the story remain true. And we never have to worry about a scientific theory, evolution, or any other theory, coming along that falsifies these deeper points. Augustine thought that the creation story could easily be read in a metaphorical way to illustrate a deeper point, but this would not be the case with the resurrection, for instance, which is clearly presented as something that literally happened. In addition, we must point out that we cannot allow an argument that says science shows that human beings do not rise from the dead to refute the resurrection (or any other claim to the miraculous) because this argument assumes in advance that naturalism is true, and so is question-begging; or to put it another way, it assumes that God does not exist, and so could not override the laws of physics in some special cases, such as in the case of the resurrection. It is circular reasoning to rule out miracles in advance before the existence of God has been decided, a mistake many modern theologians, including Bultmann, seem to have fallen into.[20]

2. The status of human beings: does evolution show that man is not "special"?

It is argued by many, and suspected by others (including some religious believers), that evolution might undermine the special status of human beings in creation. Naturalists Richard Dawkins and Edward O. Wilson, among others, have argued for this view. Dawkins, as we have seen in the previous chapter, argues that evolution undermines the notion of teleology in nature because human beings are fully produced by the evolutionary process, just like all other species, and so differ only in degree from them. Wilson has pioneered the field of sociobiology, the study of the biological basis of social behavior, using evolutionary principles as a guide, and comparing human behavior and animal behavior in a series of intriguing speculations. He suggests that human beings are shaped more by their genetic inheritance, and their environment, than by anything else, and that there is no such thing as free will. Morality, therefore, is also the product of culture, which in turn is mostly the product of genetics; in addition, moral behavior must be explained in terms of its evolutionary advantages.[21] Along with Michael Ruse, he has argued that "ethics ... is an illusion fobbed off on us by our genes to get us to cooperate [with each other]."[22]

Let us tease out the many issues raised by this complex topic by considering several more specific questions.

a. *Is the human species necessary or accidental?* The question of necessity and contingency in philosophy in general is a quite fascinating one, and it comes up again when one is considering various scientific theories. The question is aimed at exploring what about our universe, including the existence and nature of life, *has to be the way it is, and could not be otherwise*? The question is often asked about the laws of physics, about the overall architecture of the universe, about the specific species that exist, about the relationship between the species, and about the biological structure of the species. Must these features of the universe necessarily be the way they are, or might they have been different? Could, for example, the laws of physics have been different? Could we have ended up in a universe in which Newton's law that "for every action there is an equal and opposite reaction" is not true, and where some other relationship between material bodies holds? As regards evolution, could a whole series of different species have evolved than the ones that actually did evolve? Might it have been possible for human beings not to have evolved at all, or perhaps we might have had a different biological structure (six fingers on each hand perhaps)? It is important to be clear about what this question is asking. It is not asking could God, or whoever designed the universe, have designed it differently. God probably could have designed the universe in many different ways. The question is asking: given our study of science and the natural processes that produce effects in the universe, might these processes have produced something different than what they did in fact produce? If the process of evolution had gone differently, could it have been the case that human beings might not have existed at all? *Could* the process have gone differently?

This is what thinkers like Dawkins, Sagan, Wilson, and Stephen J. Gould are suggesting. They hold that the theory of evolution not only shows that the creation story in the Bible is false, but that in general it shows that the religious view of the world is *not true*. This is because the theory of evolution suggests that human beings are not special in the way that most religions argue they are. The existence of the human species is due to the "blind forces" of natural selection, and not due to design or necessity. Human beings were produced by exactly the same natural processes that produced all of the other species. It is also true, according to these thinkers, that the human species did not have to emerge from this process, its emergence was simply an accident of natural selection. If we replayed the tape of life, as Stephen J. Gould has put it, we would end up with different species than the ones we have now, and almost certainly there would be no species of *Homo sapiens*. Gould argues that if we examine the processes of evolution closely, they do not seem to show evidence of design.[23] Quite the contrary, Gould argues, the whole process seems to show evidence of randomness, chance occurrences, dead ends, and lucky breaks. Evolution involves a lot of waste, many adaptations do not work, some species survive but in difficult circumstances, etc., all evidence, it is claimed, against evolution having any order or design behind it.

In short, these thinkers are saying that if we examine the actual process of evolution, it appears to operate by chance, and not design, and given this, the products of evolution, including our species, would come to exist by chance as well. This would mean that not only did *Homo sapiens* not have to exist, but also that we did not have to occupy the place in the tree of life that we do in fact occupy, that we did not have to have the biological and anatomical structure that we have. In addition, our species may become extinct, or be surpassed by other species that evolve to a greater degree of sophistication than us (millions of years into the future). This is because there is an element of chance operating in nature that is outside of our control, despite the fact that we are the only species to understand the process of evolution, and to have some (but not total) control over it (a disease could wipe out our species, or severely restrict our progress, and open the door for another species to surpass us). Yet, this discussion is not complete without further consideration of the fact that human beings have consciousness and free will, and the status of these features in the evolutionary story, and without further consideration of what is meant by saying that nature operates by "chance." The issue of whether the human species is accidental or necessary brings up the crucial question of the role of chance in nature.

b. *Does evolution occur by chance*? The concept of chance is always lurking in the background in any discussion of evolution but is seldom brought out in detail. But many evolutionary biologists are clear in saying that the process of evolution involves a lot of chance, as Gould's view above illustrates. But what does this mean? In answering, we must be careful to distinguish between what we might describe as the surface view of chance and a deeper metaphysical account of chance. On the surface, evolutionary biologists, such as Gould, argue that it certainly appears as if the evolutionary process is significantly governed by chance. For instance, in the development of a particular species, like chimpanzees, it is a matter of chance which features are constitutive of the environment that (the ancestors of) the chimps find themselves in, features which in turn affect their development, that is, their chemical, biological, and anatomical makeup. For example, it is a matter of chance that the environment the chimps' ancestors lived in was relatively free of stormy weather because stormy weather would destroy the ancestors' source of food, and severely affect the survival of the species. This means that it is really just a matter of luck that the chimps survived at all. It might seem that there must be some necessity in the process of how the chimp evolved because his biological structure will significantly determine the future structure of his descendents; for example, if he can walk upright then it would not be a matter of chance that his descendents could escape certain predators; however, we must not forget that the fact that he can walk upright is itself a matter of chance, as is his whole structure (and the structure of the predator). So, it would seem that, once we keep this point in mind, all of the species and their features that emerge from the evolutionary process are due to chance.

So the process of evolution appears to operate significantly by chance, and this would contradict the idea that the process is designed, or directed. We need to emphasize that this is not a metaphysically driven conclusion, that is, it is not just a naturalist like Dawkins saying that he does not think that evolution is designed or planned; it is supposed to be a type of scientific claim that is justified by examining the data and empirical evidence for evolution itself. The claim that evolution occurs by chance, in short, is supposed to be driven by the scientific evidence, and not by one's worldview.

However, the issue is even more complicated, and to see why we need to look beneath the surface. Philosophers have often considered the question as to whether there is any genuine chance in the universe (leaving out for the moment human free will, a crucial topic that we will come back to in the next section). The first point to consider here is the laws of physics. The universe operates according to physical laws, and these laws always hold. We have mentioned a few of these laws in earlier chapters, such as Ohm's law, Newton's laws, the laws of electricity, etc. These laws have been progressively discovered and codified by science over the centuries, and it is a remarkable fact that the universe follows laws like these, regularities and consistencies in nature that determine how nature operates. In considering the question of chance, we therefore need to identify the key question more accurately. That question is: is there anything that happens in nature, or indeed in the universe as a whole, that is not governed by the laws of physics? The answer to this question in modern physics is generally no, especially at the atomic level (we will come back to the subatomic level later). What this means is that whenever anything happens in the universe, there is a cause for it, and the cause operates according to, or obeys, or can be explained in terms of, the laws of science. It would be difficult to do science if we believed that events did not obey physical laws. But this means that there is an underlying determinism in how nature behaves.

So let us apply this conclusion to evolution. Did the chimps' food source occur by chance or was it caused? It was caused. The cause was probably something as simple as seeds blowing over the area because of high winds, a lot of rain fell in the area too, and so trees grew where the chimps ended up living, and became a source of food. If this had not happened, the chimp would not have survived, and so forth. Did that devastating storm which occurred in one particular year, and which had a significant cumulative effect on the biological structure of various species, happen by chance? No, there is a cause for why a storm occurs that we can explain scientifically. There is in fact a complete causal story for why species have the biological and anatomical structure they have (although we have little idea of the specifics of this story in particular cases, and never will have). There is also a complete causal story to explain the type of environment in which they live. So, when we speak of chance in evolution, we are speaking too loosely. We are often confusing our inability to describe how something happened, or to predict what will happen, with the view that when it happened it happened by chance (i.e., that its prior cause did not occur by necessity). What we should be saying is that we can't explain exactly how things happened, or predict what will happen, because we don't know the full causal story due to gaps in our knowledge, not because there is no full causal story, *and not because each step in the causal chain is contingent (i.e., did not have to happen the way it did, in fact, happen)*. We overlook the fact that for *every effect* that occurs in biology, there is a specific cause of this effect, *including for every supposedly ("chance" or "random") mutation*! But evolutionary scientists sometimes forget this when they are talking about the process of evolution.

We cannot reconstruct the causal story about how things happened in the past because the subject matter is simply too vast and too complicated for us to be able to explicate its full causal history. We cannot reconstruct the full causal history of the existence of the Amazon river, for instance, but we do not doubt that in an account of its full causal history each effect will require *its specific prior cause*, right back to the beginning of the causal chain. Not for a moment can we entertain the view that one piece of the causal chain, say the Ice Age carving out the river bed, could not have happened *given its specific prior* cause (a specific prior cause that had *itself* to happen, *given its* specific prior cause, and so forth). It is the same with the evolution of the various species, the same for any mutation in genes that is causally responsible for evolutionary change.

We can use the analogy of the balls on a pool table to illustrate this point. When one "breaks" the pool balls around the table with the cue ball, the location each ball ends up in is not a matter of chance, though we often speak loosely as if it is. But what we really mean is that we can't *predict* where the balls will go, but not that where they go is unpredictable in itself, that is, happens by chance. Where each ball goes is precisely determined by factors such as its speed and weight, the speed and angle that the other balls hit it, by the size, shape, and structure of the table, etc. Ball A (given its characteristics) has to end up in a certain precise location *given the cause of its movement* (being hit by Ball B with its characteristics on this particular table, etc.). The cause of A's movement can only be changed if B is changed, and B can only be changed if the cause of its movement is changed, and so forth. (This is why it is possible to construct computer models to play pool accurately and fairly—meaning that if in a computer pool you hit the ball at the wrong angle it will not go into the pocket!) It is the same in nature. Here is another example to illustrate the same point: a friend of mine missed an important meeting a few days ago because the fan belt on his car broke when he was on his way to the meeting. He said it was just a matter of chance that it broke when it did! We talk this way all the time, but in the context of this discussion, we need to note that it was not a matter of chance that the fan belt broke when it did, it was a matter of physics. The belt breaking was a function of the precise amount of wear on the belt, in addition to the type of material the belt is made of, and the stress it was placed under at the time; given all of these things, it had to break when it did, even though we could not predict precisely when this would happen. So it is with nature.

If we examine Gould's point about replaying the tape of life in the light of these considerations, we have to ask his question more precisely. We are not now simply asking if we replayed the tape, would we end up with the same species (and the same everything) that we now have? We have to ask if we replayed the tape, *with the same starting conditions, ingredients, laws of science, timeline, etc.*, would we end up with the same species (and the same everything), that we now have (again leaving human free will out of consideration for the moment)? In other words, suppose the tape of the universe were to be replayed starting from the exact same initial state—the exact same big bang—would we end up with the universe having the same history up to at least the appearance of *Homo sapiens*? I think the answer to this question is yes. It is like asking if we set up the same pool table with the balls all in the same place, and then break them at exactly the same angle, same speed—everything the same, in short—would they all end up in the same locations on the table as before? Again, the answer is yes. This is how physics works, and why we can have confidence that happenings in nature (and indeed in the area of technology) will behave today the way they did yesterday, will behave the way they are supposed to behave most of the time. This is true unless the variables change, which only means that the causal conditions change. But no prior cause can change, or be otherwise than it was (B must hit A at a precise angle and speed), given *its* prior cause, which also cannot change. Each effect must be what it is given its prior cause, which suggests a determinism about nature. This is why events in nature can still be explained in terms of the laws of physics. All of this shows us that it is not at all clear that the process of evolution (the events which contribute to evolutionary change) happen by chance; indeed, it is not clear whether there is any chance at all operating in the natural process. Many thinkers have been sloppy in talking as if there is a major element of chance in the process. The only way to change the course of history is to change the initial conditions, which brings us inevitably back to the question of *how the initial ingredients came about in the first place, to the question of the origin and nature of the big bang*. That is to say, these considerations bring us back to cosmological and design arguments for the existence of God (arguments we will discuss in detail in later chapters).[24]

The topic of chance is further complicated by the findings of quantum mechanics which seem to suggest that at the subatomic level, nature might operate by chance, though this conclusion is very controversial. Quantum mechanics seems to reveal a difficulty in determining the precise nature and measurement of subatomic particles. Some argue that our inability to pin down the behavior of subatomic particles is due to the fact that *our* experimental interaction with the particles, by means of technology, affects their behavior, and this is why they can't be clearly measured, rather than because of any inherent instability or unpredictability in the particles themselves. We will discuss this view in a later chapter, but I don't think it affects our conclusions here for two reasons. The first is that even if there is an indeterminacy at the level of subatomic particles, there is still determinism at the atomic level, and this is the level evolution is operating at. In other words, the laws of physics still apply at the atomic level, and are extremely reliable, and so the process of evolution, like all processes, is still subject to them. The second point is that when evolutionary biologists like Gould and Dawkins talk about chance in nature they are not talking about an indeterminism or an unpredictability (in principle) at the quantum level. This level does not usually enter into explanations on evolution, which deals with much larger entities, like the molecular makeup of cells, the anatomy of species, fossils, habitats, environmental features, and so forth. These evolutionary biologists are talking about chance in the way we suggested above, in the sense that *the causes of events* could have been different, and so the species that emerged might have been different. However, what they are mostly talking about is unpredictability and not chance or indeterminism in nature; they sometimes appear to be suggesting that nature does not always quite follow the laws of physics, as if events in evolutionary history do not have a cause, when in fact they should be more careful, especially given the implications of what they are saying.[25]

c. *What is the role of consciousness and free will in all of this?* The subject is made even more complicated by the emergence in nature of human consciousness and free will. Free will is a human quality that is not subject to the laws of physics, and so would introduce an element of genuine chance in nature. The question of how human consciousness arose has proved extremely problematic for evolutionary biology, and it has obvious relevance to the question of whether nature is fully deterministic or not. Religious thinkers generally hold that human consciousness and free will are essential features of *Homo sapiens*, are part of God's design; these human characteristics also demarcate a clear difference in kind between human beings and other species, and are a part of human nature, part of the essence of man. This is because, although other species do have some form of consciousness, none have reasoning or logical ability, the capacity to do abstract thinking, or to use complex forms of language. Free will is another quality that clearly marks out human beings as distinctive, and that constitutes a very strong argument against determinism being true for the whole of reality. This is because free human actions cannot be subject to the laws of physics, because then they would not be truly free; indeed, a scientific account of free will is a contradiction in terms. In addition, free will is the basis of morality, responsibility, theories of punishment, and even democracy. So, the fact that human beings have free will, many philosophers and theologians have argued, is strong evidence that the process that gave rise to human beings could not have been purely physical in nature, or at least cannot be fully explained by means of physics. (We will return to the topic of human consciousness and free will in much more detail in the next chapter.)

The religious believer is not necessarily committed to any specific theory as to how consciousness emerged in the development of the species, and theistic philosophers have held a variety of views on this interesting question. The most popular view historically has been that God created the mind alongside the body in some way that is mysterious (that is, that science in unable to explain), that consciousness did not emerge fully from physical processes. Therefore, the physical development of the species, including *Home sapiens*, could have occurred in different ways, one of which might be evolution. On this view, it would follow that not everything that exists is physical, and not everything can be explained by science, specifically human consciousness cannot be explained by science. This is in opposition to the naturalist view which holds that at some point in evolutionary history brains began to form through the process of natural selection (in the way described in the early part of the chapter), and that at a certain level of brain complexity, consciousness was produced by the brain, and is therefore, as the materialist argues, a by-product of the brain. The materialist further argues that we will eventually discover how to explain consciousness scientifically, despite the fact that it appears right now to be a very difficult problem. Some theists, such as Nancey Murphy, have recently argued that there is no difficulty in a religious believer holding that consciousness could emerge in this way from a purely materialistic process (a view known as emergentism, or nonreductive physicalism), but that it would still need the creative power of God to bring this about.[26] This view holds that mental life can occur only under certain physical and biological conditions, but that it is irreducibly distinct from them. Despite this position being more compatible with the theory of evolution, it has not generally found favor with theistic philosophers, mainly because it is regarded as giving too much credence to naturalism.

3. Evolution and the universe: is evolution an argument against design in the universe?

Evolution is sometimes presented as an argument against design, not just in nature, but in the universe as a whole. This can be understood in two ways. One way is the way argued for by Richard Dawkins. Dawkins holds that evolution, in the way discussed above, is an argument against design in nature, and he seems to think that it follows from this that there is no design in the universe at all. He believes that the structure of the universe, and the laws of physics, apparently does not need an explanation, that the forces of physics are "blind."[27] He also says that before Darwin it was not possible to be an intellectually fulfilled atheist, which seems to suggest that Darwin's theory answers all of our questions about design in the universe, not just in nature.[28] Dawkins thinks that evolution can explain all of the apparent design we see in the universe, including the laws of physics, and so there is no place for a teleological approach to reality. The second way that evolution can be used to explain design is that of Carl Sagan. As noted in the previous chapter, Sagan has proposed the theory of "cosmic evolution," the basic concept of evolution applied to the universe as a whole, whereby all present states of the universe (when looked at from any discipline) owe their nature to previous states. In this sense, cosmic evolution is part of a search for a unified theory that would explain everything that exists (but not ultimate origins, of course).

Many theistic writers believe they have a very strong response to these often speculative arguments, and also point out that we must be careful to keep the theory of evolution distinct from what is often claimed in its name (something that Dawkins, Sagan, and others have not always done). The confusion between evolution and naturalism, between science and atheism, is all too evident in the work of these writers, and can often give science a bad name in modern discourse, a bad name it does not deserve. Many theists draw attention to the fact that there are questions that evolution and any other naturalistic accounts of design cannot help us with. For instance, evolution cannot explain the *origin* of matter and energy. Evolution cannot help us with perhaps our two biggest questions on the subject of God's possible existence: (1) how did the universe come to be, what is its ultimate cause?; and (2) how the design of the universe came about, "design" here understood as the regularities present in the underlying laws of physics (an argument we will come back to in detail in Chapter 6). Evolution also cannot explain the origin of life; it explains how life evolves after it came into existence and is located in a specific type of environment.

A majority of theistic philosophers argue that because evolution cannot answer these crucial questions about the origin and nature of the universe, and so cannot answer ultimate questions about the origin of the species either, that it is no threat to religious belief. It is true that it would show that the biblical story of Genesis is not literally true, but this point was accepted by many long before the theory of evolution, including by St. Augustine, as we have seen. But this fact does not affect the deeper philosophical points behind the creation story. Evolution, advanced as an explanation for every fact about human beings, and so as an argument for naturalism, runs into what seems to be insuperable difficulties in trying to explain the origin of the universe, the order in the universe, and key facets of human life such as the origin of mind, and the nature of morality and free will. Religious philosophers and theologians who argue this way argue that evolution was directed by God, or designed by God, and that human beings are, therefore, at the top of the evolutionary tree by design and not by accident. In short, human beings differ in kind, and not just in degree, from other animals. (This view is sometimes called "theistic evolution," though this description is still contentious.)

We have seen therefore in this chapter that evolution need not be seen as a threat to religious belief, although it would be in conflict with a fairly strict biblical literalism. For there are many facets about the universe, and about the human condition, that evolution cannot explain (and to be fair that it is not *officially* trying to explain). It is also a mistake to claim too much for the theory of evolution because this approach only ends up giving science a bad reputation leading many to think that science as a discipline is actually hostile to religion. This only succeeds in distracting us from a careful study of the theory of evolution, and the evidence for it, as well as its religious, philosophical, and moral implications.

I hope our discussion in this chapter shows that not only is the topic of evolution and religion fascinating in its own right, but that nobody who is really interested in the debate between science and religion, and especially in the implications of scientific theories for questions about religious belief, and about worldviews more generally, can afford to be ignorant of this matter in the twenty-first century. I hope it is also obvious that we should not be afraid of this debate, or reluctant to engage in it, as theologians from many different religions sometimes are, because it should be clear that science offers us nothing on the ultimate questions. As theologian John Haught has suggested, from the religious point of view we should be inspired to try to figure out another small part of God's creation by studying modern scientific theories, including evolution, and exploring their religious implications![29]

5 Science and the Human Person

Chapter Outline

A challenge to the traditional understanding of the human person	120
The nature of consciousness	121
Human free will	128
Immortality	134
Artificial intelligence	136
The search for extraterrestrial intelligence	142

Our reflections in previous chapters have raised many exciting questions about many topics, but perhaps none more so than about the nature of human beings, and about our place in the overall scheme of things. In this chapter, we will focus more specifically on the consequences of various implications of the religion-science relationship for our reflection upon, and understanding of, the nature of the human person. Changes and advances in scientific understanding are applicable not only to the physical universe, but also to us, because in an important sense, human beings are physical beings too, and the physical side of our nature is also subject to scientific study, to some extent at least. This conclusion alone has weighty consequences, and not just in obvious areas of study such as medicine and health-related fields, but also for deeper philosophical matters concerning our consciousness and free will, our ethical and political values, and how we live together in societies. Our understanding of morality is closed tied to our understanding of the human person, and our political values are closed tied to our moral values. One's moral values almost always presuppose some philosophical view of the human person; indeed, this is often the root of our moral disagreements because one's position on moral issues often depends on which philosophical theory of the person one finds most persuasive. It follows, therefore, that any significant changes in our understanding of ourselves as human persons will have a significant effect on many other areas of our experience. In short, the foundation of the moral and political order is usually some philosophical or religious view, or perhaps a combination of views, of the human person, and our understanding of the human person is increasingly being influenced by current developments in science, in an often contentious debate and dialogue with philosophy and theology.

Let us bring together some of the more significant ideas relating to this theme that have come out of our previous chapters before we go on to identify more specific questions about the human person that have begun to exercise various thinkers, and that have great significance for religion. The first idea we should focus on is an idea that became prominent after Newton—that we live in a mechanistic universe, where the universe is seen as a large machine that operates according to the laws of science, something akin to a giant clock. This idea prompted speculation that everything in the universe operates causally in essentially the same manner (and so can be studied in essentially similar ways), such as gravity, planetary motion, volcanoes, rainfall, the movement of particles which constitute the structure of physical matter, and *human beings*. Human beings are physical beings, so perhaps we too can be analyzed as particles in motion, operating according to physical laws. This idea also goes hand in hand, second, with a strong commitment to scientific progress, and the ever-increasing and expanding nature of science as a discipline, along with the hope that the scientific method can be turned to the study of almost any subject (as long as the subject is physical in nature). As we have already seen, thinkers like Darwin and Freud argued that human beings are proper subjects for scientific study, and proposed fascinating theories aimed at contributing further to our understanding of ourselves.

A third development that complements this new confidence in science is the great success of the discipline already surveyed in Chapter 3. It is important to emphasize that many thinkers held the view that science could likely also be successful in many of these new areas of study (human origins, medicine, psychology), as well as in more traditional areas (the physical universe, the study of actions and events, matter and motion, etc.). This was taken as further support for the view that a scientific study of the human person was also *morally* justified. Of course, fourthly, it is only a short step from this attitude to the (minority but no less significant) philosophical worldview of naturalism, that we should *commit* to the view that everything that exists, no matter how sophisticated or how complex it appears to be, is ultimately physical in nature, and so, at least in principle, is an appropriate subject for scientific study. It is but a short step, some argue, from the general successes of science to the expectation that eventually science will unravel *all* of the mysteries of the universe, including the mystery of life and of the nature (and ultimate origin) of human beings. We have already presented an overview of this attitude in Chapters 2 and 3 in the work of Dawkins, Sagan, Crick, and their forerunners, Laplace, Diderot, La Mettrie, Freud, and perhaps Darwin.

A challenge to the traditional understanding of the human person

The idea of a mechanistic universe, along with the theory of evolution, raised important questions about the human person, and on many levels seemed to present a challenge to traditional religious views. The traditional religious view, well exemplified and developed in detail in the work of St. Thomas Aquinas, was accepted by the vast majority of thinkers, so much so that it is accurate to say that it was the standard way of thinking about human beings up until the nineteenth century. This view of the human person provided the intellectual foundation for many different areas of life, for example, in morality, politics, education, law, and theories of punishment. Proponents of this view held that God designed the universe according to a particular design plan. This means that the existence of the human species is necessary and not an accident of nature, even if it is true that the all of the various species came about through the process of evolution. According to this view, human beings therefore differ in kind, and not just in degree, from other species. Human beings are intended by God to be the most advanced, developed species, and this gives us a metaphysical priority and value when compared with other species (though it does not mean that other species, and even nature itself, have no value). Proponents of this view point to specific characteristics of human beings to defend the view that human beings differ in kind from other species. These characteristics include the fact that human beings have consciousness, are capable of abstract thinking, logic, and complex problem solving, the fact that human beings are moral agents, the fact that we have free will, and are capable of language, and our other remarkable intellectual, spiritual, and moral capacities and achievements.

We will discuss these features of human beings in detail in the sections that follow, but it is important to note that this view of the human person is under challenge today, at least in intellectual circles, especially from the proponents of naturalism, who often appeal to the latest scientific theories to support an alternative view. The most radical version of this naturalistic, secularist outlook holds that human beings differ only in degree from other species, that we are higher up on the evolutionary tree not by design (because there is no designer) but by chance. In addition, the same (natural, accidental) process that produced other species also produced us, so while it is true that human consciousness is far superior to a monkey's consciousness, this is due to the "blind" forces of nature, and not to any design plan. It could have been the case that monkeys or some similar species evolved with a consciousness comparable to ours in terms of ability, or even with a superior one, or some other totally different species could have evolved with a higher level of intelligence. All of these outcomes are subject to the vagaries of a natural process that is not designed, not planned, but entirely random, and down to chance and luck in its final outcomes. As evolutionary biologist, G. G. Simpson put it: "Man is the result of a purposeless and materialistic process that did not have him in mind. He was not planned. He is a state of matter, a form of life, a sort of animal, and a species of the Order Primates, akin nearly or remotely to all of life and indeed to all that is material."[1] Supporters of this view conclude then that human consciousness is only an advanced form of the rudimentary consciousness that we see in other species, such as dolphins, dogs, and chimps. It is not of a different order to that form of consciousness, does not differ in kind from that form of consciousness. A contemporary materialist, Paul Churchland, has spelled it out clearly for us: "We are creatures of matter and we should learn to live with that fact."[2] Our reasoning and logical ability can be understood in the same way, as can our capacity for language. Moral agency will prove more difficult to reinterpret, even as a research project in principle, as we will see presently. But before we get into the topic of moral agency, we need to look further at the complicated question of consciousness.

The nature of consciousness

Philosophers have long been exercised by what is called the body/mind problem in the philosophy of mind. Students are often puzzled when first introduced to this problem because they were not aware that there is a body/mind problem! But many thinkers have been interested in what turns out to be one of the most significant problems in philosophy because so many important issues depend upon the answer. These issues include immortality, the existence of God and of the supernatural order, free will, artificial intelligence, even the debate between theism and naturalism (secularism). As the debate between religion and naturalism has become more pronounced in recent times, it is no accident that the body/mind problem is one of those problems in contemporary philosophy that is getting a great deal of attention. Reflections about the nature of mind also often bring in evolution, neurological research, and other topics relating to the mind and its activities. We will try to navigate carefully through this absorbing, but complex, topic in what follows.

The main puzzle in the philosophy of mind concerns the relationship between the body and the mind. There is obviously some connection between them in the nature, experiences, and life of a human being, but what exactly is the connection? Is it possible for us to learn something more about the connection? As noted in Chapter 2, the "mind" here refers to consciousness, ideas, concepts, thoughts, reasoning ability, logic, memories, imagination, even emotions. The "body" refers to the human brain, specifically the physical stuff of the brain such as the hemispheres, lobes, cortexes, neurons, cells, membranes, dendrites, and their associated molecular and chemical composition. There are three main views on the relationship between the body and the mind. The first view, briefly mentioned in Chapter 2, is called dualism, and was strongly defended in the work of René Descartes, whose arguments we will concentrate on here.[3] Descartes provides one of the best-known accounts of the relationship of body to mind in the history of ideas, and some version of it (though there are important differences between versions) was held by most major thinkers, including Plato, Aristotle, Augustine, Aquinas, Locke, Reid, and Kant. Descartes argued that the body and the mind are two distinct entities, two substances. The mind, on the one hand, is a mental, even spiritual entity, a nonphysical entity; the brain, on the other hand, is a physical entity. This dualistic view holds that the mind is an independent entity in its own right, is not produced by the brain, and does not necessarily depend upon the brain for its existence. The dualist holds that the body and the mind have a relationship akin to the relationship in a car engine between the alternator and the battery. They are distinct, but related, entities; one does not produce the other, and if one was removed from the engine, the other one would still exist. Although this is not a perfect analogy, it does give us a good sense of the dualist position.

The dualist further and crucially argues against *reductionism* in the understanding of the brain/mind relationship. Reductionism is the attempt by some philosophers to explain one set of usually problematical and apparently nonphysical phenomena in terms of another set of usually simpler, more easily understood physical phenomena; in effect, the attempt is to explain the more difficult entity, the mind, in terms of a more simple entity, the brain. Descartes held that reductionism cannot succeed because the mind is a distinct entity whose properties cannot be explained in scientific terms, and so even if we did come to fully understand everything scientifically about the brain, we would not fully understand everything about the mind, just as with the battery and the alternator (though we would probably know a bit more about the mind based on our knowledge of its interaction with the brain).

Descartes and other dualists make a crucial further point. This is that the mind has causal power over the brain, which is a clear indication of its metaphysical status as an entity in its own right. This is best illustrated by considering a few simple examples. First, let us consider the physical and mental processes that you undergo when you feel hungry. Your stomach sends signals to your brain, and you start thinking—as part of your conscious thought processes—about food! You might begin thinking that it is time to get lunch, consider where you will get it, and what you will eat. Will you eat in the college cafeteria, like you usually do (a prospect that may not fill you with joy), will you have the chicken sandwich you had yesterday, or will you select a roast beef sandwich for a change? The dualist argument is that the brain prompts the mind to think about food along these lines, but when one thinks through the options and decides what to do, the mind *causes* the brain to send signals to the body to actually cause one to move to the cafeteria. The mind and the brain interact, and both have causal power over each other. In addition, it will not be possible to figure out the nature of the causal interaction between brain and mind because the mind is nonphysical and we have no way of studying the nature of the nonphysical.[4] This analysis also introduces the crucial further question of free will, which we will come to in a moment. A second example to illustrate the causal power of the mind concerns higher level thinking, such as might be involved in thinking about wiring a house for electricity, in how to set up an experiment in chemistry to test for poison in a plant, in how to solve an equation in mathematics, in how to reconcile the fact of the evil in the world with the existence of an all-good God. These are all problems that require abstract thinking, thinking that will result usually in some kind of causal activity on the part of the person doing the thinking, for example, the electrician will actually wire the house following the plan he worked out abstractly, and the chemist will set up and run the experiment according to his abstract analysis of the problem, and so forth. Everyday, commonsense examples such as these, the dualist holds, show clearly that the mind is more than the body, that it is not reducible to the brain, and that it has causal power over the brain.

This dualist approach to the body/mind issue is opposed to materialism, the other main position about the body/mind relation. Materialism is the view that the human mind is either a complete physical entity, or even if it might have some nonphysical properties, these depend upon the brain. Some philosophers take a strong view of materialism and argue for mind/brain *identity*. This is the view that the mind and the brain are the same thing, they are identical. It is not that these philosophers deny that consciousness, thoughts, and logic exist; they simply hold that these features are not nonphysical; they are, rather, sophisticated, complex *physical* operations of the brain. Although we don't fully understand how they work yet, we will in the future through further scientific research. Others take a more moderate view holding that although some features of mental life might be nonphysical, these are still produced by the brain, and therefore are completely dependent upon the brain (this position is sometimes called modern materialism or epiphenomenalism).[5]

The specifics of the debate between dualists and materialists involve a theoretical analysis of mental properties and activities, and the development of philosophical arguments to show that these activities and properties cannot be explained by physics and science, in the case of the dualist, or that it is scientifically plausible that they could be, in the case of the materialist. One argument often appealed to by the dualist is the argument from personal identity. This argument is based on the fact that each of us has our own individual, unique personal identity, an identity that endures over the course of our lives, a continuing self, despite all of our bodily changes. We know that all of our bodily cells are continually being replaced with new ones, yet you are still the same person you were when you were 3 years old, or last week. The dualist explains this by saying that we have an enduring, nonphysical mind whose existence is not dependent upon bodily changes, although dualists have often differed as to which part of the mind is responsible for our identity, with some saying it is our consciousness, others that it is our souls, which contain our consciousness (an issue we will come back to below). The dualist also argues that on a materialist view, there is no convincing way to explain personal identity because one would be forced to say either that, despite the fact that we are made of matter and energy, somehow an enduring self could "emerge" from all of this which would be the basis of our subjective continuous experiences, our memories, feelings, and mental habits, or that there really is no enduring self, that it is an illusion of some kind. Neither view, according to the dualist, is rationally believable.

Most materialists, following David Hume, have responded by arguing for the latter alternative. Hume proposed the "bundle theory of the self," which was based on his claim that we never actually experience this enduring "I," but are "a bundle or collection of different perceptions, which succeed each other with an inconceivable rapidity, and are in a perpetual flux and movement ... nor is there any single power of the soul which remains unalterably the same,"[6] and therefore, according to Hume, there is no real substantial self. Many other creative reductionist theories have been put forward in recent times (e.g., by Derek Parfit[7]); most of them entail that people do not exist, that is, that there is no enduring self, but only a body with changing conscious states, perceptions, feelings, etc. Many of these views are founded on making a distinction between maintaining a continuity across our various successive psychological states, and a deeper notion of self, to which the psychological states belong. It is then argued that the former can occur without having to be part of an underlying permanent substance, and are all that is necessary for providing an explanation of personal identity. This line of research has proved notoriously difficult for reductionists to develop even theoretically, let alone empirically, and the counterintuitiveness of denying that we are people with real enduring identities places a serious question mark over all materialist accounts of the mind/body relation.[8]

The dualist also appeals to the argument from intentionality. This argument is based on a recognition of something we often take for granted in our ordinary, everyday experience of our mental life, and of the activities of mind. The mind has very peculiar, indeed quite remarkable features. One of these is intentionality, which is a property of our thinking. We can appeal to a thought experiment to illustrate the unusual mental property of intentionality. Think about your watch for a moment; form a picture of it in your mind. If someone asks you: what are you thinking "about?", you will answer, "I am thinking about my watch." You are not thinking "about" your coat or your shoes. The ideas and pictures in your mind are said to have intentional content, that is, they are "about" or "of" something out there in the real world (in extra-mental reality, or the world outside the mind). This is true for most of our beliefs, concepts, ideas, arguments, and so forth. It is always intelligible to ask someone who is thinking: what are you thinking *about*? The dualist claims that intentionality cannot be explained in physical terms, because it makes no sense to say that the atomic or molecular structure of a physical object (e.g., brain cells) could be *about* another object distinct from it. Nor does it make much sense to say that a physical object could produce a nonphysical effect that would have as one of its features the phenomenon of intentionality. The materialist would need to explain the existence of intentionality in a scientific way involving an account of the workings of the human brain. What is required is an explanation in terms of physical properties, and scientific causal laws. The dualist argues that this cannot be done.

Intentionality is a very difficult problem for a materialist view of the mind, because it draws attention to a feature of mind that we do not see in the world of matter, particles, and the laws of physics. It would take the breaking of new bounds in science to explain how a physical object could be "about" something. Nevertheless, materialists must hold, if they are to remain materialists, that intentionality has a physical explanation. It is just that we have not discovered it yet. The second reply of the materialist is to suggest that intentionality might be some kind of illusion, in the sense that the "aboutness" is actually *of the mental state*, is somehow contained fully in the mental state, not the object in the world (an "aboutness" that would still have to be explained). This type of response would usually be offered as part of an anti-realist theory of knowledge (such as those discussed in Chapter 3).

The philosopher Robert Adams has offered a different argument for the unique nature of the mental, based on what are sometimes called "qualia."[9] Qualia is a technical term in the philosophy of mind for various feelings and experiences that human beings undergo in the course of ordinary life, for example, what it is like to experience pain from a toothache, what the experience of fear is like, what the experience of seeing red is like, and so on. There is no doubt that qualia are real; but are they nonphysical, mental properties, or physical properties? Adams argues that there seems no way in principle to explain qualia in physical terms. Take, as an example, your experience of seeing red. Suppose for the sake of argument, Adams argues, that we grant to the materialist two hotly debated and very controversial points: that the experience is correlated with a corresponding brain event (every time you see red, you are in brain state A, leaving aside for a moment what it actually means to say we are in a brain state), and further, let us also agree that the brain state causes the experience of red, something most materialists hold. Nevertheless, Adams argues, the brain state is not the same thing as the experience of redness, and if materialism were true, we would still need a scientific causal explanation for the experience of redness. How would we go about getting this? Adams says that all we can do further is to learn more about the brain state that produces the experience of redness. But suppose we discover all there is to know about the brain state, would this explanation tell us what the experience of red is like? It seems not. We would almost have to undergo the experience of seeing red as a result of studying our scientific account of it, and this is not plausible! Adams suggests, as does philosopher Thomas Nagel, that it does not seem possible logically to give a third person (objective, scientific) explanation of what is a first person subjective experience, such as the experience of seeing red, or of feeling pain, or of what it is like to be me, of what Nagel describes more generally as "the subjective experience of consciousness."[10] These philosophers present this as an intractable problem for materialism, and as a strong argument in favor of the view that the human mind, and so the human person, cannot be entirely reduced to physical properties and causal laws.

Materialists often reply to these and similar difficulties about explaining features of the mental in terms of physics by appealing to what I like to call the "scientific faith" argument in the philosophy of mind. This involves beginning essentially from a premise or from a supposition of naturalism, and then arguing that the mind must be physical. One then confronts difficult problems, like the problem of qualia and of our subjective experiences, by arguing that, although these problems appear to be both logically and practically very difficult right now, we will eventually solve them when we have more knowledge of how the brain works. This argument is based on an appeal to inductive evidence that since we have worked with many things in the past, for example, lightning, that we thought we could not explain, but for which we eventually did find a scientific explanation, it will be the same with the recalcitrant features of the mind. The dualist does not deny that the scientific faith argument is a good argument in general in science (when applied to lightning) but denies that it is a good argument when applied to complex features of the mental, such as consciousness, intentionality, qualia, and (as we will see in a moment) free will. This is because human consciousness and its properties are obviously not just more physical objects that need an explanation; rather, they seem to have no basis in physical matter, such as atoms and causal laws. Therefore, to treat consciousness as if it was just another physical object is far-fetched. It is also not legitimate logically to assume a starting point of naturalism if the question of the status of the human mind is yet to be decided.

Human free will

Another essential feature of the human person is free will. Free will is not only an indispensable concept in the religious view of the world, but it is also a central feature of any view of the world, even though we don't always focus on it explicitly in our moral, social, and political arrangements, but usually take it for granted. But it takes only a moment's reflection to realize what a truly remarkable and complex property of human beings free will is, and this is why many thinkers believe that the existence of free will is a decisive argument against any theory of materialism about the human mind. Free will may be defined as the ability of human beings to make a genuine choice between alternatives, a choice that is not determined by scientific laws operating on atomic or molecular particles or combinations of particles in the brain. Although there appears to be some cause and effect processes involved in free will, there also has to be an essential noncausal aspect to it, otherwise it would not be free will.

We can try to illustrate this point with a concrete example. Let us return to our earlier example of feeling hungry and examine it from the point of view of the phenomenon of free will. As in our previous example, one feels hungry and, speaking very generally, this biological event sends signals through the nervous system to the brain, and the brain then causes us to start thinking about food. I may start thinking, like I did today, that it is lunchtime and that I will go to a nearby barbeque restaurant, where I will order the combination plate of ribs, ham, roast beef, turkey, and a variety of side dishes! I will not order the rib sandwich today, because I had it on a recent visit. But then, I remember that the restaurant does not offer the combination plate at lunchtime, so I decide that I will have the roast beef instead. I prefer roast beef to turkey, and the roast beef sandwich at this restaurant is very good. I then get up from my desk and start walking toward the restaurant in order to have lunch. Now let us attend closely to what has happened here. My body has initiated the process of me thinking about food. I have gone through a fairly complex mental operation involving ideas, thoughts, images, and reasoning concerning food. I have made several *decisions* involving logical reasoning about where I will have lunch, what I will have for lunch, and when I will have lunch. These decisions then enable me to exercise causal power over my brain and body in order to physically move my body to the restaurant to have lunch.

The decisions I have made are arrived at freely in some mysterious way as part of the mental process of thinking about lunch. But I do have reasons for them; for example, the reason that I am having a roast beef sandwich is because I like roast beef, and this restaurant has excellent roast beef. Yet, these reasons do not causally compel me in the scientific sense to choose roast beef; I could quite easily go to the restaurant and order a turkey sandwich—there is nothing to prevent me from doing this. Unlike say a machine that might be programmed to appear to be making a certain decision (the decision appears free but really is not), I am really free to make a decision. Proponents of dualism and those committed to the doctrine of free will argue that there is no possible way to give a scientific account of free will because this is a contradiction in terms. It would be in effect asking for a scientific, causal account of something that is not subject to a causal explanation. What we can therefore say about free will is that it is real, but outside of physics, and beyond the scientific method. This is not a critique of the scientific method, but a recognition that this method is limited to the physical realm, and that there are some things beyond the physical realm.

This is a simple case taken from ordinary human experience, but free will is present in so much of what we do as human beings. I can begin thinking about various abstract problems, say the problem of evolution and religion, I can decide to go to college, to pursue a certain career, to take up bowling, or countless other endeavors; all of these decisions are based on my belief in and experience of free will. In fact, free will goes even deeper than this in our experience. For free will is also the basis of morality, since the whole enterprise depends on human beings having a genuine choice between good and bad actions. Likewise, moral responsibility, punishment, and even democracy itself all depend on the prior belief that human beings have free will. The dualist argues that since human beings have free will, then materialism is false. This is a very thorny problem indeed for materialists who are faced with saying that, since all of our actions are rooted in our brains and central nervous systems, then all our "choices" would be explicable in terms of scientific causal laws, operating on bits of matter. We would be like sophisticated robots, whose very operations are determined by causal sequences operating according to scientific laws. In short, there is no room for free will in a naturalistic universe. This radical view is known as determinism, as noted in Chapter 2.

Determinism is usually defined as the view that every current event in the universe and state of the universe is determined by previous events and states of the universe. Applied to the physical world, this would mean that the current state of our galaxy, the Milky Way, was caused by previous states of our galaxy, and that these states in turn were caused by preceding states, all the way back to the big bang. In short, nothing can occur in the universe that is not brought about through causal interaction with previous events. There is no chance in the universe, in the sense that an event could occur that has no cause. We may not know the cause of a specific event, according to the determinist, but it always has a cause. Applying this thesis to the world of nature on the earth, and specifically to the process of evolution, this would mean that there is a prior cause for every species that exists (as discussed in the previous chapter). For example, there is a causal story, which the theory of evolution attempts to tell, about how whales came to have the structure they have, and this story involves all of those prior events and causes which eventually resulted in the emergence of the whale, with its distinctive structure. Now what does this deterministic theory say when applied to human beings, and specifically to the workings of the human mind?

The determinist argues that since the mind is completely physical in nature, it operates according to causal laws operating on physical matter, as we have already noted, and so this means that every present state of the brain is caused by preceding states.[11] In this way, the mind operates like any other organ in the body, for example, like the heart. The current state of one's heart is determined by its structure and by the causal states that operate around it in a specific environment. Preventative medical treatment aimed at the heart is an attempt to alter these causal states. This holds for everything, the determinist, suggests, including the human mind. It also applies to so-called free decisions. Recall our examples above illustrating free human activity. The determinist argues that these actions are not really free—that there is a causal process going on that results necessarily in the action that we take, and our belief and our feeling that our actions are free are therefore illusory and mistaken. For example, when we consider which sandwich to eat for lunch, the determinist argues that our "choice" between a chicken or a beef sandwich is in fact caused, and so we are compelled to do what comes at the end of the causal process, just as a photocopying machine must print the page when you press the print button (assuming it is working properly, i.e., the causal sequence is all in place). We may think we are making a free choice, and of course we believe that we are free, but we are really not. The determinist does not claim to know how this process works. It is obviously enormously sophisticated and complex, and determinists see it as a research program for the future, to be developed as we come to know more and more about the human brain and its activities (the view of Francis Crick, discussed in Chapter 3). This position, as Holmes Rolston points out, "moves determinism over to the realm of promises, not observations."[12] This "promise," if it is ever fulfilled, will likely involve a combination of genetic and environmental influences (for more on genetics, see Chapter 8). It is not that determinists want to deny free will; it is more that they can't see any way to fit it into a worldview that holds that everything is physical in nature, and governed by causal laws. It is not possible for the determinist to allow for even a very restricted domain of genuinely free decisions, because this little area of free will would still be outside physics, and would therefore show that determinism and naturalism are false.

It is not surprising that determinists have been disturbed by not only the counterintuitiveness of their position, especially as regards the phenomenon of free will, but also about the enormous consequences the doctrine of determinism would have for human life in general. Because of this, they feel they have to put forward some other explanatory account of human action and decision-making that offers something more than simple determinism. Some thinkers have developed what are called compatibilist theories of human freedom as a way of offering a more realistic account of human decision-making. Compatibilism is based on the view that although determinism is true, we may still be able to have some semblance of free will. One of the most sophisticated versions of this view is to be found in the work of John Fischer and Mark Ravizza.[13] These authors are particularly worried about moral responsibility, and claim that central to moral responsibility is the notion of "alternative possibilities" in the various moral situations in which we find ourselves. If a person has no choice in a situation, we would not normally hold him morally responsible for his subsequent action. Determinism undermines moral responsibility because it holds that we do have no choice when faced with alternatives, but are caused to follow one course over the other. The Fischer and Ravizza view revolves around trying to draw a meaningful distinction between cases where we do something "freely" in ordinary experience (but of course the action is not really free), and cases where we might do something because we have been hypnotized, brainwashed, duped, or coerced. Is there a meaningful difference on a determinist thesis between "deciding" to have lunch at a particular restaurant oneself, or being hypnotized and therefore compelled by the hypnotist to have it at that restaurant?

The answer seems to be no if determinism is true. This is because if determinism holds then I am not acting freely on either scenario when I "choose" to visit a particular restaurant. Compatibilists like Fischer and Ravizza always fail to attend in detail to what is meant by causal determinism. If causal determinism holds, then all current events are determined by past events and the laws of nature *including* my brain states, reasoning processes, logical deductions, beliefs, desires, and "*decisions*." Therefore, if one assumes causal determinism, I would have *no* choice about whether to order the sandwich in either case, the case where I appear to choose it freely, or the case where I am operating under hypnosis. The only difference between them is the actual causal process involved, but crucially there is a *complete* causal story to be told in each case, with the same action as the end result (like either a flood or a strong wind causing a tree to collapse). Compatibilist theories are interesting, but it is hard to see how they could be true since there is an apparent contradiction at the heart of them, but one must resort to something like them in order to deal with this problem for materialism. It is not unfair to say that they are somewhat desperate attempts to retain some semblance of free will in a deterministic universe.

We have been looking at the matter of free will primarily from a metaphysical point of view, but let us not forget that one can also look at the issue from a more psychological point of view as well. Indeed, we have seen in Chapter 2 how thinkers like Sigmund Freud tried to give a psychological basis for much of human action. In the context of our discussion here, we can see that what Freud and others are claiming is that many human actions that might appear to be free, or the result of a rational (and free) decision-making process, might in fact have psychological origins—meaning psychological causes—outside of our control. It is obviously important to ask the question about not just how do we actually move this theory into the realm of fact, with detailed examples and case studies of how it works—something that psychology as a discipline has struggled mightily with over the years—but also, and more pertinent to our discussion in this chapter, as to whether these psychologists are denying that human beings have free will. It seems that they did not look at their theories of psychological reductionism from the point of view of free will. It is also probably accurate to say that they were not denying free will, though it is obvious that their views have large consequences for the topic of free will, consequences which they have failed to consider adequately. For example, if free will exists it would mean that not everything can be explained in terms of physics, which would be a strong argument against Freud's view that all actions can be explained in terms of psychological reductionism. It also would mean that Freud's overall atheistic view that everything has a scientific explanation, including the human mind, is not true.

As a final question related to this topic, we must consider the subject from a logical point of view because there is a logical contradiction at the heart of all deterministic views about human freedom. We can draw on the work of another psychologist, B. F. Skinner, to illustrate this point. Skinner is usually regarded as the most influential psychologist of the twentieth century. In his book, *Beyond Freedom and Dignity*, he defended a type of determinism that he thought we could use to mould individuals, particularly as infants, into better citizens.[14] Since human behavior is determined by a combination of our environment, biological structure, and genetic makeup, we might be able to discover, when we know more about how all these processes work and interact with each other, what "inputs" (e.g., childhood upbringing, educational system, external rewards and punishments, etc.) in a person's life and experience would produce the correct "outputs" (i.e., most desirable actions from a social, moral, and political point of view). Human beings could be treated like car engines: given the structure of the engine, which we do have a detailed scientific understanding of, if you operate your car in the right environmental conditions, use the right oil, fuel, replacement parts, and so forth, you will get optimal performance, whereas if you use the wrong oil, or fuel, or parts for repairs, you will get poor performance.

There is one fatal flaw, however, in this interesting thesis. It assumes that the person choosing the "inputs" chooses them freely! For if this were not the case, the experiment could not succeed because, since all human actions are caused, and there is no free will, then any "inputs" chosen to influence the environment of infants could not be chosen freely. The "choice" of inputs would, in fact, be causally determined by the environment and physical structure of the person responsible for choosing the "correct inputs"! So, the thesis is fundamentally contradictory because it is based on the contradictory claims that determinism is true of infants but at the same time it requires free will to get the process going. We can apply this criticism more generally to determinist theories. Proponents of determinism are trying to convince people that determinism is true; they want people who believe in free will to give up this belief, and to accept the view that determinism is the correct thesis about the process of human decision-making, the way things really are in the world. However, if determinism really is true, this would mean that the proponent of determinism did not freely arrive at this view, but was in fact caused to hold it. It also means he was caused to argue for the theory of determinism in his work, and that if someone comes to be convinced by his arguments they too were caused to do so, and did not do so freely because the arguments convinced them! All of these scenarios are widely implausible, and are part of the reason that free will has remained a central feature of human beings' understanding of themselves, and a feature that plays a central role in religious views of human life and the universe.

Immortality

The foregoing reflections lead us to consider the question of immortality, the question of whether some of all of our nature will survive our bodily death. This is an essential belief of most religions, although there are different theories of what form the afterlife might take. Religious philosophers and theologians believe that dualist arguments show that the mind is nonphysical, and so it has a certain independence from the brain, and it follows that it is possible that we may be able to survive bodily death. Given the radical difference between the body and the mind, discussed in the previous section, the argument is that although the mind and the brain certainly work together in this life, there is no logical objection to saying that at bodily death the mind could survive. Since the mind also involves our consciousness, ideas, and memories, this would also be an argument that it would be *us* that survives—that our personal identity would be maintained in the afterlife. Sometimes materialists reply by invoking the "brain injuries" argument. This is the argument that when the brain is injured, there is often a corresponding loss of mental function, and this shows that the mind is dependent on the brain for its activities. The dualist replies that this argument would show that, in this life, the brain is a *necessary* condition for mental life, but it does not show that it is a *sufficient* condition for mental life. Nor would it follow that after death the mind could not operate without the body. The arguments discussed in the preceding sections, the theist argues, point to the fact that the mind is more than the brain. So, it could still be the case that the mind can function on its own, without needing brain events, and that this can happen in an afterlife.

This brings us to the notion of the soul, and its relation to the body and the mind. Many philosophers have held the view that the soul and the body are distinct entities; the soul is nonphysical, and the body is physical, and the soul is what animates—in the language of Plato, Aristotle, St. Thomas Aquinas, and many others—the matter in the body. St. Thomas puts this by saying that "the soul is the principle of life."[15] Some also hold that it is not just human beings that have souls, but perhaps lower animals and even plants could have a type of soul in the sense that they are alive, and it is the soul that gives them animation. Aristotle, for instance, held that there are three types of souls, the nutritive or vegetative soul, which is to be found in plants and some animals, and is responsible for assimilation and reproduction; next, there is the sensitive soul, which is to be found in animals, and which possesses sense perception, desire, and local motion. Finally, there is the human or rational soul, the highest form, which contains the powers of the other two forms, and which is responsible for our powers of reasoning and deliberation, which are aimed at truth.[16]

Not all of the philosophers mentioned agree on whether the soul can exist independently of the body. Aristotle thought it could not, but he did propose that thought (and perhaps the mind) could exist independently of the body. Plato, St. Augustine, and Descartes argued that the soul could exist independently of the body, as did St. Thomas, but he argued that it would not be its natural state, that eventually it would be reunited with the resurrected body by means of divine action. The relationship between the soul and the mind is more complicated, and many traditional religious thinkers, in particular, did not fully work out their views on this matter. Some hold that the soul contains consciousness, others hold that consciousness is the same thing as the soul, but at very least on either view it would mean that in the afterlife, one's conscious mind and its states would survive, and so one's personal identity would be preserved.

These different views on the relationship of mind to soul have also influenced different views of the afterlife.[17] We can only sketch here a few different positions as a way of whetting the appetite of those interested in pursuing this fascinating topic further. As we have noted, one of the main Western views is that the mind alone is sufficient to guarantee one's personal identity in the afterlife. A second view is that the body will be resurrected, and will eventually be reunited with the nonphysical mind. Eastern religions, however, usually defend some account of reincarnation (a view we also see in ancient thinkers like Plato and Plotinus). There are a variety of views on what forms reincarnation can take. The central claim, however, is that the soul survives bodily death and is then reincarnated in another body. Reincarnation therefore requires a belief in dualism. The process of reincarnation can go on for centuries, before the soul eventually escapes the cycle of birth, death, and rebirth. This is what it means to achieve salvation. Eastern religions also have a different understanding of the nature of the afterlife. Buddhist and Hindu thinkers have often explained the afterlife as a place where the individual consciousness is absorbed into an undifferentiated "Oneness." We can invoke the metaphor of regarding one's consciousness as being in a jar in this life in order to understand this view better; death then is as an escape from the jar into an overall Oneness, which is the ultimate reality.[18] This is in contrast to Western views of immortality, which have stressed strongly the fact that the individual retains his or her individuality in the afterlife—this is why questions of personal identity are important—and achieves a personal relationship with God.

The soul and the afterlife are essential features of the religious view of the world because they provide the link between this world and the next world. It seems essential for human beings to survive death in some form if salvation, as understood by most religions, is to have any meaning. Salvation revolves around the idea of human beings following a proper spiritual and moral path in this life, and then entering into a personal and eternal relationship with God in the next life. If this view is to make sense, there has to be an afterlife, even though we sometimes disagree about what one needs to do to achieve salvation, and about the precise form the afterlife may take. But, from a purely philosophical point of view, the religious thinker argues that the immateriality of the intellect can furnish a set of good reasons to believe that the physical world is not all there is, and so the possibility of immortality becomes more plausible. It is also significant that it is precisely the most significant features of human beings, intelligence, free will, and moral agency, that have resisted scientific explanation, and that are responsible for our main conceptions of ourselves, for our moral and political capacities (no matter what our worldview is). The last point is that in looking at what we call the cumulative case argument for the existence of God—all of the separate arguments taken together (including the design arguments and the first cause arguments which will be discussed in later chapters)—these arguments reinforce each other, and so the arguments for the immaterial nature of the intellect and free will strengthen the conclusion that materialism and naturalism cannot be the true theory about the nature of reality.

Artificial intelligence

The question of the nature of mind, and of the relationship between body and mind, has important implications for the growing study of artificial intelligence. The attempt to create artificial intelligence in machines also raises yet further questions about our nature as conscious, thinking beings. In order to further explore the subject of artificial intelligence, let us separate out two issues at once. First, there is the technical project of trying to build a machine that can perform all or most of the intellectual functions that we can perform, such as thinking, reasoning, imagining, being creative, perhaps talking, etc. Although scientists have made great strides in this area, they are nowhere near producing a thinking machine, a machine that can think or converse like human beings, for example. Machines that can play chess and play recorded slogans, or even manufacture electronic voices, do not count here, because we are talking about reproducing human mental activities such as working on an abstract problem that requires logical inferences, carrying on a conversation, considering imaginative scenarios, understanding one's interlocutors, and so forth. But although we are unable to make machines that can perform these kinds of mental activities now, who knows what we might be able to achieve in the future? Someday, we may be able to build machines similar to Data in *Star Trek*, a machine that can perform many of the intellectual functions that we can perform. We could also construct such a machine to look like us, and program it as closely as possible to act like us. If it becomes possible to create a machine like Data in the future, how will we react to such a machine, treat such a machine, work with such a machine? We need to emphasize that we are not so much interested in whether it is technically possible to build such a machine, though this too is obviously an important matter. But we will assume for the purposes of our discussion in this section that it is technically possible. This leads to our second point which is that, assuming that it is possible to build a machine like Data, what implications would it have for our understanding of the nature of human beings? Would it show, once again, that we are not as unique as we think we are; more specifically, would it show that our capacities are not as unique as we regard them because we can build machines that can do what we can do? Would artificial intelligence have any implications for free will? For our understanding of human nature?

Philosophers interested in these questions should be distinguished from computer scientists who work in the area of artificial intelligence, because the former are not interested so much in the technical project of developing an intelligent machine, but are more interested in what an artificially intelligent machine might tell us about the nature of human intelligence. Computer scientists (with some exceptions, of course) are not as interested in this question. Philosophers wish to know, more specifically, what the study of computers and their programs might yield about the workings of human intelligence that would throw light on the latter. They are greatly attracted to the analogy between computer hardware (the machine itself, hard drive, computer chips, etc.) and its programs (software), on the one hand, with the brain (hardware) and the mind (software), on the other; some propose as a working hypothesis that mind is to brain as computer software is to computer hardware.

The dualist and the materialist have different views on artificial intelligence, as one would expect. The dualist holds that it might be possible to build machines in the future that can perform many of the intellectual activities that we can perform (indeed Descartes himself raised this possibility[19]), but the machine would only be *simulating* human mental operations but not actually *replicating* them. To simulate human activities means that the machine *acts* like it is doing mental operations, but it really is not. For example, it might act like it is understanding mathematical equations and reasoning logically about them, when in fact it is not, it is simply going through a mechanical and digital process that involves the operation of a combination of wheels, pulleys, electronic circuits, and digital chips, all operating according to physical laws. The machine is not "understanding" anything, there is no "mind" or "reasoning" involved, at any level. We must also be careful to note that we are only talking metaphorically when we say things we can't help saying—that the machine "acts," "processes information," "is only doing," and so on. These active human verbs imply that the machine is thinking or reasoning, perhaps that it is some kind of individual entity, but the dualist urges that this is only a way of talking, not a description of what is going on in the machine. It is similar to saying that one's car is being "stubborn" as a way of indicating that it is difficult to repair.

Artificially intelligent machines, the dualist claims, would be only more sophisticated versions of current computers; their internal operations would be no different than that of a photocopier, which is following a causal process from the moment one presses the start button to the moment the photocopied page appears. It would be the same with androids no matter how sophisticated these operations appear. Artificial intelligence may succeed in simulating intelligence, and understanding, and perhaps even imagination, but it will not succeed in replicating it, that is, in producing machines that actually are capable of understanding, thinking, and imagining. For machines have no minds, no matter what their external operations may suggest. Just like when a simulated human voice at the other end of the telephone tells you to hang up, there is "nobody there" in the machine. This is because all of these mental operations in human beings are nonphysical operations, and cannot be explained by physics alone, as we saw in our discussion above. Understanding, for example, is a mental operation, which involves the areas of consciousness, reasoning, intentionality, and free will, and it cannot be explained at the physical level, so therefore it would not be possible to build a physical machine that actually had consciousness or understanding because the nonphysical nature of these activities is an obstacle that cannot be overcome.

The materialist view, on the other hand, because it already holds that consciousness is physical, has to automatically take seriously the view that it might be possible to develop machines that, in some way, have real minds, real understanding, real intentionality, and real reasoning skills. This is because materialists already hold that the mind and its activities consist primarily of physical matter, and that mental activities are nothing more than sophisticated physical operations involving matter, energy, chemicals, and causal laws. Of course, no materialist claims that we could build machines that would be made out of the same stuff as human beings (at least not yet), but given that mental activities are either physical activities, or can be explained totally in terms of physical activities, it might be possible to construct a machine that reproduced the exact same physical activities; in such a case, we might have to say that the machine is really thinking. It would be analogous to asking if there is any essential difference between a DVD player that is made entirely of metal parts and one made entirely of plastic parts; if they can perform the exact same functions, we would have to say that both are DVD players. Since the plastic player can play DVDs, we have to say that it is a DVD player. The question is whether it is the same with human beings? Say we overcome the technical problems and produce a machine that can do intellectually what we can do, would we then have to say that the machine is intelligent because it can do intelligent things? The dualist says no because the machine is not really performing anything, is not understanding, and is not thinking, but this answer is not open to the materialist. It is not so much perhaps that the materialist wants to defend artificial intelligence, but more that he would have to take it seriously in a way that the dualist would not.

The British mathematician, Alan Turing, was interested in the question as to how machines might be judged to be intelligent. What would the machine have to be capable of doing so that we would come to the conclusion that the machine was genuinely intelligent, and not just following programs? Suppose a machine could carry on a conversation with a person, or could perform an experiment in science, or write a story, would that be enough to say that the machine is intelligent? Turing proposed what has become known as the "Turing test" for machine intelligence, a test that measures intelligence by how the machine acts more so than by what is going on inside its "head."[20] He proposed setting up an experiment with a human being in one room and the machine in another, and a second human being who is allowed to carry on a conversation with both by asking questions and receiving answers, and who also does not know that one of his interlocutors is a machine. Turing held that if the second human being could carry on an intelligent, although simple, conversation with the machine through messages carried back and forth, and so could not tell that it was a machine, then we would have to say the machine is intelligent.

This is an interesting test, but one flaw in it is that this would be simulation of human intelligence, but not necessarily replication of human intelligence. The machine would still be following programs and instructions and performing mechanical and digital operations but would not actually be thinking, or understanding, or willing, etc. Many people working in artificial intelligence seem to overlook or ignore this key common sense criticism of an approach like Turing's behavioral approach. Yet Turing and others would argue that if a machine came along that could act like Data in *Star Trek* it would be very hard for us not to treat the machine as intelligent. Day to day interaction with the machine would cause us to judge it more in terms of its behavior than in terms of its internal workings, and this would mean that we might come to regard its internal workings as not as significant metaphysically as we initially thought. This approach is an offshoot of the behaviorist approach in psychology more generally which attempts to explain and understand human actions in terms of outward behavior rather than inward states, but it suffers from implausibility because we do all know that we have internal states, such as reasoning, beliefs, ideas, anxieties, and so forth. We also attribute internal states to others in terms of their behavior; not only that, the internal states are crucial to the essence of the person, and they are the cause of the external behavior. So, why not adopt the same approach with machines?

Despite being a strong, indeed ardent materialist, philosopher John Searle constructed the famous Chinese room example as a powerful objection to the whole project of artificial intelligence.[21] Searle imagines a case where you, an English speaker, are locked in a room, and are given three batches of Chinese writing; the first batch consists of a script; unknown to you, the second batch is a story in Chinese; and the third batch is a series of questions about the story. You are also given a set of rules in English for manipulating the contents of the script according to their formal shapes; the rules tell you how to answer questions (from batch 3) about the story (batch 2), using the script (batch 1). However, you do not know a word of Chinese. Searle argues that in this example you are operating in the same way that a computer operates. You are manipulating symbols according to a set of rules (the "program"); you might look like you understand Chinese to an outsider (i.e., you would pass the Turing test), but of course you do not understand Chinese. But suppose we change the experiment so that you now have before you batches in English, but everything else remains the same. In this second case, you do *understand* English! Searle uses this example to show that since in the first case you do not understand Chinese, then neither does the machine, and so the computer model does not explain understanding. It is not necessary that we know how to explain the nature of human understanding in order for this example to work. We just need to know that, whatever the machine is doing, there is no understanding involved, and so understanding cannot be explained in terms of machines and their programs.

To the behaviorist objection above that if the machine appears to be understanding, then it really is understanding, and to the objection concerning other minds (that we only attribute "minds" to others based on their behavior and so why can't we do this with machines), Searle argues that it is not necessary to know that other people have cognitive contents. Instead, we need to focus on what I am attributing to them when I attribute cognitive states to them, and the answer is that it is not just computational processes because the Chinese room example shows that such processes can exist *without* cognitive states. Searle sees at least two problems with the "mind is to brain as program is to hardware" analogy: first, the program is purely formal, meaning that it operates syntactically by moving symbols around according to preprogrammed rules (which are themselves digital and mechanical operations); second, mental states exhibit features of intentionality and understanding, but machines do not.

Despite these interesting attempts to explain the human mind in physical terms, it seems that the essence of what it is to be a human being strongly resists a physical explanation. So many qualities and characteristics of humanity, such as consciousness, rationality, understanding, moral values (compassion, empathy, tolerance, for instance), and free will, all that we hold dear as the foundation of human life, and without which our personal and political lives are impossible to conceive, prove very problematic for materialist approaches to the mind. Of course, these qualities and characteristics are also often defining features of the religious approach to reality. They support the view that human existence is unique among all the species, despite the way the species came about; their existence and nature also supports the view that morality is part of the essence of human life, and the possibility of an afterlife.

The search for extraterrestrial intelligence

The topic of the nature of a human beings, when coupled with some of the possibilities suggested by evolution, leads us naturally before we bring this chapter to a close to consider the difficult but interesting question of the possibility of life on other planets. This is a tricky question to have any certainty about, of course, but we can raise several important points that may help us gain a clearer understanding of the topic. We also need to consider how the topic is relevant when thinking about the nature of human beings, and our overall understanding of reality.

The first point to make is that we have no evidence of life on other planets, and indeed the search for extraterrestrial intelligence, called the SETI project, is often regarded by many as a waste of time and money, time and money that could be better spent doing something more productive. (This is the point of view in the stimulating film, *Contact*, starring Jodie Foster as Ellie Arroway, at the beginning, but that point of view changes later when a message is received from outer space!) The feeling is that, while there may be life out there on other planets in distant galaxies, these are too far away for us to discover, given our present state of technology. Yet Ellie's reasoning in *Contact* (which is based on the novel by Carl Sagan) certainly gives us pause: given that there are 400 billion stars in our galaxy alone, if only one out of a million had planets, and if just one of those had life, and if just one in a million of those had intelligent life, there would be millions of civilizations out there in the universe. It might be, those who support the SETI project argue, that although we do not have the technology yet to reach other planets where intelligent life exists, the alien civilizations might be more advanced and might have developed technology that enables them to travel through galaxies at high speeds (or send messages through space), and so perhaps they could contact us! Although we have only started sending out these messages recently (since the early 1960s) and they would take a very, very long time to get to a distant galaxy (our neighboring galaxy, Andromeda, is 2.5 million light years away, and a light year is almost 6 trillion miles in distance!), aliens might have sent their messages out millions of years ago, and so some of these messages could be coming into our galaxy just about anytime now!

The second point is to ask whether any further considerations can be brought to bear on whether any of this is likely or not. A naturalist like Carl Sagan holds that it is possible because he wishes to argue that evolution not only can explain the origin of the species but also the origin of life. Sagan, Christian de Duve, and others extend the theory of evolution to the origin of life itself through the process of abiogenesis, as we saw in Chapter 3. These thinkers extrapolate that the same process could occur on other planets in other galaxies, and so there might be other civilizations out there. Sagan further thinks that because the environment and building blocks of life on other planets would inevitably be different than those on earth, quite different species would likely have come into existence on those planets, and this would confirm that human existence is not unique, that our biological structure is not necessary, but only accidental. The theist argues that all of this assumes too much that is excessively improbable: that living things originated from nonliving things, that evolution happened by chance, that life-forms of our complexity could originate by chance, and that our higher faculties, consciousness, reasoning, free will, and the moral domain all consist of matter, and are accidents of nature, rather than the products of design.

But despite Sagan's view being far-fetched, we need to consider the question of what would be the implications for humanity if we did discover other life-forms, especially intelligent life-forms, on other planets? The answer may depend on the type of alien species encountered. It is possible that the discovery of alien species would further strengthen the cumulative case argument for the existence of God. If one takes the anthropic argument, in particular, seriously (an argument we look at in the next chapter), and appreciates the extremely small probability of our universe being suitable just by chance to support intelligent life, this is a further argument that life on earth was designed, or was intended. This conclusion of the anthropic argument would also apply to life on other planets: there would be a very low probability that it could originate by chance. Therefore, if it turns out that there is life on some other planet, this would be perfectly consistent with the argument from design. Naturalists like Sagan believe that if we discover life on other planets, this would confirm the hypothesis that life originated out of nonliving things here on earth, and this would be further confirming evidence for an atheistic or naturalistic interpretation of evolution. However, this is question-begging because we would have no direct evidence of life originating from nonlife (this would still remain a hypothesis). But based on the evidence from the big bang, the possibility of life occurring on any planet in our universe is so incredibly low in terms of probability that its existence better supports the conclusion that a designer is responsible. This conclusion would also seem to apply to the discovery of life on other planets.

How the discovery of life on other planets would affect our understanding of ourselves will probably depend a lot on what the alien life is like. If we discover human beings on another planet, it would be hard not to interpret this fact as a further support for a religious view of the world. It would not be believable to think that it just so happened that the kind of life that developed (by chance) on both planets turned out to be exactly the same. But suppose that the alien species had a different biological structure, body structure, etc., from us but still had the same logical and reasoning ability as us, along with free will and moral agency? (This is how most science fiction films portray alien species.) This scenario could easily support a religious conclusion because it would show the centrality of reason and morality in intelligent life, features which suggest a Designer. Only if the alien species were radically different from us in almost every respect—biology, reason, and morality (it is hard to conceive of intelligent life without a system of reason at least similar to ours)—might one see it as an argument in favor of naturalism.

Yet, even on this point we should be cautious because of the possibility that God's creation may be vastly more spectacular than we had hitherto thought. It would diminish the centrality of human life in a way if we found intelligent beings on other planets that were not human, but not the majesty of intelligent life in general as existing in the universe, and not the view that life is created according to a particular plan for a particular reason. Let us not forget that the alien species would share our ultimate questions: what is the cause of the universe, and of the order in the universe? This point is illustrated by a captivating moment in the film, *Contact*, when the lead character Ellie asks the alien how everything got here, and he answers: "nobody knows." Indeed, how *could* he know the answer, unless he could show how something comes from nothing, how the laws of physics originated, how life originated, how consciousness, reason, free will, and morality originated? Other civilizations, if they exist, will have the *same* ultimate questions as we have, which illustrates once again the inadequacy of naturalism, and of the attempt to press science into its service.

We have seen in this chapter that many have resisted attempts by naturalists to co-opt science in support of various forms of materialism and reductionism. Religious believers have mostly rejected reductionism in all its forms, as indeed have many scientists. It is important to be aware of the limits of science, and to appreciate that naturalists are inclined to claim far more than the results of scientific research on various matters actually warrants (e.g., in relation to consciousness and the origin of life), a position which once again is an indication of their *commitment* to naturalism as an article of faith, rather than as a view which is driven by scientific evidence. Once we recognize that some (agenda-setting) scientists are wont to work from a position of metaphysical naturalism, rather than methodological naturalism, there is plenty of room for a complementary relationship between religion and science on the interesting questions raised in this chapter relating to the human person. Religious thinkers will be fully supportive of science, but will argue that because theism is the best overall explanatory theory of reality, that science will find its natural place within this position, so we can all work together in trying to understand the depths of reality, and the meaning of human life.

6
Design in the Universe

Chapter Outline
William Paley's argument 147
The "laws of physics" argument from design 152
Design at the beginning: the anthropic argument 158
Intelligent design arguments 163

When considering matters of science and religion, the subject of design is never very far away. It is relevant to the question of whether there is an intelligence behind the universe, to the question of the ultimate purpose, or *telos*, of human life, to the topic of the connection between evolution and design, and to the question of whether the various processes and events that constitute the beginning of the universe (the big bang) show empirical evidence of design. In fact, arguments that appeal to the concept of design have been very popular in the history of ideas, among a wide range of thinkers in different disciplines, and they have often been at the heart of the attempt to do natural theology. Natural theology is a subdiscipline of the philosophy of religion. It involves examining any evidence for the existence of God that can be found in the physical universe (including from the study of life), and then attempting to draw some conclusion about whether or not God's existence can be inferred on the basis of the evidence found. Natural theology has usually reached a positive conclusion on this matter. Various forms of the design argument have been at the heart of natural theology, and have been offered as support for the view that there is an overall purpose to human life. The arguments of natural theology are also invoked as a support for the claim that evolution and religion are compatible, no matter what people on various sides of contemporary controversies might claim to the contrary.

The idea that the universe might be the product of design goes right back to the ancient Greeks who were impressed with the apparent orderliness and purpose in the things we see around us in the world. In fact, the pre-Socratic thinkers regarded this orderliness as one of the main features of our experience that needed an explanation, and this was a motivation for many of their informed speculations about reality. But it was not just the ancient Greeks who thought they could see order in the universe, for, just as with our everyday intuitive sense that the universe must have some cause, the idea that the universe shows signs of design cannot fail to occasionally cross the mind of anyone who seriously reflects about its nature and origin. The question of whether our universe, with its complex structure and makeup, is the product of an intelligent mind is one we naturally consider. Most would acknowledge that the universe does on the surface at least show some evidence of design or order, and this is why the question of whether it is designed or not is a natural one to ask. It does not follow, however, from the fact that the universe seems to exhibit order or design, that it actually is designed. This is why we need to take a more careful look at what we mean by "design," as well as at which features in the universe might be said to exhibit design, and in what ways these might point to a designer. The design argument, or the teleological argument, comes in different forms, each with its own group of champions. In this chapter, we will examine four of the main versions of the argument, and their relevance and implications for the religion-science discussion. These arguments are: (1) William Paley's argument based on the subtle complexities of nature, an argument he illustrates with his famous watch analogy; (2) the modern "laws of physics" argument from design, which makes a significant appeal to the evidence of recent science; (3) the anthropic, or fine-tuning, argument, also based on an appeal to recent scientific evidence, in this case from the big bang theory; (4) the contemporary argument from intelligent design, which again appeals to empirical evidence, particularly from microbiology, and which at the same time is a critique of natural selection, one of the key concepts of the theory of evolution. Consideration of these four arguments will also reveal the pervasiveness of the concept of design in myriad areas of our experience and interaction with the universe.

William Paley's argument

One of the best-known versions of the argument from design can be found in eighteenth-century philosopher William Paley's book, *Natural Theology, or Evidences of the Existence and Attributes of the Deity* (1802).[1] Paley's argument has received new attention in the last 30 years because of the ongoing cultural disputes involving evolution and religion, and now more recently, intelligent design (especially in the United States). Paley was much impressed by the view that the universe appears to exhibit a type of order; he argued that one could reason from this order to an orderer, or a designer, who was responsible for the design we experience at the heart of our universe. In talking about "order" or "design," Paley was mainly interested in understanding this concept in terms of "purpose." His approach has echoes of Aristotle's idea of final cause, the view that objects have a specific purpose in nature. Paley believed we could detect a type of design in nature in ordinary empirical ways, and that this design suggested that the universe and the objects in it had a particular purpose. Many find Paley's approach intuitively very plausible because he argues that because we can see design, it is reasonable to suggest that there may be a designer. It seems obvious, many people will agree, that when we examine the universe it is natural for one to think that it has been designed, despite the fact that there is occasional evidence that would militate against this conclusion as well. For example, when the astronauts looked out from their *Apollo 8* spaceship at the vast expanse of space on December 24, 1968, and relayed pictures of the earth from the spaceship (and then read from the book of Genesis), they were struck from their unique vantage point (as all watching on TV were too) by not just the fact that the universe exists at all, but also by its beauty and ordered structure. We note the planets in their orbits, we observe a certain consistency about nature, we marvel at the order of the seasons, we note that the universe can sustain life, that nature appears intelligible to the human mind, etc. But, while all these empirical observations suggest the idea of design, we need to think more deeply about whether they really are examples of design. Do they represent, or can they be elaborated as representing, design in the universe, in the same way that examining the parts of a car engine will reveal design, a design that clearly supports the conclusion that there is an intelligence behind a car engine? Paley argued that they do.

As an illustration, Paley uses the example of finding a watch on a heath. Supposing that we had never seen a watch before, Paley argues that we would conclude, after examining it carefully, that it was designed by a mind. It is too intricate an object to have come about by chance, which is the only other alternative; it clearly seems to have been put together for a purpose (to tell time). It is reasonable to argue this way about a watch, he suggests, but it is not reasonable to argue this way about a stone. This is because of the intricate nature of the watch, which we discover upon examining it. Paley argues that even if we had never seen a watch made, this would not weaken our conclusion that the watch has a designer, nor would the fact that the watch sometimes goes wrong, because "it is not necessary that a machine be perfect in order to show with what design it was made."[2] Paley continues that no man in his senses would accept that the structure of the watch was the result of a series of "chance occurrences" in nature.

But, Paley continues, if this is a reasonable way to argue about a watch, it is also a reasonable way to look upon nature itself. There are very intricate, complex, ordered operations in nature, and they could easily be said to have a purpose. Paley was particularly impressed by the physiological aspects of animals, and offered the example of the complex ordered operation of the human eye as evidence of clear design in nature. Animal habitats, he held, also seem perfectly designed for the animals that live in them. In addition, these animals seem to have a purpose in nature, as Aristotle argued, from which they never deviate. Indeed this argument also applies to human beings. Paley points out that every observation he made concerning the watch "may be repeated with strict propriety concerning the eye, concerning animals, concerning plants, concerning, indeed, all the organized parts of the works of nature."[3] Therefore, it is reasonable to conclude that there is a designer behind nature, that there must be a mind who thought up various purposes that would be part of nature, and put them into practice, as it were, just as the watchmaker did with the watch.

The basic reasoning behind this version of the argument from design is straightforward. The premise of the argument is that the universe shows evidence of design or order. This order is detectable through ordinary empirical ways, for example, we examine the physiological structure of animals and humans, and we note the intricate nature of these structures (resembling the intricate nature of a watch). The conclusion of the argument is that, since there is evidence of design, this means that there is probably an intelligent designer of the universe. The argument is an inductive or probabilistic one; it does not say that the design in the universe offers conclusive proof of a designer, but only that it is a very reasonable conclusion.

The design argument is also an argument from analogy. The analogy is based on a comparison of the universe and its design with human artifacts (e.g., a watch, a car engine, a furnished room) that we have designed. Paley employs the analogy in this way: given that we can see design in many artifacts in the world (watches) and their environments, and we know that intelligent (human) minds are responsible for this, then so too, if we find design in the universe (animal and human structures and their environments), we can similarly infer that an intelligent mind is behind this design. It will not be the same type of mind because although there are similarities between human and natural designs, there are also significant differences. (We can make a watch, e.g., but we can't make a rabbit.) Like most analogies, the analogy emphasized here does not claim to be perfect in every respect. But it is strong, according to Paley and supporters of the argument, and enables us to conclude that the cause of the universe is most likely God, the intelligent designer.

There have been various attempts at a rebuttal of the argument from design, but it was not until the theory of evolution came along that some thinkers thought that they had an effective way to respond to Paley's argument. This was because the theory of evolution offered a naturalistic explanation for precisely the type of design and order that Paley had focused on. At least this is how contemporary thinkers see the theory of evolution and its relationship to Paley's argument; yet this particular understanding of evolution as an attack on design was not as prevalent in Darwin's day, where the implications of the theory were developed more slowly. But, the contemporary secularist, in particular, as we pointed out in Chapter 1 in our discussion of positive atheism, is seeking a way to justify his secularist view of reality so he often turns to the theory of evolution, and gives it a more secularist reading than the evidence for the theory actually warrants. This is why a contemporary secularist like Richard Dawkins can say that he can't imagine anyone being an atheist before 1859 (the year *The Origin of the Species* was published).[4] Before this date, in Dawkins' view, Paley's argument rightfully held sway with most people. But after Darwin, things are different.

Critics of Paley's argument agree with him that there is an order of sorts apparent in nature, but go on to argue that it most likely has a naturalistic, scientific explanation. Therefore, the move to a supernatural explanation is redundant because it is not warranted by the evidence. The theory of evolution shows that the various species evolved *naturally* and by *chance* in the way Darwin described (discussed in detail in Chapter 4). But if all of the species originated by chance according to the process known as natural selection, this means that no species has to exist, no species is necessary, no species has to have the nature that it actually has. It also means, most importantly, that the point that fascinated Paley so much—that species seem so perfectly designed for their particular habitats—now has a *natural* cause. The "design" is only apparent, and is due to the "blind" forces of natural selection, which involve the struggle in nature between competing species, the survival of the fittest, the shaping of environmental conditions by chance events in nature, and so forth. While it looks like the structure of the finch, for example, was designed so that finches could survive in their habitats, this biological structure was not designed at all, but evolved in naturalistic ways over time. The same is true of the human eye, an object so complex in its operation that it has fascinated many. Although the eye is analogous with a watch in some respects, as Paley claimed, the eye is not designed, but came about due to the chance processes of natural selection operating over a very long period of time. Not all species survived, of course; and many others have undergone transformative changes over millions of years.

The theory of evolution is proposed as an effective reply to Paley's version of teleology, which emphasizes the suitability of habitats for their species, and the remarkable complexity of biological structures, as support for the claim that nature seems to have been designed for a purpose. Evolution would seem to be a successful reply to any argument of this type because it seems to be an argument against Aristotle's final causes and also against his view that each object consists of matter and form, where the form is the essence, or nature, of the object, which the object then fulfills or exemplifies in its natural development. The theory would provide us with a natural explanation for the purposes in nature that Paley concentrated on. Evolution, therefore, can be seen as a theory which indirectly attacks the notion of teleology, at least as it applies to the origin and nature of species, and many thinkers were only too glad to interpret it in this way, though (as we noted in Chapter 4, and will come back to again in the next section), it is by no means entirely clear that it does undermine the view that nature is teleological.

A problem for this use of the theory of evolution is that the theory applies only to biological systems. It is unable to explain the *origin* of matter and energy, and this is a mistake that some well-known contemporary scientists often make, like Francis Crick and Richard Dawkins. As we will see later in this chapter, they often talk as if evolution not only explains the origin and nature of species, but as if it can explain the origin of *everything*, including the universe.[5] Well-known scientists sometimes let their exuberance for the theory of evolution dominate their supposed commitment to dispassionate reason and evidence! But evolution is unable to explain the existence of the universe, and the underlying order in the universe. Dawkins, and others, overlook the point that evolution is not a theory about the origin of matter and energy. It only takes a moment's reflection to realize that in order for evolution to occur, it is necessary to have already present existing matter, and also some kind of environment, in addition to a set of laws that regulate how everything behaves. Sometimes we overlook the obvious logical point that evolution cannot occur unless something first exists! And so, evolution *logically cannot* be an account of the origin of the universe. The theory of evolution is not enough to solve the main problem facing a naturalistic account of origins: where did the first matter and energy come from, matter and energy that govern significantly what *can* happen as the universe "evolves"? This brings us to consider the underlying order in the universe, and so to the "laws of physics" version of the design argument.

The "laws of physics" argument from design

The philosopher, Richard Swinburne, has pioneered a more modern version of the argument from design, often called "the laws of physics" or "the laws of science" version. Scientists, including Paul Davies, have also invoked this argument.[6] Swinburne distinguishes between two different ways of thinking about design, what he calls regularities of copresence, or spatial order, and regularities of succession, or temporal order.[7] All instances of design in the universe fall into one or other of these categories. Regularities of copresence, on the one hand, refer to patterns of spatial order at a particular instance in time, such as a town with all its roads at right angles to each other, or a section of books in a library placed in alphabetical order. Regularities of succession, on the other hand, refer to patterns of behavior of objects such as their behavior in accordance with the laws of nature, or the laws of physics. Swinburne refers to Newton's law of gravitation that all bodies attract each other with forces proportional to the product of their masses and inversely proportional to the square of their distance apart as an example. A working car exhibits instances of both kinds of order: many of the parts are arranged so that the car, at some instance in time, obeys the instructions of the driver, and at the same time, there is the underlying order whereby all the parts of the car are always following or obeying the laws of physics (in, for instance, the cars mechanical and electrical operations). Swinburne points out that up until the present time, many thinkers took the regularities of succession for granted, and generally focused on the regularities of copresence, which they constantly marveled at. There is no better example of this than Paley's appeal to the orderly operation of animal and plant life in nature, such as the human eye, and also in man-made machines, such as watches.

However, there are two problems lurking for any argument from design that is based primarily on an appeal to the regularities of copresence. The first is the one that we have already discussed above, the risk that the regularities of copresence—the order we can see on the surface in many parts of nature, such as the eye, the habitats of the species, the structure of plants and animals—may be explained in some other naturalistic way, and so the need to appeal to a designer is redundant. This is exactly what happened to Paley's argument when the theory of evolution came along, as we have seen. The theory was proposed as a natural, scientific explanation for those regularities of copresence that many, including Paley, marveled at in nature. The second problem for Paley's version of the argument is that there are many examples of spatial disorder in the universe as well, such as the arrangement of mountain ranges around the world, the natural condition of grasslands on the U.S. plains, the weather patterns in the North Pole, or the chaos of ocean waves interacting with landmasses. This second problem is perhaps not as serious as the first since the proponent of the argument can still hold that the order in the universe outweighs the disorder (as Paley himself pointed out), but nevertheless, it may weaken the argument overall.

However, the "laws of physics" version of the design argument avoids these problems because it appeals to an underlying order that is present even in regularities of copresence, no matter how these regularities appear to the naked eye, and *no matter what scientific explanation is produced to explain them*. We know from our work in science that there are "regularities" that occur in nature, empirically detectable patterns in how nature behaves. These have been codified and established as the laws of science, which include the laws of physics and chemistry, perhaps the two most basic sciences (along with mathematics) for understanding the physical universe. Examples of the laws of physics would include Newton's law of gravitation, as just noted; Kepler's laws of planetary motion (his first law states that the planets circle around the sun in elliptical orbits, with the sun at one focus of the ellipse); Ohm's law relating to electrical circuits (mentioned in Chapter 3), and many others, both simple and complex. A simple law from the point of view of the ordinary person might be that an object with a greater mass will crush an object with a lighter mass if it lands on top of it, all other things being equal. Or that an object with a lighter color will be harder to see against a lighter background than a darker object. Or that water will weaken the composition of wood over time (and so the farmer paints his fences every few years with wood preserving chemicals). These are ordinary everyday facts that we are familiar with in our experience, and, even though most of us may not often think of them as being governed by or produced by the "laws of science," their existence is remarkable from a philosophical point of view because they indicate that there is an underlying order in the universe.

Swinburne argues that it is a quite remarkable fact that our universe follows laws consistently, with no exceptions. And so it seems reasonable to think that this underlying order in the universe was caused by an intelligent mind. This argument relies on the fact that if our universe really is a chance occurrence, and is absent of any design, how is it that we live in a (scientifically) lawful universe rather than a lawless or chaotic one? It would be an amazing coincidence if the universe just so happened to be structured in this lawful way. These laws make life as we know it possible: they make travel possible, medicine possible, mathematics and science possible, and even life itself possible. In addition, these laws help us to understand how things work, and to improve our situation in the universe over time. It could have been the case that when we examined the world we found that there were no or very few laws. We might have found no consistent relationship between wood and water for example, or no consistent laws in biology, a situation that would compromise the whole area of medicine. One might object that if there were no or very few physical laws in our universe, then human life would never have evolved either, and so we would not be here to ask these questions. This is almost certainly true, but it does not alter the fact that this is the kind of universe that very likely would have existed—a scientifically lawless one—if the universe really were a product of chance. There is, therefore, an ultimate order to nature, which, as Swinburne explains, suggests a designer.

Swinburne believes that the move from the design represented by the laws of physics to the existence of an intelligent designer who is responsible for putting these laws in place is a reasonable one. He relies on the argument from analogy that is present in many versions of the design argument. He argues that there is no possible scientific explanation or other natural explanation for the underlying order in the universe, and so the hypothesis of a designer is the only possible explanation. The reason for this conclusion is that we know the causes of some regularities of succession, for example, a dancer moving her body when she performs a dance in time to music, or the notes of a song sung by a singer.[8] But producing the order that we find in the universe itself would require much more power than we have; it also would require intelligence and free choice. Swinburne explains the analogy this way: A's are caused by B's (human artifacts are caused by us); A*'s are similar to A's (the order in the universe is similar to the order we can put into the world); therefore, A*'s are produced by (a) B* similar to B's. This analogous form of reasoning is used all the time in ordinary logic and in science. It echoes what is essentially the same point made in St. Thomas Aquinas's fifth argument for the existence of God, which puts the matter this way: "An orderedness of actions to an end is observed in all bodies obeying natural laws, even when they lack awareness. For their behavior hardly ever varies, and will practically always turn out well; which shows that they truly tend to a goal, and do not merely hit it by accident."[9]

We should not underestimate the fact that many people take the laws of physics for granted when thinking about the universe (including many scientists)[10]; when thinking about design, many of us tend to think in terms of regularities of copresence rather than in terms of regularities of succession. Sometimes the two types of order are confused, as in the work of Richard Dawkins. In his book, *The Blind Watchmaker*, Dawkins is attempting to argue that the order in the universe is only apparent, that the order we see is in fact the product of blind chance, and comes out of an initial state of disorder. He appeals primarily to the theory of evolution as a way of explaining the order in the universe. But what about the order exemplified in the laws of physics underlying the behavior of physical matter and energy? Dawkins uses the metaphor of the nonrandom arrangement of pebbles of various sizes on an ocean beach to explain how this order in our universe came about:

> If you walk up and down a pebbly beach, you will notice that the pebbles are not arranged at random. The smaller pebbles typically tend to be found in segregated zones . . . the larger ones in different zones. The pebbles have been sorted, arranged, selected. A tribe living near the shore might wonder at this evidence of sorting or arrangement in the world, and might develop a myth to account for it, perhaps attributing it to a Great Spirit in the sky with a tidy mind and a sense of order. . . . [But] the arranging was really done by the blind forces of physics, in this case the action of waves . . . They just energetically throw the pebbles around, and the big pebbles and small pebbles respond differently to this treatment so they end up at different levels of the beach. A small amount of order has come out of disorder, and no mind planned it.[11]

Dallas Willard has described this argument of Dawkins' as an "order out of chaos" mysticism, an approach to an explanation of recalcitrant features of the physical world that involves not asking the normal questions we would ask about physical events. Commenting on this example, Willard points out that "nothing whatsoever has come out of disorder in this case"[12] because the interaction of the pebbles in the waves is a perfectly orderly process obeying the laws of physics, as is the process of the pebbles falling out onto the beach. The pebbles may appear to fall in a pattern on the beach because big pebbles and small pebbles react differently to the motion of the waves. So, someone walking along the beach might think that the order in the pebbles was due to a child playing with them (i.e., to an intelligent mind). However, in terms of Swinburne's distinction, the pebbles on the beach represent a regularity of copresence, and in this case we have a natural explanation for this regularity, the interaction of the waves and the pebbles, governed by the laws of physics. But the interaction of the waves and the pebbles is a regularity of succession, and *this* regularity has still not been explained, otherwise we would be saying that the laws of physics explain the laws of physics! As Willard goes on: "Moreover, *we* know for sure that *Dawkins himself* knows this. What afflicts him at this point can be very simply described. He is in the grip of the romanticism of evolution as a sweeping ontological principle, bearing in itself the mystical vision of an ultimate *Urgrund* of chaos and nothingness of itself, giving birth to the physical universe, which is all very fine as an aesthetic approach to the cosmos, and vaguely comforting. But it has nothing at all to do with 'evidence of . . . a universe without design,' as [his] book suggests."[13] Dawkins may be right in claiming that evolution can explain the type of order Paley was talking about, regularities of copresence, but it cannot explain the order that is the basis of the laws of physics version of the design argument. Dawkins therefore, as Willard notes, is claiming far too much for the theory of evolution, more than the theory itself ever tried to claim, for the theory officially does not purport to explain the laws of science!

It is obvious that evolution cannot give us an explanation for the laws of physics, because evolution, like all scientific theories, must *presuppose* these laws. Evolution is a theory of change, explaining how species change over time in particular environments. But the key point is that these changes will happen in accordance with the laws of physics. The matter and energy involved will behave, or follow, or obey the laws of physics in ways we have discovered in science. So, for example, when a storm destroys the food source of the chimps, this is because of the physical laws that govern the interaction of wind and rain with various types of plant; or when finches with longer beaks become dominant this is because they can better forage out food than their competitors with different beak structures, and so forth. These are all basic laws of nature that we progressively discover, codify, and elaborate by means of the various sciences. Evolution is not an explanation of them; rather it operates according to them. It is these laws that the second version of the design argument is based on. As Charles Taliaferro has noted, "Reigning accounts of biological evolution (and their successors) do not address questions about why there are any such evolutionary laws at all, or any organisms to begin with."[14] And as Willard concludes, "Let us say quite generally then that any sort of evolution of order of any kind will always presuppose preexisting order and preexisting entities governed by it. It follows then as a simple matter of logic that not all order evolved."[15]

Is the analogy involved in this version of the argument from design a good one? The reader has to make a judgment as to whether the supposed similarity between the order we know we can produce in the world, especially the point that this order is caused by intelligence, does carry over in a consideration of the universe itself. If it has order in it, does this mean there is an orderer? Would it be stretching reason too much to think that there might be a natural explanation for the order present in the laws of physics? David Hume, and many others, have raised questions about the appropriateness of the analogous reasoning used in the argument from design. Swinburne considers a number of Humean objections, and tries to rebut them.

The first objection put forward by Hume is what I call the "one world objection," the objection that because of the uniqueness of the world, it is illegitimate to conclude that it is analogous to human artifacts. Hume thinks that if we had several worlds that we knew were caused by gods, then, by analogy, we could reason to the probable cause of any new world under discussion as being a god. This critical point should make us look carefully at how objects are being compared to see if the similarities outweigh the differences. This is a good point, but Swinburne holds that the analogy involved in the design argument is a careful analogy, even though the argument acknowledges that the order in the world and the order produced by humans obviously can't be analogous in all respects.

Hume raises another popular objection against the argument: that if we are going to say there is a designer based on the evidence of design in nature, shouldn't we be able to explain the designer? But supporters hold that, although the nature of the designer is obviously very important, it is a logically distinct question from the question of whether there is a designer. The main aim of the argument is to show first that there *is* a designer, and then later we may be able to say something further about the nature of the designer, both positive (the designer has power, and knows mathematics and logic) and negative (the designer is not like man). This last point is important because sometimes this objection is pressed by Hume and his followers to say that we should conclude that the designer is like man, if we are going to employ the analogy of the human mind creating things. But again the point is that analogies are not perfect, no analogy says that objects are alike in every respect, and there are obvious differences between the world and human artifacts (a watch, an engine) to enable us to conclude that the power and intelligence of the designer is on a vastly different scale to ours. We can't make a world, but the designer of the universe can, and so there is justification for concluding that the cause of the universe cannot be a human being. We may not be able to say that the designer is the God of traditional theism (we would need other arguments for that), but the argument would have established quite a bit if it could minimally show that there is a designer.

Another objection to the design argument is to say that the order in the universe came about by chance. This objection is suggesting that it is reasonable to believe that the order in our universe has no cause; it is simply an accident of the history of the universe; that we could just as easily have had a universe without order (and in which life could not arise); the type of universe we end up with is no more predictable than throwing a can of alphabet soup off a table, and observing the results. The letters in the soup can land in an almost infinite variety of patterns on the floor. Among the possibilities are that they will spell out nothing meaningful or coherent, but if they happen to fall in such a way that they spell out "Arsenal play the most entertaining soccer" then this too just happened by chance! However, if one walked into a room and saw a spilled can of alphabet soup spelling out this message, one would immediately think that someone had rigged it this way, that is, that the message was spelled out by an intelligent mind! The reader has to judge whether it is reasonable to reach a similar conclusion about the underlying order that is present throughout the universe.

Design at the beginning: the anthropic argument

Let us begin our consideration of the anthropic argument with a thought experiment. Suppose you had no knowledge whatsoever of plumbing systems, had never seen one, were totally unfamiliar with the movement of water through a series of pumps, pipes, hoses, and valves for various purposes. Let us also suppose that you are taking a walk in the mountains, and you come across what is in fact a complicated irrigation system for watering an area of the valley below. But you, of course, have no idea what it is. Everything else you have seen on your trip through the mountains appears, upon reflection, to have arisen naturally, such as the land masses and river beds, trees, rocks, slopes, streams, flora, and so forth. The irrigation system might have arisen in the same way, but somehow it seems different, so you begin to take a closer look. First, you examine the individual parts, the valves, pipes, adapters, t-junctions, pumps, motors, etc., and you notice that each one has to be just the way it is in order for the system to work. The adapters, for instance, have to be just the right size, the right thickness, running in the right direction, and made from the right material, to function; any deficiency in any one of these features, and the adapter will fail. You also notice that all of the parts of the irrigation system have to be present together at the same time and in a certain pattern so that the system can work to irrigate the side of the valley. These two points, that each part has to satisfy very specific conditions, and that all of the parts must be present at the same time in order for watering to occur, lead you to the conclusion that the irrigation system could not be a chance occurrence, but has been designed by an intelligent mind for a particular purpose.

The "anthropic argument" for the existence of God claims that the same reasoning can be applied to the beginning of the universe (the argument, originally suggested by astrophysicist, Brandon Carter, is named to emphasize the privileged position of human beings in the universe). The argument has been advanced by John D. Barrow, Frank J. Tipler, John Polkinghorne, Paul Davies, and many others.[16] The main idea in the argument is an appeal to the nature of the big bang, specifically to the fact that it appears "fine tuned" to produce a universe that would eventually lead to the emergence and survival of life, and to the arrival of conscious observers who can understand many of the processes that gave rise to their existence. The argument appeals to the latest work in cosmology, astronomy, and astrophysics, which tells us that, given the nature of the processes involved in the big bang, the probability of the right conditions occurring on earth for the support and sustaining of life is extremely low, so low as to be almost incalculable. Proponents of the anthropic argument hold that there are several features that had to be just right in the big bang for the universe to be capable of supporting life. Otherwise, the universe would have no life.

These initial conditions that are necessary for the emergence of life are causally independent of each other; in addition, the probability of each one occurring is itself extremely low, never mind all of them occurring together to make the existence of life possible. The conditions include the following: the degree of gravitational force in the universe, the strong and weak nuclear forces, the isotropic distribution of matter and radiation, the ratio of matter to antimatter, and the presence of stable elements that are heavier than helium. The strong nuclear force, for instance, is a force that exists in the nucleus of atoms; it enables the atoms to stay intact against the powerful forces of repulsion that exist in the protons of the atom. If this force were just a slight bit stronger, our universe would be dominated by helium atoms, and it would not be possible for hydrogen to exist, and therefore water, and therefore life.[17] William Lane Craig points out that if the strong force were increased by as little as 1 percent, the nuclear resonance levels would be so altered that almost all carbon would be burned into oxygen; but an increase of 2 percent would preclude formation of protons out of quarks, preventing the existence of atoms. However, if the strong force were weaker by as little as 5 percent it would unbind deuteron (a stable atomic particle), which is essential to stellar nucleosynthesis, leading to a universe composed only of hydrogen. It has been estimated that the strong nuclear force must be within 0.8 and 1.2 of its actual strength or all elements of atomic weight greater than four would not have formed.[18]

Stephen Hawking has also argued that a reduction in the rate of expansion of the big bang of one part in a hundred thousand million millions would have led to a recollapse of the universe, while a similar increase would have produced a different universe than the one we have. He also notes that if the electrical charge of the electron has only been slightly different, stars either would have been unable to burn hydrogen and helium, or else they would not have exploded (and there would be no sun and so no life).[19] Similar arguments have been made relating to the other features mentioned which were all present at the big bang. Most significantly, their presence in just the right way (e.g., the right degree of strong nuclear force), and the presence of all of the other necessary conditions at the same time, is a quite remarkable fact. As Craig has put it: "When one mentally assigns different values to these constants or forces [present at the beginning of the universe], one discovers that in fact the number of . . . universes capable of supporting intelligent life is very small. Just a slight variation in any one of these values would render life impossible."[20] Although the probabilities of all of this happening just the way it did are hard to calculate with any degree of accuracy, there seems little doubt that the general point is true—that the probabilities involved are incalculably low, even if presently we can't be precise about the exact figures involved.

Proponents of the argument hold that when one reflects on what all of this implies, one is justified in concluding that the evidence from our study of the early stages of the universe suggests the conclusion that the universe was designed specifically to make life as we know it possible. This argument does not say that the existence of *any* universe was improbable, but that the existence of *our* universe was so improbable as to be not worth taking seriously. We only have two alternatives—that it was deliberately set up by an intelligent mind to support the existence of life, or that it is simply a remarkable coincidence that it should support life. The latter alternative is hard to believe given the staggering improbabilities involved. The physicist Freeman Dyson put this point by saying that it almost seems "as if the universe in some sense must have known that we were coming."[21]

This argument is not the same as the laws of physics argument, although the laws of physics are obviously present at the big bang as well. The laws of physics would be part of the underlying order present in the structure of the universe, right back to the big bang. The anthropic argument is based on an appeal to what we might describe as a second level of order that is present at the big bang. So, there are really two levels of order present in the early stages of the big bang, the underlying laws of physics, and the nature of the actual ingredients that are necessary for life to emerge on earth (assuming that the emergence of life on earth is a quite remarkable fact). This is analogous to saying that there are two levels of order present in a car engine: the underlying laws of physics that make any consistent operations of matter and energy possible in the engine (and so make it possible to create the conditions that produce the explosion of fuel and oxygen that moves the piston, to take one small instance of an engine's operations), and then the order or design placed in it by the engineers using various elements to produce an operating machine, such as mechanical parts, wiring, electrical, and fuel systems. Without the laws of physics, this design is not possible, but even with the laws of physics, the explosion will not happen unless the parts of the engine are arranged in a certain way. So, it is with the beginning of the universe; the underlying laws are there but the parts that exist also have a certain structure, *and* a certain relationship to each other, that all seem designed to facilitate the creation of *our* universe, and the later emergence of life.

Some critics respond by appealing to the "multiple universes" theory. The basic claim of this theory is that our universe is only one among many alternative universes. Looked at from this point of view, the probability of at least one of these universes being able to support life would, therefore, be higher! Michael Martin advances this argument:

> . . . [T]he improbability of life may be the result of many gods or of impersonal creative forces. Moreover, cosmologists have developed an alternative naturalistic explanatory model in terms of so-called world ensembles. They have conjectured that what we call our universe—our galaxy and other galaxies—may be one among many alternative worlds or universes . . . given enough universes it is very likely that in some of these the complex conditions necessary for life would be found.[22]

The reader should ponder these alternative explanations of design. Is the conjecture of "world ensembles" too speculative, too ad hoc to serve as an effective rejoinder to the anthropic argument? Does it ignore the rational significance of undisputed scientific evidence contained in the big bang? Or, is it a reasonable suggestion required by the ever outward search for scientific explanations of unusual phenomena? Sometimes students especially will often raise a different objection to this version of the design argument. They sometimes invoke an argument that has also been suggested by Stephen Hawking: that since life on earth obviously exists, the universe had to have been the sort of universe that would produce us, and so when we look back at the beginning conditions we would obviously find that they are very suited to support life, because it is these ordered conditions that produced us![23] Again, this is true, but it doesn't alter the fact that there might have been no order in the big bang such as to produce life. It could have been the case that almost *any* combination of ingredients in the big bang would have likely supported the existence of life. Instead, we find that the ingredients necessary to produce life are extremely hard to come by—recall the low probabilities—and yet they emerged from the big bang. As J. J. C. Smart has noted, "It is the fine tuning that (partially) explains the existence of observers, not the existence of observers that explains the fine tuning."[24] It would also be the case that, if the initial conditions in the big bang were just slightly different, in the way described above, that we would not exist, but this does not alter the scientific facts that show that it is necessary to have several very precise ingredients for our universe to produce life, and that we have them! It is easy to see why we have them if we consider that things might have been designed that way, but if we think they came about by chance, then their existence is almost unbelievable.

The existence of these ingredients is not just improbable in the sense that it is remarkable that life happened to emerge in our universe, a type of life that can look back and understand (to some degree) its nature and origin, the type of universe it is in, and so forth. This is the sense of improbable we use when we say that it was improbable that, although the tornado destroyed the town, it did not hit the house where the people were taking refuge. An event like this is improbable but does not necessarily suggest design. The sense of improbable in the anthropic argument stems from the fact that when we examine the initial conditions of the universe given in the big bang, we can see from our study of these conditions that it very unlikely that life would emerge, and yet it did. Of course, it is logically possible that our universe could have formed in a certain way by chance. This conclusion cannot be totally ruled out; yet we must also reflect on whether or not it is a probable conclusion. This is the central insight of the anthropic argument, and it is yet another way in which work in modern science can be employed to support an argument for the existence of an intelligent designer, another way in which science can be used to support rather than to undermine religion.

Intelligent design arguments

In the past 10 years, a new form of the argument from design, referred to as intelligent design (ID), has forced its way into the debate about design in the universe. It is an approach that also raises questions about the boundaries of science as a discipline, as well as about the process of natural selection and the link between science and naturalism. Intelligent Design generates a lot of heated disagreements, more than many of the other equally disputed topics we are discussing in this book. There are several reasons for this. The first is that some critics believe that ID is really a form of creationism in disguise, a way of trying to smuggle religious views into science. However, it is not correct to describe ID as a form of creationism because of two crucial points: first, proponents of the theory allow the *empirical evidence* to drive their arguments unlike creationists who usually begin from a religious perspective and allow the Bible to drive their main points; second, supporters of ID do not officially identify the intelligent designer as God, but conclude only that there is an intelligent designer based on the evidence. Sometimes critics will respond to these points by saying that their real *motive*, however, is religious; yet, from a philosophical point of view, the motive behind an argument is not that significant, because logically one should look at the argument itself, rather than the motive of the person who presents the argument. The argument must stand or fall on its own merits, and be analyzed in terms of its logical structure and subject matter. This is true as much for an argument for intelligent design that one may think is motivated by religion as it is for an argument in favor of evolution that one may think is motivated by atheism. We do not discount the theory of evolution because some people who passionately advocate it may be doing so in order to promote atheism; similarly, we can't discount ID theory based on our perceptions of the motives of its advocates.

A second reason for why ID generates heated debate is because it is not only a theory proposing that there is an intelligent mind behind the universe but, as we will see presently, it also offers a critique of the theory of evolution at the same time as it develops its own position (unlike the other arguments we have looked at in this chapter, with the possible exception of Paley's). This has led some to call for the teaching of Intelligent Design theory alongside the theory of evolution in high school biology courses, as a rival hypothesis. Proponents of this view hold that it is a form of discrimination to exclude intelligent design just because many scientists reject it. They argue that ID is held by many serious scholars, and so is entitled to a place at the table. This had led to often bitter public disputes surrounding ID theory in several U.S. states, including Kansas and Ohio, leading to much acrimony on both sides. Unfortunately, these hostilities inevitably poison the atmosphere, and often make a genuine discussion of the absorbing issues involved hard to achieve because both sides are suspicious of each other's motives. The strongest rhetorical criticism that the anti-ID people make toward ID is to say that it is a dishonest attempt to sneak religion into the school curriculum, while the strongest rhetorical criticism from the ID side is that the anti-ID people are more concerned with promoting atheism than with a rational and fair debate, and are hypocrites for continually talking about free speech while at the same time censoring ID theorists! From our point of view in this book, the public policy side of the dispute as it applies to education is ultimately a secondary matter, since we are primarily concerned with the philosophical, religious, and scientific questions raised by the theory of Intelligent Design.

A third reason for the hostility to ID is that it is a theory which raises interesting questions about the definition and boundaries of science itself, as we will see. In particular, it asks the question as to whether the conclusion that there is an intelligent designer might be seen as a *scientific* conclusion. If so, this would expand our usual understanding of science. Needless to say, this move is greatly resisted by critics, and leads to the debate sometimes being conducted in a way that completely ignores the actual issues under discussion.

One side tries to shut down the debate before it begins by dismissively saying that ID is not science, and the other side replies that this barb illustrates again that modern science is just another form of atheism, with scientists trying to exclude any criticism of their theories by using an ad hoc definition of science that is indistinguishable from atheism. Using our distinction from Chapter 3, ID proponents accuse modern science of promoting metaphysical naturalism instead of methodological naturalism. Let us look more closely at the arguments of ID theorists, and along the way we will come back to some of these points again.

The leading ID theorists are Michael Behe, William Dembski, and Phillip Johnson, all of whom have presented interesting versions of the argument.[25] We will focus primarily on Behe's version of the argument here. Behe's argument can be understood in terms of three general points. First, he argues in his book, *Darwin's Black Box*, that evolutionary principles, especially the process of natural selection, cannot explain the complexity of the living cell at the molecular level. Behe argues that the cell is "irreducibly complex," by which he means that it needs all of its various complex parts in place *all at once* in order to operate, and perform its specific function. If this is true, it would be a critique of natural selection, which says that each specific part of an organism developed individually and gradually over time because its existence gave some selective advantage to the organism at each stage of its development. Behe uses the analogy of a mousetrap to illustrate his point. Just as a mousetrap needs all of its parts in place at the same time to function as a mousetrap, it is the same with the cell at the molecular level. Behe cites the example of the bacterial flagellum, which he argues is unlikely to have arisen by the gradual process of successive modifications caused by natural selection and random mutation as argued for by the theory of evolution. Three parts are required for the flagellum to function, the paddle, a rotor, and a motor (Behe uses a mechanical model to explain how the flagellum works). As he explains it:

> The flagellum is a long, hair like filament embedded in the cell membrane. The external filament consists of a single type of protein, called "flagellin." The flagellin filament is the paddle surface that contacts the liquid during swimming. At the end of the flagellin filament near the surface of the cell, there is a bulge in the thickness of the flagellum. It is here that the filament attaches to the rotor drive. The attachment material is comprised of something called "hook protein." The filament of a bacterial flagellum, unlike a cilium, contains no motor protein; if it is broken off, the filament just floats stiffly in the water. Therefore the motor that rotates the filament-propeller must be located somewhere else. Experiments have

> demonstrated that it is located at the base of the flagellum, where electron microscopy shows several ring structures occur. The rotary nature of the flagellum has clear, unavoidable consequences . . . [it] must have the same mechanical elements as other rotary devices . . . Because the bacterial flagellum is necessarily composed of at least three parts—a paddle, a rotor, and a motor—it is irreducibly complex. Gradual evolution of the flagellum . . . therefore faces mammoth hurdles . . . no scientist has *ever* published a model to account for the gradual evolution of this extraordinary molecular machine.[26]

Behe goes on to argue that many features of biological systems are irreducible complexities, and that they are even likely to be far more complex than current research shows. He thinks that one cannot explain these complexities by saying that these systems could have developed gradually by means of the modification of an earlier system through the process of selection because the earlier system too, if it was functional, would have been an irreducible complexity. Some might claim in reply, to take the human eye as another example (one we considered in Chapter 4), that the various parts of the eye evolved because they individually performed some selective advantage for the organism over the years. Yet the function each part performed would not be connected with sight, because for sight to occur we would need the eye itself, and all its interrelated parts working together, in addition to connections to both the optic nerve and the brain. But Behe argues that the eye itself is an irreducible complexity because it requires all of its parts working together at the same time to perform its function, just like the mousetrap. His conclusion therefore is that irreducible complexities look very difficult to explain by means of natural selection. So, this first claim of ID theory is also at the same time a critique of the process of natural selection, but it does not necessarily deny other claims of the theory of evolution, such as that all species are genetically related (common descent).

The second step of ID theorists is to conclude that the complexities already described at the cellular level are such that it is reasonable to conclude that they are the product of an intelligent designer. The irreducible complexities in nature (as in the eye) are analogous in this step to a mousetrap or a car engine; they are so complex that it is unreasonable to think they came about by a natural process. The third step is to argue that this is a *scientific* conclusion, not a philosophical or a religious conclusion, and so ID would be part of science, not philosophy or theology. The reason ID theorists hold that ID is a part of science is because the claim that molecular biology shows evidence of design is an *empirical* claim, based on an investigation of living cells through various experiments in molecular biology. In short, ID theorists hold that they have examined the human cell scientifically and allowed the evidence of what they found to drive their conclusion. They sometimes compare ID to other disciplines that operate in a similar way and that are generally regarded as scientific, for example, forensics, archeology, and the search for extraterrestrial intelligence (SETI). They often appeal to the movie, *Contact* (1997), referred to in the previous chapter, to emphasize that their conclusion that the human cell is designed is just as scientific as the conclusion made by the scientists in that movie that the message they received from outer space came from an intelligent mind.

A number of interesting criticisms have been raised in response to intelligent design. The first has been the most common and loudly argued criticism, but also probably the least significant from the point of view of the truth of the theory. This is the criticism that intelligent design is not science. Critics make this charge because they hold that a scientific theory should be falsifiable, testable, involve measurable data, lead to predictions, and so forth (the criteria we considered in Chapter 3). Yet ID does not seem to meet these criteria because there seems no way to study the nature of the designer, or to test the claim that there is a designer. The designer hypothesis seems to be outside of science, as science is normally understood. This is a strong criticism of ID, though not a fatal one because it is mainly a criticism of how ID is to be *classified*; it is not a refutation of its main claims. Yet while one can argue that ID forces us to have a useful debate about the delimits of science, it still seems reasonable to say that it would confuse matters too much if we expanded the definition of science to include ID. It would be better from the point of view of having a reasonable discussion about all of these interesting matters to argue that while ID may provide an attractive argument for an intelligent designer, we should not insist that it be regarded as part of science. This would be a more productive approach. (Some have also argued that ID does not satisfy the definition of science because it is not falsifiable, one of those features thought by many to be a key part of a good scientific theory. However, this is not true: ID could be falsified if evolutionary biologists could produce a clear natural explanation for one of Behe's "irreducible complexities.")

A second criticism of ID is more serious. Biologist Kenneth Miller, and many others, argue in response to the first main claim of ID that natural selection *can* explain the complexity of the cell. Miller argues that the cell probably performed *different* functions in the past when it lacked some of the features it currently has (features that then later evolved because of natural selection, and gave the cell, and the organism, some further advantage it did not have earlier). In short, when natural selection led to the emergence of new parts of the cell, the cell most likely took on a *new* function that the one it then had. One example Miller cites is the type III secretory system (TTSS), which allows gram-negative bacteria to translocate proteins directly into the cytoplasm of a host cell. The proteins of the TTSS may seem to have little to do with the bacterial flagellum, but Miller cites research that shows that the TTSS proteins are homologous (similar because of their shared ancestry) to proteins found at the base portion of the flagellum, suggesting that "a smaller subset of the full complement of proteins in the flagellum makes up the functional transmembrane portion of the TTSS."[27] This would be an argument against Behe's view because it would mean that this part of the flagellum, the TTSS system, could work in isolation from the other parts of the flagellum, and so the flagellum would not be irreducibly complex. These counter cases are still at the early research stage, and much depends on whether the gaps in explanation can be filled in, because supporters of ID point out that specific examples to illustrate Miller's arguments are pretty thin, and still disputed.

This is one of the problems with natural selection overall as we saw in Chapter 4. There are so many unknowns about the precise steps of natural selection in specific cases that it is often hard to reply to criticisms like those made by proponents of ID with the kind of detail that people would need to be convinced. So, there is something of a standoff. However, Miller is confident that natural selection is a very good explanation for how cells got their "irreducible complexity," and he does raise very interesting cases as a challenge to ID. Behe, in particular, has responded to Miller with the general point that evolutionary biologists display an all too familiar tendency in the discussion of the evidence for evolution—a willingness to jump the gun in the face of criticisms by claiming more for the theory than the evidence actually shows in those particular cases under discussion. An instance of this approach is to be found in the criticism of ID by James A. Arieti and Patrick A. Wilson:

> The fact that *multiple* functions may be selected for in a series of ancestral environments renders irrelevant the holistic or irreducibly complexity of a current structure. A bird's wing, for example, might be considered irreducibly complex relative to the function of flying: if its surface were reduced or its feathers rearranged, shortened, or removed, the wing would no longer serve that particular function. The catch is that parts of the wing *may well have served different functions in different ancestral environments*. Feathers, for example, may have served as heat-regulators before they became long enough for flight. Evolution is opportunistic. It takes advantage of available structures adapted for one function and

co-opts them into a different service. None of this requires foresight, intelligence, or teleology.[28]

There is no doubt that this is an interesting argument against ID that one must take seriously. But one obvious weakness in it is that it is based on contrived, speculative examples, not real life cases that have been documented. So, when Arieti and Wilson conclude that evolution is opportunistic like this, Behe and supporters of ID respond that it might be, but this point has not been demonstrated because the cases they cite to support this conclusion are based on speculation not facts. In short, Arieti and Wilson have not earned the conclusion that evolution "takes advantage of available structures adapted for one function and co-opts them into a different service" because the example they cite as an illustration is not based on a real case.

An extension of the previous critical point is that ID is "god of the gaps" argument, an argument that is logically suspect. The point is that an intelligent designer is invoked to explain complicated cellular processes at the level of microbiology, but that eventually we will find a full scientific explanation for the "irreducible complexities," and the hypothesis of an intelligent designer will be redundant, and also embarrassing. Just because we don't know the explanation now, Miller argues, it does not follow that we will not find it out in the future. Although not a decisive objection in general to the design argument, many think that ID is particularly vulnerable to this criticism. To assess whether it is or not, one must make a judgment on whether Behe has a good argument that current science cannot explain the complexities, and also whether it is likely to be able to do so in the future.

An important part of Behe's case is his claim that a natural explanation for the irreducible complexities is exceedingly unlikely to be forthcoming because of the nature of the problem (he has argued that the problems for natural selection will only get worse). (The same point is made by supporters of the laws of physics argument—that it is not plausible to believe that a natural explanation for the existence of the underlying laws will be forthcoming.) This raises the question of how do we know when we have reached the limits of scientific explanation? Obviously, this question has to be handled very carefully, and on a case-by-case basis, because if we conclude too quickly that there is no possibility of a scientific explanation for a phenomenon, we run the risk of later being proved wrong. Yet if we refuse to ever consider the possibility that there might not be a scientific explanation, we run the risk of adopting a naturalistic approach in science, that is, of ruling out design explanations by definition.

In response to this problem, some thinkers, most notably Phillip Johnson, claim that modern science, in refusing to consider the view that scientific research might reveal evidence of design, is *atheistic by definition*.[29] Johnson is well known for arguing that modern science is essentially atheistic or naturalistic in practice and outlook. Although I think that Johnson has done a great service in pointing out the atheistic tendencies of modern science, and has chastened many scientists to be more careful when discussing the nature and limits of their discipline, I think he oversteps the mark when he says that science is *essentially* atheistic. As noted in Chapter 3, science does generally adopt a working assumption toward the physical realm called *methodological naturalism*, which means that only physical, testable explanations will be considered and pursued (and so ID would be ruled out). But, as we also noted in Chapter 3, it is a simple logical fallacy to conclude from this that the *only possible explanations* for any aspect of reality are physical ones (this would be metaphysical naturalism). It is obviously important to keep the two views distinct in one's work as a scientist, something that modern science writers, as we have seen, have not always been successful at.

When one is thinking about whether ID is a "god of the gaps" argument one must be careful not to allow an assumption of metaphysical naturalism to influence one's thinking, just as one should not be too quick to rule out the possibility of a scientific explanation either. Perhaps the best way to walk this line is to recognize that science confines itself to physical explanations, but to accept that this does not exhaust the explanatory possibilities in relation to the universe and the human person. The discipline of philosophy, or the realm of the rational, is broader than that of science, and is free to consider that some areas pointed to by reason might be outside of science (as science is normally defined), but are nevertheless important for all that in our attempts to explain our universe and the human person. These areas include the topics of the ultimate origin of the universe, of life, of consciousness, and questions concerning the laws of physics, the soul, and the objective moral order.

God and the Universe

Chapter Outline

The universe and the big bang theory	172
God as first cause	174
The significance of relativity and quantum mechanics	180
How does God act in the world?	185

Our reflections on the different ways the concept of design may play a role in our attempts to understand the meaning and purpose of human life, as well as its significance for our thinking about the world around us, eventually leads us to what is sometimes called the "cosmological question": the question of how the universe got here in the first place. It is a question that has exercised philosophers ever since Plato, but it has become especially intriguing in the light of path-breaking work in astronomy and astrophysics in the twentieth century. The big bang theory of the origin of the universe, in particular, has brought renewed force to the cosmological argument, the attempt to demonstrate that the universe must have a first ultimate cause, which is God. The cosmological argument will be the focus of the first part of this chapter. We will also consider briefly how strange, even mind-boggling, scientific theories, especially the theories of relativity and quantum mechanics, might affect our understanding of reality, especially in relation to the various regularities in nature as expressed in the laws of physics, and what impact these findings might have on our understanding of the big bang, and on our search for a Creator.

It is not enough to argue that God is the first cause of the universe; religious philosophers and theologians need also to reflect on the nature of God.

What kind of God is suggested by the various arguments of natural theology, including the first cause argument? We will conclude the chapter with further reflection on another fundamental question we have hinted at in earlier chapters, but which we must now address more fully: how might we understand God's interaction with creation? This is a crucial matter in the relationship between science and religion. Many thinkers have been interested in this question, yet were often uncertain as to how to answer it. In earlier chapters, we have seen this topic arise in the medieval view of God and his relationship to the world, in relation to the theory of evolution, in our reflections on chance, and in relation to the question of how the laws of physics work. So, it is appropriate to conclude the chapter with a brief consideration of some of the ways that God might be understood to interact with his creation.

The universe and the big bang theory

The universe we live in is remarkable in any number of ways, but one of the features that can't fail to impress us is the sheer size of the cosmos. Our own galaxy, the Milky Way, which consists of most of those stars we can see in the night sky, is around 100,000 light years across, and about 1,000 light years thick (recall that a light year is the distance light travels in a year, which is nearly 6 trillion miles!).[1] The Milky Way contains at least 200 billion stars. The earth is the only planet in the Milky Way that has life; it revolves around the sun, which is about 8 light minutes from earth (93 million miles); many of the other stars that we see in the sky are several light years away (e.g., the brightest star, Sirius, is 8.6 light years away). (Don't forget also that when we observe these stars and galaxies in the sky, we are observing them the way they looked when the light left them, so if a star is 8.6 light years away, we are observing it the way it looked 8.6 light years ago, which may not be the way it is today.) We also know, thanks to the work of American astronomer, Edwin Hubble, that ours is not the only galaxy; Hubble also figured out a way to measure how far other galaxies are away from us, and, because of his pioneering work, we now calculate that there are at least a 100,000 million galaxies in the universe!

Following Hubble, astronomers discovered by means of applying the Doppler effect to light that most of the galaxies we can observe are moving away from us. The Doppler effect refers to the fact that stars produce light of a shorter wavelength if they are approaching an observer and of a longer wavelength if they are moving away. This means that, when one looks at the light through a prism, there is a blueshift when the light is approaching and a redshift when the light is receding.[2] Astronomers discovered that there is a redshift visible in the observation of galaxies which means that they are moving away from us, and therefore that the universe is expanding. This theory of the expanding universe is often illustrated by comparison with an expanding balloon. If one thinks of the balloon as the universe, and paints dots on it to represent the galaxies, and then blows up the balloon, one has an insight into what it means to say that our universe is expanding. The discovery that the universe is expanding was revolutionary, because before that scientists, including Newton and Einstein, had assumed that the universe must be static.

This brings us to the question of the beginning of the universe, the question of the initial blowing up (and initial existence) of the balloon (the big bang). It also raises the question of the rate of expansion of the universe: are the forces of gravity strong enough throughout the universe to halt the expansion and bring it crashing back on itself (the big crunch), or will it continue expanding forever? We don't know the answer yet to this latter question because we are working only with estimates of the distances to outer galaxies, and because it is also believed that there is a large amount of dark matter in the universe (matter which we can't see, but which would have an effect on the forces of gravity). Stephen Hawking has noted that the present evidence suggests that the universe will continue expanding, but that even if the big crunch were to occur, it would not be for another 10,000 million years (so we can relax for the moment!).[3]

It follows from these observations and calculations concerning the expanding universe that at some point in the past there must have been a big bang, the beginning of the universe, the point at which the explosion and expansion started. This occurred between 10 and 20 billion years ago when the distance between the galaxies was zero. At this time the density in the universe and the curvature of space-time would have been infinite; in mathematics, this point is called a singularity. One might not have to worry about singularities too much if they only occurred in mathematics, but Einstein's theory of general relativity predicted that there could also be singularities involved in real physical quantities, such as when the density of matter or its temperature become infinite, and this is thought to have happened at the big bang.[4] In 1964, two American physicists, Arno Penzias and Robert Wilson, discovered background microwave radiation throughout the universe (dating to 300,000 years after the initial explosion), which was thought to be produced by the heat of the big bang. At the big bang, the universe is thought to have had zero size and also to have been infinitely hot. The big bang would be the beginning of space and time, and the beginning of the laws of physics. Before the big bang, there was nothing. In the first 3 minutes after the big bang, the temperatures would have fallen significantly, and the universe would have become less dense as it expanded. The neutrons and protons that make up helium, hydrogen, and lithium would have begun to emerge by means of the interactions between basic particles and hot gases, operating according to laws like gravity, the strong nuclear force (which holds atoms together), the weak force, and the electromagnetic force (referred to in the previous chapter in our discussion of the anthropic argument). It is estimated that it takes about 300,000 years for atoms to form. It takes another 300 million years before stars and galaxies form (i.e., about 12–15 billion years ago), some of which were recently pictured by the Hubble telescope. Our sun was formed about 5 billion years ago, with the earth emerging out of its matter and gases about 4.5 billion years ago; then the first life-forms began to appear on earth about 4 billion years ago (as discussed in detail in Chapter 4).

This all too brief account of cosmic origins and development still conveys the enormous size and complexity, as well as the majesty and beauty, of our universe. And although some of the details are still speculative, some still controversial and some hotly disputed, the general outline of the story is accepted as true by the vast majority of cosmologists and astronomers. So, while it is true to say that the big bang theory has not yet been fully established, it has supplanted its earlier rival, the steady state theory.[5] This is what science now tells us about the beginning and structure of our universe. But what about its ultimate origin? What caused the big bang itself to happen? This is a question that seems to be outside of science, and one that philosophers have been thinking about for centuries. It is a question that is the inspiration for the first cause, or cosmological, argument for the existence of a Creator, a very popular and influential argument in the history of thought, an argument to which we now turn.

God as first cause

There are different versions of the cosmological argument, and we first consider the more contemporary version (often called the kalām argument, after the kalām tradition in Islamic philosophy, where the argument was popular). This argument had been advanced by St. Bonaventure (1221–1274), who was a contemporary and often philosophical sparing partner of St. Thomas Aquinas; and by contemporary philosopher, William Lane Craig, who appeals to the big bang theory, and other scientific evidence, in his version of the argument. It is also an argument that has enormous popular appeal, and that plays a part in the reasoning of most religious believers when they think about why they believe in a Creator, even though they may never have studied the argument formally, could not explain it clearly, and indeed may never have heard of the argument!

The best way to approach this argument on a common sense level is to take a (natural) event in the universe and to ask how was it caused? Since we have been talking about the big bang, let us ask how the first atoms were formed in the aftermath of the big bang? We can give what philosophers sometimes call the local cause as the answer. This is the answer scientists would give, the one mentioned above, whereby the atoms were formed because the early matter had cooled enough so that the nuclei of atoms could capture electrons, aided by the strong nuclear force, and so forth. But the philosopher wants to know the ultimate cause of the first atoms, how atoms got here in the first place. This is a much more puzzling question, of course, yet it is a perfectly reasonable question to ask about the process that led to the beginning of the universe.

We are invoking a chain of prior physical causes to explain the existence of atoms. But how did this chain of causes get started, or where did it come from? There are two possible answers to this question: the chain either has a beginning in time, or it goes on forever backwards into the past, which would mean that the universe has an infinite past. St. Bonaventure argued that the latter view is logically impossible, and so the universe must have a beginning, a first event.[6] He formulated a series of unsolvable logical puzzles that would result if we were to accept that an actual infinite chain of physical events could exist in the real world (and not just in the mind as a theoretical possibility). Bonaventure's argument has been modernized and further developed in recent times by William Lane Craig.[7] As well as appealing to logic to support his case, Craig also appeals to the latest scientific research, especially the big bang theory, and the second law of thermodynamics. The big bang theory, just described above, strongly supports the conclusion that the universe had a beginning in time. The theory is well confirmed, and represents good scientific evidence that the universe had a beginning. It shows that there was a first event, and therefore that history (and time) has a finite past (it makes no claim about the future).

There is another scientific theory that lends further support to the conclusion that the universe had a beginning. This is the evidence from the second law of thermodynamics. This law says that the entropy in the universe tends to a maximum. Entropy is the measure of total disorder or chaos in a system. What this means in practical terms is that in a closed system, processes will eventually run down and die, given enough time. A closed system is a system that contains everything that exists in it, and which has nothing outside of it. The universe is such a system, and the eventual running down of the universe is called the "heat death" of the universe. Now the question is, according to Craig, why has the universe not experienced this heat death yet? The obvious answer is that the "heat death" of the universe would take about x billion years, and so far only less than x billion years have elapsed. Craig's point, however, is that this answer is not acceptable if one believes that the universe has an infinite past! This is because we would already *have had* an infinite amount of time elapse before the present moment, and that should be more than enough time for the heat death to occur! The second law of thermodynamics therefore, like the big bang theory, supports the view that the universe had a beginning.[8]

Craig goes on to argue that although infinities are useful concepts in mathematics and set theory, these are potential infinities, not actual infinities, and he agrees with Bonaventure that the notion of an actual infinity does not make logical sense when we move from talking about it in the abstract to consider concrete cases. His best-known example to illustrate this point involves an imagined library with an infinite number of books, where the books are stacked on the shelves in alternate colors, red, black, red, black, and so forth. The library would have an infinite number of red books and an infinite number of black books, and an infinite number of total books. But logically this means that it would have the same amount of books in total that it also has in a single color, which is absurd! Odd conclusions also follow if one were to check out a book or to add new books to the library, for these subtractions and additions would have no effect on the total number of books in the library, which is an infinite number. Craig is suggesting that once we begin to imagine what would have to be the case for an actual infinite series of physical events to really exist out there in the real world, we begin to see that it leads to logical absurdities. This is an indication that the notion is not intelligible. He also draws attention to another obvious logical problem for the claim that the universe has an infinite past. If this were true, how would we ever get to today, since it is not possible to cross an infinity? We can appreciate this argument better perhaps if we imagine ourselves standing far off in the past, with the assumption that the past is infinite, and looking toward the future. The point is not how do we get from point A to point B. The answer to that question is straightforward, and involves a finite amount of days. But if we ask how did we ever get to point B at all, and if the answer is supposed to be that we crossed an infinity of events, this is absurd. The same problem applies to point A as well, of course, or to *any* point in history one cares to take.

The next step in the cosmological argument is to argue that this first event, the big bang, must have had a cause. The big bang is somewhat of a unique event, being the first event, and so it is clear that the question about what caused it cannot be answered by science. Because we are talking about the first event in the universe, we cannot give our usual answer to the question of the cause of an event, which would involve invoking an earlier physical (local) cause. This is a logical conclusion that applies no matter what the first event turns out to be. Yet, if we are to be rational, we must conclude that no matter what the first event is, it must have a cause. Otherwise, we would have to say that it has no cause at all; that it came into existence without a cause, just appeared, as it were. But this goes against all of our reason, scientific work, and experience with empirical evidence. As Dallas Willard has noted, "even if it were neither self-contradictory nor counterintuitive to suppose that something originated without a cause, the probability of it relative to our data would be exactly zero. There is . . . not a single case of a physical state or event being observed or otherwise known to originate 'from nothing.'"[9]

So given this important point, the third step is to argue that the cause of the big bang is God. This conclusion is arrived at by reasoning about what the cause may be like from our available evidence. We can argue, first, that the cause must be *outside* of the physical order, must be *nonphysical* in some very important sense. The cause of the big bang can't itself be yet another physical cause, because we can always ask what caused this (earlier, prior) physical cause, so we would not be answering, but only postponing, the ultimate question. This is because we know that no physical event can be the cause of itself. Supporters of the cosmological argument also hold, second, that the cause of the universe must be very powerful indeed in order to be capable of creating a universe like ours, and thirdly, that the cause is also likely to be an intelligent being of some kind. This is a more reasonable alternative than saying that the cause is an impersonal force, or a nonphysical, nonintelligent entity. One can appeal to the design argument here also as further support because intelligence is also suggested by the order and beauty in the universe (as we saw in the previous chapter), and so the various arguments for the existence of God can reinforce each other in this way. The creation of a universe like ours, not to mention the existence and nature of life, including human life, would seem to require by any reasonable standard a phenomenal intelligence. Fourth, the cause of the universe must also be a necessary being, a conclusion that brings us to St. Thomas Aquinas's version of the argument.

St. Thomas disagreed with St. Bonaventure on the issue of whether the universe must have had a beginning. He believed that one could show that the universe must have a cause whether it is eternal or has a beginning in time, a question he regarded as open (though obviously today he would have to acknowledge evidence supporting the big bang theory). His argument is based on an appeal to the intriguing metaphysical notions of contingent and necessary being. A contingent being is a being that is not the cause of itself. In order for it to exist, it must have had some prior cause, otherwise it would not exist. In addition, a contingent being cannot last forever; at some point it will pass out of existence. A series of contingent beings linked together by cause and effect is called a contingent series. St. Thomas then applies these concepts to our universe. The universe, he holds, is made up of individual events none of which is the cause of itself, and so the universe is, therefore, a contingent series. But a series of events like this requires an ultimate explanation for its existence, *no matter how many members are in the series*. We can explain the local cause of any particular event, or sequence of events, by pointing to prior causes in the series, but this will not, as St. Thomas argues, help us to explain the existence of the *whole* series. We logically cannot find the cause of the whole contingent series within the series of events even if it is an infinite series.

This brings us to what many regard as the essence of the cosmological argument: the conclusion that it is reasonable to conclude that *a necessary being exists*. Critics of the argument, including Richard Dawkins, frequently misunderstand this point.[10] Dawkins thinks that the theist just postulates that God is the cause of the universe, but St. Thomas is arguing that the existence of a necessary being is not a postulate, but a plausible cause of the universe. This is because, logically, there are only two possible answers to the question of how did the universe get here. The first is to say that it was created by a necessary being, a being who always existed (and so who was not brought into existence by a prior cause). Any other answer involving contingent beings would not provide us with an explanation of the universe, because we can always ask what caused this (contingent) being, and so forth. St. Thomas knows that it is reasonable to wonder how a necessary being could exist, but the main point of his argument is to illustrate that a necessary being *must* exist. That even if the concept looks odd at first, it is the most reasonable answer to our question about the ultimate origin of the universe. Otherwise, we would have no way to explain the existence of the universe. When we reflect on the issue of the cause of the universe, we will see that we inevitably run into the probability of a necessary being. The second possible answer to our question is to say that the universe has no ultimate cause, has no explanation, that it is just here. But the human mind strongly resists this answer because it is so difficult to accept on a number of levels, the main one being that it is not logical. St. Thomas is asking: is it reasonable to think that our universe came into existence without a cause? The answer is no, and our reasoning points to a necessary intelligence behind the universe, rather than to a beginning that has no cause, an infinite past that has no cause, or either a beginning or infinite past that have only a contingent cause.

Critics have responded to the cosmological argument in predictable ways. A variety of objections have been raised to Craig's logical paradoxes. Paul Draper has suggested that the absurdities generated by Craig's examples only seem to work if one *assumes* that the concept of an actual infinity is absurd. Perhaps if we took the concept more seriously, Draper argues, we would have to look at things differently.[11] Perhaps, but the big bang theory is strong independent evidence for Craig's conclusion. Another point is to say that the concept of a necessary being is unintelligible. But supporters argue that the cosmological argument shows that the concept is intelligible, and that one should be careful about assuming that physical existence is the only kind of existence if the existence of God has not yet been decided. The concept of a necessary being is also the best answer for dealing with the objection "where does God come from?" because a necessary being is a being that always existed. The cosmological argument is an argument that shows that physical existence is very likely *not* the only kind of existence one can have; indeed, it is an argument about this very question. Supporters hold that it is an argument that points clearly in the direction of a necessary being.

Bertrand Russell argued that the universe might be just a "brute fact."[12] A brute fact is supposed to be a fact that does not need an explanation; it is just there. But the concept is quite vague, and may be an ad hoc move concocted simply to block the cosmological argument. It could mean that the universe does not need an explanation, or it might mean that although it needs an explanation, there is none available. If it means the former, then it seems false on any reasonable investigation of the nature of the universe. If it means the latter, then it seems to stop the debate about the existence of God too early, and implicitly suggest that by definition physical existence is the only kind of existence.

One can detect a kind of bias toward the "brute fact" (or similar) view of the beginning of the universe in the work of several major scientists and intellectuals, but it is a bias for all that. Supporters of the cosmological argument rightly draw attention to the key point that it is very hard to believe that our universe came into existence without a cause. And the first cause argument shows that the cause cannot be anything that we would usually count as a cause, and must be outside of the physical order. This is a strong point in favor of a religious view of reality being true, even if it does not settle denominational or doctrinal questions. If one is convinced by the cosmological argument, as many are, then it is incumbent on one to think about the reconciliation of religion and science, incumbent on one to consider how religion and science must work together in trying to understand creation.

The significance of relativity and quantum mechanics

So far, we have been talking about the world primarily in terms of classical Newtonian physics. This is the scientific point of view that regards reality as particles in motion, operating according to the laws of physics. In Chapter 2, we saw this view come into its own after Newton, and gain significant impact with the Deists of the eighteenth century, among many others. It is also a consequence of this view that the universe is deterministic in the way we discussed in our account of evolution and chance in Chapter 4 (recall the example of the pool table). Those who argue for the theory of cosmic evolution (discussed in Chapter 3), also assume a deterministic universe, that is, that every current state of the universe is caused by preceding states, and that every future state can in principle be predicted based on its present state, and an application of the physical laws of the universe. Newton's view also regarded space and time as absolute properties, that is, they are true properties of the universe (in the realist sense described in Chapter 3), and are the same for everyone everywhere. More specifically, he thought that the motion of objects relative to one another, or relative to different observers of the objects who were themselves in motion, would have no effect on the time the observers would see the objects. For example, this means that if two flares are set off a few seconds apart, an observer who is moving away from them will measure the same time between them as the flare setter. This is indeed the common sense view of space and time, the one we all take for granted in our everyday lives and do not question for a moment.

However, Albert Einstein's theory of relativity challenged this view of space and time. The theory of relativity is notoriously difficult to grasp, as well as being extremely counterintuitive, (and involves enormously complicated mathematical formulae), but fortunately we only need a brief overview here of its conclusions and their philosophical significance. Let us first summarize the theory of special relativity, which was suggested to Einstein by the Michelson-Morley experiment of 1887, which showed that the speed of light is the same in all directions of the universe. Einstein argued that there is a causal relationship between space and time so that two observers who are in motion relative to one another could have different observations about whether two distinct events occur simultaneously, especially if they were traveling at very high speeds.[13] One consequence of this is time dilation, which means that time becomes relative to the observer of an effect. To return to our example of the flares, if the two flares are set off a few seconds apart, the observer who is moving away from them will *not* measure the same time between them as the flare setter, according to the theory of special relativity. This effect is not noticeable at the slow speeds we experience in ordinary life, but it is very significant if the speeds approach the speed of light. Time dilation would appear to make time travel possible, at least into the future, because a consequence of it is that since there is a causal relationship between space and time, at speeds close to that of light, time slows down. This would mean that if a man could travel out into space at speeds approaching the speed of light, his aging process would slow down relative to that on earth, so that if he were to return to earth he would have aged more slowly than those who remained! Those who remained might be long dead by the time of the traveler's return, and so the traveler would get a look into the future. Time dilation has been established in clocks (atomic clocks on the space shuttle, for instance), but not directly so far in living organisms (where its extreme counterintuitiveness still leaves it open to question without direct confirmation). The general theory of relativity argues that the universe should be regarded as a space-time continuum, in which the presence of mass causes a curvature of space, thereby creating a gravitational field. This theory supercedes Newton's theory of gravity because Newton said that gravity was a force between bodies, whereas Einstein showed that it is a field, similar to a magnetic field. The conditions in the gravitational field determine the movement of stars and planets. General relativity has been tested by various experiments, and, among many other things, allows us to estimate the age of the universe.

It is not clear that the theory of relativity has any special significance for the religion-science connection because it does not seem to pose any significant challenge to the religious view of reality, and indeed it underscores an important part of the design argument, the significance of the laws of physics. This is because relativity theory requires that the laws of physics hold and operate in the same way throughout the entire universe, supporting the view that nature outside free human actions is deterministic. Einstein expressed this point by saying that "God does not play dice with the universe," a sentiment which also underscores his disagreement with certain elements of quantum mechanics, which we will come to in a moment. However, some thinkers suggest that special relativity does introduce an element of metaphysical relativism into the universe, the consequences of which are still largely unexplored, and others suggest that relativity theory might have some significance too if we consider God as an observer of the universe, though again it is not clear how to develop such a notion.

However, another scientific theory came along in the early twentieth century called quantum mechanics, which seemed to raise a challenge to the theory of relativity, and to our understanding of the macroscopic world. Quantum mechanics deals with the interactions and structure of subatomic and atomic particles, such as the quanta, neutrons, electrons, quarks, photons, etc. Particle physicists study the energy and momentum of these particles, among other things.[14] It has been a very successful area of research, becoming the basis for transistors, lasers, modern electronics, and nuclear energy. But there are problems associated with studying subatomic particles that do not apply in the ordinary macroscopic world of our experience. The main problem is that when we study a subatomic particle, because it is so small, it is affected by the methods we use to study it, specifically by the energy from the light source (light energy does not affect our study of large objects, such as tables and chairs). This means that when we are studying the particle as observers we are also changing it, affecting how it behaves. The energy from the light wave that is used to study an electron, for example, will affect the *motion* of the electron in a way that cannot be predicted; if a longer light wave is used to avoid this problem, then the measurement of the *position* of the electron will be affected. In short, we cannot know both the position and the rate of motion of the electron at the same time, a conclusion called "the uncertainty principle" by German physicist Werner Heisenberg. A consequence of this state of uncertainty is that we can't state the laws concerning the behavior of particles operating at the subatomic level with precision; they have to be expressed as statistical probabilities.

What are the implications of this theory? First, it may be incompatible with the theory of relativity, which works fine for larger objects such as large bodies, stars, and galaxies, and which relies upon the laws of physics operating consistently, whereas particles in the quantum world behave strangely, and the laws by which they operate can only be statically expressed. All of which is another reminder that our current major scientific theories are far from established. This leads us to the second implication which is that some feel that the uncertainty principle adds an indeterminacy, an unpredictability and randomness, to reality that could undermine not only many of our scientific theories, but also that would add an imprecision to our general understanding of our experience, including perhaps an undermining of the laws of physics, and the notion of design. This is because quantum mechanics gives rise to a fundamental philosophical question concerning how we are to decide if what we are observing in the electron, for instance, reflects its actual behavior in itself—the way it really is in objective reality—or whether it only reflects how it behaves when *we* are observing and studying it? However, an indeterminism is not necessarily an effect of quantum mechanics because of the two schools of thought regarding the uncertainty principle: that the indeterminacy is in the particles themselves, and is therefore an objective truth about reality, which was Heisenberg's view (the Copenhagen interpretation), or that it results only from our inadequate current attempts at measurement, the view of Einstein and Max Planck.[15] This latter view is the most rational one to adopt on the grounds that all of our experience is against the view that the behaviors of particles could be indeterminate in themselves. From a logical point of view, it is not clear that such a notion is even intelligible.

We must also not forget that the various probabilities at the quantum level are still determined. It might nevertheless be the case, though, that the world of particles is indeterminate from a practical point of view in the sense that we will never be able to overcome our problems in trying to measure and study these particles, that our techniques will always affect our results, and this would mean that our knowledge of this microscopic world would remain incomplete. This leads to our third point that at the atomic and larger levels the world does operate in a deterministic way, and this allows us to pursue objective science in a realist sense, to discover and apply laws that hold consistently, and to arrive at certain knowledge. It is the case that any indeterminacy at the subatomic level, which is hotly disputed, does not transfer over at the atomic level (at least most of the time) because the effects are so small, and so it would not affect the debate about many of the issues in this book.

We should also note, fourthly, that some thinkers have used the uncertainty of quantum mechanics as a possible way to provide a materialistic account of human freedom. Heisenberg and others argued that the indeterminacy of quantum mechanics leaves us with an unpredictability about nature; some try to make this unpredictability the basis of free will. But it is not clear how this could explain free will without having a more detailed account of how the process would work because if quantum effects are the result of deterministic processes after all then we would not really be free, and even if there is a genuine indeterminacy in nature, it is not clear that this would be the same thing as free will since the conscious decision of the agent would still be missing. A fifth consequence is the exact opposite of our previous point. Several have argued, including Stephen Barr, that the crucial role of the observer in producing quantum effects is also an argument against the view that the human mind can be explained in purely materialistic terms.[16] According to Barr, the logical structure of quantum theory requires that the intellect of the observer lies to some extent beyond the possibility of the physical/mathematical description of the total system. This is because in quantum mechanics the probabilities must be calculated by an observer, and if he too were to be subject to the mathematics of quantum theory, he would step out of the world of facts and into the world of the merely probable, meaning that the theory would only be able to say what we might find, not what we actually did find. Barr argues that what makes an observer an observer is an act of the (immaterial) intellect, and this act cannot be completely described by the physical theory without inconsistency, because "the mathematical descriptions of the physical world given to us by quantum theory presuppose the existence of observers who lie outside those mathematical descriptions."[17] Although there are considerable philosophical difficulties that accompany different interpretations of quantum mechanics, Barr's argument represents an intriguing application of it to the body/mind problem, and if true, would be yet another indication from science itself that reality resists complete physical explanations.

This point leads to a sixth consequence of quantum mechanics which is that it undermines the search for "a theory of everything," pursued by some scientists such as Crick, Sagan, and Steven Weinberg. This would be a kind of unified theory of many different branches of science that would explain everything in existence, including biology, in terms of physics, chemistry, and mathematics, a type of reductionism that would restrict scientific explanation to a few basic laws and ingredients. As Crick has put it, "Eventually one may hope to have the whole of biology 'explained' in terms of the level below it, and so on right down to the atomic level."[18] The inability of quantum physicists to predict the behavior of subatomic particles with certainty undermines this attempt, perhaps fatally. We should also note finally that the leading scientists involved in developing these theories did not think they presented any special problems for religion. While Einstein's religious views are often the subject of speculation, Heisenberg, Planck and another well-known quantum scientist, Erwin Schrödinger, all believed in God. Heisenberg also held that although science was a powerful discipline, it was limited in what it could find out about reality because some truths are outside its domain.

How does God act in the world?

All of this current work in science, in which philosophers and theologians have taken a great interest, prompts us to reflect further about the religious significance of these scientific theories. The first thing to remind ourselves of is that many religious thinkers accept the classical view of God, or some version of it, that we outlined in our discussion of St. Thomas Aquinas in Chapter 2. This is the view that says God is an immaterial being, who is omnipotent, omniscient, and omnibenevolent. He is also conceived of as morally perfect, and worthy of worship. Many argue that this is the kind of God supported by the cosmological and teleological arguments for the existence of God, as well as various other interesting arguments we can't get into in this book, such as arguments based on religious experience, and the nature of objective morality. The program of natural theology is supported in some form by a very broad range of contemporary thinkers, including scientists Francis Collins, Paul Davies, and John Polkinghorne, theologians Keith Ward and Alister McGrath, and philosophers Richard Swinburne and William Lane Craig.[19] Although these thinkers do not agree on every feature of the classical view of God, many of them are very impressed with the central insights of the first cause and design arguments: that the universe must have an ultimate cause, and that the order, intricacy, and complexity of the universe, including the emergence of human life (and the phenomena of consciousness, reason, free will, and moral agency) support the conclusion that the universe was created by an intelligent mind for a particular purpose. In considering these and other arguments, many thinkers have also been impressed by the latest work in science, and regard it as providing yet further evidence for their case, including the big bang theory (first cause argument), the nature of the big bang (anthropic argument from design), the underlying architecture of the universe (laws of physics version of design), and neurological studies (the exceptional properties of human consciousness). Lifelong atheist philosopher, Anthony Flew, recently became a believer in God, primarily because of the weight of scientific evidence in three areas: first, the fact that nature obeys laws; second, the dimension of life, of intelligently organized and purpose-driven beings, who arose from matter; and third, the very existence of nature itself.[20]

However, these thinkers do not all agree on the question of how God acts in the world. This question has two aspects to it: how is God related to the world, and how does God act in the world? The challenge is to develop a view which does not make God too remote from his creation, but also one which takes into account the consequences of modern science (though there is considerable disagreement about how to interpret this latter point). Modern theology, in particular, is perhaps too much intimidated and influenced by modern science, and often allows science to define its approach in a way that is usually inconsistent with the main theological views of God's nature. This intimidation is usually evident in two (overlapping) areas, the possibility of miracles, and the operation of natural laws. A miracle is usually defined as an intervention by God in the laws of physics to bring about an effect in the world. God's intervention in this way might be obvious to us, or it might be undetectable, brought about by subtle manipulations of the laws of nature (at the quantum level, some thinkers suggest).

However, some modern theologians, who have become perhaps too close to a naturalistic mindset, appear to rule out miracles almost by definition, and seek other ways to explain God's agency in the world. These theologians are rightly mindful of avoiding a "god of the gaps" approach where one might conclude that an effect in nature was miraculous only to have it later explained by science, but they move from this point to adopt the rather dogmatic position that God's action in the world *should* not be detectable, but *must* be hidden. Some go further, such as Thomas Tracy, to say that God must not even be regarded as acting in the world through intervention in physical laws, even in subtle ways that we are unaware of. These constraints placed on how we should understand God's actions do not seem to be motivated so much by theological considerations as by a defensive posture adopted in the face of modern science. The view seems to be that modern science appears to disallow miracles so theologians will not appeal to them to explain God's actions, except in the sense that they are not detectable, and with the further requirement that they not even involve a violation of the laws of physics.[21] But such an approach gives too much respect to scientific explanations and at the same time faces inconsistency because these same theologians usually hold that science cannot explain all of reality, that God created the universe and has considerable power, and that God answers prayers. These beliefs are inconsistent with the view that God either could not or would not interfere in nature by altering natural events in subtle and not so subtle ways.

The traditional classical view appeals to the distinction between primary and secondary causes as a way of explaining God's acting in the world. This is the idea that God creates the world out of fundamental ingredients consisting of a certain configuration of matter and energy, which operate according to the laws of science. So, God is the primary cause of the world. Human beings study the physical universe, and progressively discover a good deal of knowledge about how it works. Ordinary events in the universe are governed by scientific laws, and operate within the constraints of matter and energy (these are the secondary causes, which science studies). Most supporters of this view (with the notable exception of Descartes) have also held that God is bound by the laws of logic and reason, which issue from his nature, and which also govern the nature of the laws of physics to a significant extent. In addition, proponents hold that God does not normally interfere in the day-to-day operation of physical events (the secondary causes); yet God can perform miracles whenever he wishes, and often does so, especially by responding to prayer (it is sometimes also overlooked that the creation of the universe would itself be a miracle). Classical theism rejects the deistic view that God set the universe in motion, but then does not interfere further in creation.

For classical theists, God is the ultimate cause of the whole system in the sense that he set it up in a specific way (and continually sustains it in being), and so some argue (e.g., Brian Davies[22]) that in a real sense God defines the final outcome, and is wholly sovereign over the universe. So, God is responsible for the emergence of life through the process of evolution because, given the initial setup conditions and the laws of physics, life had to emerge when it did, and in the manner in which it did, with human beings as the most advanced species. Biblical literalists accept much of this view too, but they sometimes argue that what is often called an act of "special creation," a miracle, might occur at various points in the ongoing creation process, for example, at the point of the emergence of new species. Many thinkers do not like this latter view because it sounds like a "god of the gaps" argument, a form of argument whereby we invoke God to explain a particular event that we cannot currently explain by science. Michael Behe's argument for "irreducibly complexities" in nature (discussed in Chapter 6) is often accused of appealing to acts of special creation.

This classical view is trying to balance two points, sometimes with difficulty, that God is responsible for all that happens in creation, and at the same time that the universe operates according to a set of natural laws which do not require God's constant working in the world (but only his occasional working). The one exception is the area of free will, an area not subject to the laws of physics. Free will is a limitation that God has placed upon his power, because he cannot fully control our free decisions. This is because God cannot do the logically impossible; he cannot create free beings who at the same time are guaranteed, in the sense of being *caused*, to make the right choices. So, God gives us other resources to guide us toward the right moral path: reason, revelation, human nature, moral virtue, conscience, and the ability to influence God's will through prayer (and so God is immanent in creation, unlike in deism where he is absent). Thinkers in this tradition would explain the evil that is done by human beings (often called moral evil) by saying that it occurs as a result of free will, that is, moral evil is the price of creating human creatures who have been given God's highest gift, *viz*. freedom. No matter how bad human moral evil is, a world with it is better than the other two alternatives: a world with perfect moral beings who don't have free will, or no world at all. Classical theists have more of a problem in explaining natural evil, evil that occurs in nature, such as earthquakes, floods, droughts, and disease, forms of evil that do not appear to be connected with free will. A variety of theories have been proposed to account for natural evil, including the view that it is a privation or deficiency, a fall from grace, of something that was already good (St. Augustine), that it is an unavoidable consequence of having consistent laws in nature (so fire that gives warmth can also cause pain, an example used by C. S. Lewis), that it is a series of challenges aimed at the spiritual and moral formation of human beings as they prepare for the next life (John Hick).[23]

Many contemporary thinkers are unhappy with various aspects of the classical view of God, and have tried to modernize it in different ways, including Ian Barbour and John Haught. These thinkers have been heavily influenced by what is known as the process approach to God in philosophy and theology, an approach inspired by the thought of Alfred North Whitehead. The main concepts in Whitehead's process metaphysics were applied to religious topics by Charles Hartshorne, who proposed the view that reality is not static, but is in process, and that, therefore, God is best understood as having a dynamic, even organic, relationship with his creation.[24] This is also the view of Ian Barbour, a pioneering thinker in the area of religion and science, who has noted that one of Whitehead's central points is that processes of change and relationships between events are more fundamental than enduring self-contained objects, a powerful concept when applied to religion. Process thinkers hold that there is a back and forward between God and the world, and God, as well as his creation, develops in this relationship. And so process metaphysics understands every new event to be jointly the product of the entity's past, its own action, and the action of God.[25] This view rejects a major belief of the classical view: that God does not suffer or experience emotion, that God does not need human beings, that God does not change. Classical theists had held this view because, following Aristotle's metaphysics, if God could change, it would mean that he was not perfect (as we saw in Chapter 2). On the process view, although God sets up the whole process of creation and order, and the laws by which it operates, he too is influenced by the universe and what happens in it. Process philosophers, and many other contemporary philosophers and theologians, are partly inspired by the insight that we need a more human sense of God. They argue, for instance, that it is hard to make sense out of the activity of prayer on the classical view because prayer seems to require that at least sometimes God is moved by our prayers, and so this must mean that some change occurs in God. The same point can be made about the notions of God's forgiveness and God's love. Process theists also reject the idea that God is omnipotent because this idea has connotations of coercion; instead, they hold that God attempts to *persuade* people to follow him, for example, through love, an experience that is not subject to coercion, but that has great power to evoke a response in the human heart. The classical thinkers object to the view that God is not perfect, because they see this as a fatal compromise that would undermine religion in general.

Process thinkers do believe that God is more perfect than us, but that he is still capable of even greater perfection. They are vague on exactly how God interacts with his creatures and with nature, but Barbour has argued that if we interpret quantum mechanics to be an indication that *nature itself* is indeterminate, and so chance (and not just unpredictability) is a real part of the world, then this gives us a way to see how God presents new possibilities in nature which require the interaction of the objects themselves. God, therefore, is the source of novelty in the world, but he does not determine the outcome, and so, unlike in the classical view, God would not know the future.[26] This approach can be applied to the process of evolution, and to the emergence of various forms of life, including human beings. This is an example of God's persuasion, rather than coercion, and leaves open exciting, but as yet undetermined, possibilities for what could happen in the future (e.g., in terms of whether new, more advanced life-forms could evolve), as theologian John Haught has intriguingly argued.[27]

According to process thinkers, because God is not omnipotent, he is not able to solve all problems, including the problem of evil in the world, and so they claim that this problem dissolves somewhat. Moral evil is due to human free will, and occurs alongside the development of higher levels of life that exhibit self-awareness, reason, and moral agency. Natural evil is part of the process of realizing greater value as the universe works through various possibilities, because God suffers along with us, and allows us to understand and cope with suffering. Yet this approach does not explain how the natural order, in which evil occurs, came about in the first place, and in what ways God might be ultimately responsible for it. For even if we grant process theologians like Barbour the interpretation of quantum mechanics that stresses the indeterminacy of nature itself, it would still seem to be the case that nature was set up this way by God, and that, even if he is not omnipotent, God should be able to eliminate natural evil, or greatly minimize it, since he is causally responsible for the structure that produces it. Another problem facing views that appeal to quantum mechanics as a way of making room for God's agency is that surely they still involve God's miraculous intervention in nature, even if it is hidden from us, because God would still be manipulating causal action at the quantum level in order to bring about one particular outcome rather than another. So, theologians proposing this view would not be eliminating miracles after all, or explaining God's acting in the world in a way that does not require his intervention in natural laws.

There are many thinkers who have offered interesting accounts of God's action in the world, and of how theology and science can work together, among them Arthur Peacocke, Wolfhart Pannenberg, Nancey Murphy, Philip Clayton, and Howard Van Till.[28] While we don't have space to pursue these views here, it is important to note that while these thinkers often disagree on issues like the nature of God, the way in which God acts in the world, and which account of God best reflects the biblical account, they all agree on one of the key themes of this book: that science and religion can and should be in dialogue, that the dialogue model best reflects the correct relationship between religion and science. Recent work in science, as we have noted in this chapter, opens up some intriguing possibilities for thinking about God and creation, and whatever disagreement there is over the details, there is no indication that science can explain all of reality, or that it must be in conflict with religion and theology. On the contrary, the more we discover about the universe, the more necessary the dialogue between religion and science becomes, the more the "ultimate questions" become difficult to avoid, the more they call out to us for our considered response.

8 Science, Religion and Ethics

Chapter Outline

Mapping the human genome	194
Stem cells and cloning	201
Conclusion: some lessons for scientists and religious believers	207

We have seen throughout this book that it is essential to appreciate the difference between naturalism and religion. Although naturalism is often put forward as an alternative worldview, it is a crucial—indeed we might say decisive—point in the religion-science relationship that most scientists are not naturalists, and this opens the way for scientists, philosophers, and theologians to pursue the path of dialogue rather than the path of conflict. Nevertheless, despite these important distinctions, it is accurate to say that naturalism has at times given science a bad name because people read the work of popular science writers like Dawkins, Crick, Sagan, or Wilson, or watch science documentaries in which thinkers like these have significant input, and form the mistaken impression that modern science is on the side of atheism. And, if we are to be honest, we must acknowledge that modern science has a strongly naturalistic bent to it, which serves only to exacerbate the tension between science and religion. Francis Collins, former head of the Human Genome Project, has noted that there is a kind of unwritten law within the discipline of science that one does not discuss religious or spiritual matters. There is a reluctance to talk about the (in some cases obvious) religious implications of one's scientific work (especially in the areas of cosmology, evolution, genetics, and neurology), and also a lack of enthusiasm for bringing up one's own particular religious worldview. This explains perhaps why there are so few major scientists today who are prepared to discuss the interaction between their work in science and their religious beliefs in the admirable way that Collins himself has done.[1]

This cultural bias within the discipline of science today—the opposite bias to that present in the time of Newton, for example—means that scientists themselves, unwittingly perhaps, often foster the view that their discipline is antireligious in some deeper way than merely not considering religious explanations as they go about their work as scientists; modern scientists sometimes give the strong impression that they are metaphysical naturalists at heart. They can do this, for example, by talking about religious beliefs as if they are in the realm of the irrational (or the nonrational), as if religion is "subjective" and science "objective," as if we should even turn to science for guidance on important ethical questions. These tendencies in modern science have led many people who would otherwise be sympathetic to science to look upon the whole discipline with suspicion, even with hostility. And so the "conflict model" of the relationship between science and religion (and morality) has become dominant, thereby stifling dialogue between science and its interlocutors, dialogue that many would find fascinating, timely, relevant, and enlightening. It should be noted that Collins is right that this reluctance to dialogue mostly comes from the sciences; religious thinkers and philosophers have generally proved more open to engaging questions of mutual interest with scientists, than *vice versa*.

So much credence is given to the claims and impressive advances of science in modern life by all of us (see Chapter 3) that it often seems like nothing can compete with it; we might be tempted to acquiesce in a kind of scientific hegemony over the whole of knowledge, over the whole of society, culture, and ethics. But we should be much less enamored of science in general, and should adopt a more chastened perspective, when we look beneath the surface and realize that it offers us nothing on the ultimate questions, and that it cannot help us in the whole matter of values. Science can show us how to extract stem cells from embryos, how to clone a human being, how to genetically enhance a child's physical appearance, but it cannot tell us whether any of these practices is moral or not. Neither can it help us with the development of moral character, nor with the right way to raise our children, nor with how to organize political society. The question of the right way to live, both individually and in community, is vitally more important than the truth of any scientific theory. In fact, there is a now fairly widespread and growing view that modern science is an amoral discipline. This means that scientists, regularly operating with huge government and private grants, and under pressure to forge ahead with their cutting edge research, often do not want to be bothered by questions about the morality of what they do, or by those who raise these questions. It is an unfortunate fact that scientists and science organizations do sometimes too quickly disregard the moral scruples of the public with regard to some scientific procedures, are reluctant to allow morality to get in the way of their research, and sometimes show contempt for legitimate moral concerns raised by society.

In this final chapter, we will explore the broad topic of science and ethics in an attempt to identify and elaborate on some of the key ethical concerns raised today by the newest scientific research, and how scientists, religious thinkers, and philosophers might handle them. Among the issues discussed will be the human genome project, stem cells and cloning, genetic engineering, and the implications of latest scientific research for our conception of human nature. Our task in the space available is not to present definitive answers to difficult and complex ethical matters (that would take a book in itself), but to provide an overview of the latest scientific techniques, to identify the ethical issues raised by them, and to consider some religious (and secularist) responses to these matters. We will bring our reflections to a close by identifying some important lessons for scientists and religious thinkers that stem from our reflections in this book.

Mapping the human genome

The mapping of the human genome is one of the most exciting and path-breaking areas of scientific research in recent memory. We know from work in genetics and molecular biology that each species has a set of biological instructions that are contained in the molecules and cells of each organism. These molecules are called deoxyribonucleic acid, or DNA. Friedrich Miescher, a German biochemist, discovered DNA in 1871, but it was almost a century later before further research led to the unraveling of the structure of the DNA molecule, and recognition of its critical importance for understanding the biological organization of organisms. In 1953, four scientists, Francis Crick, Rosalind Franklin, James Watson, and Maurice Wilkins, discovered the double helix structure of DNA—a twisting ladderlike sequence that contains the biological information, or "genetic codes," that are passed from one generation to the next in sexual reproduction.

DNA is found in molecules inside a special area of the cell called the nucleus; the DNA molecule is tightly packaged, and is known as a chromosome.[2] Chromosomes, which are really bundles of DNA, contain strands of DNA material called genes; the genes contain instructions to make proteins, which are the building blocks of life. Chromosomes come in pairs in an organism, one half of each pair contributed by each parent, so an organism inherits half of its DNA from the male parent and half from the female parent. The complete set of DNA in an organism is called its genome (which includes all of its genes). The actual chemical building blocks of DNA are called nucleotides, which themselves consist of three parts: a phosphate group, a sugar group, and one of four types of nitrogen bases. To form a strand of DNA, nucleotides are linked into chains, with the phosphate and sugar groups alternating. The four types of nitrogen bases found in nucleotides are: adenine (A), thymine (T), guanine (G), and cytosine (C). These are repeated millions or billions of times throughout a genome. The order, or sequence, of these bases determines what biological instructions are contained in a strand of DNA. For example, the sequence ATCGTT might code for blue eyes, while ATCGCT might code for brown eyes.[3] This means that the particular order of As, Ts, Gs, and Cs is extremely important because, not only does it determine particular features of an organism, it even determines the type of organism it is (i.e., which species it is a member of).

The gene carries the vital information necessary for the formation of proteins that are required by organisms. Proteins determine or heavily influence many features of the biological and behavioral characteristics of an organism, including its physical appearance, how well its body metabolizes food or fights infection, and even how it behaves. Proteins themselves are composed of smaller units called amino acids. (It was amino acids that the Urey-Miller experiment referred to in Chapter 3 succeeded in creating by artificial means.) The size of an individual gene may vary greatly, ranging from about 1,000 bases to 1 million bases in humans. The complete human genome contains about 3 billion bases (or sequences of letters) which includes about 20,000 genes on 23 pairs of chromosomes (each pair in the form of a double helix). A mouse genome also has 3 billion bases, and a worm has about 100 million.

The Human Genome Project was founded in 1990, first led by James Watson, and then by Francis Collins.[4] The specific goals of the project were to identify (or map) all the approximately 20,000–25,000 genes in human DNA, to determine the sequences of the 3 billion chemical base pairs that make up human DNA, to store this information in databases, and to address the ethical, legal, and social issues that arise from the project. The project was completed in 2003 (the results are available to the public on the internet), an achievement that Collins believes "will be seen a thousand years from now as one of the major achievements of humankind."[5] Collins describes the makeup of the genome as "the language of God," God's blueprint for life in the universe. He also points out that naturally occurring mutations in DNA cause variations in the biological structures of species; these are estimated to occur at a rate of 100 million base pairs per generation in humans. Most of these mutations occur in parts of the genome that have no consequence to us, but some occur in more vulnerable parts and are generally harmful. The mapping of the human genome moves us a step closer to identifying these various mutations and to eventually correcting them. This process is known as gene therapy.

Collins and his team also found that the amount of DNA used by our genes to code for various proteins is only about 1.5 percent of the total (the rest is sometimes called "junk DNA," because it does not seem to have any function), and (as discussed in Chapter 4), he argues that at the DNA level, all of the species are 99.9 percent identical, which is further evidence of a common ancestor. The larger goals of the human genome project, of course, are to add to the store of human knowledge, and to use this knowledge to benefit humankind in a variety of areas, including: in medicine—to diagnose, treat, and some day prevent by means of gene therapy the thousands of disorders that affect us (e.g., detection and treatment of genetic diseases, such as cystic fibrosis or sickle cell anemia); in agriculture—to develop disease, insect, and drought-resistant crops, and healthier, more productive, disease-resistant farm animals; in energy production and the environment—to create new energy sources, and reduce pollution; and to help in other areas such as crime detection, paternity cases, organ donations, etc.

Work on the human genome project, though fascinating and full of tremendous potential for curing disease, obviously has serious religious and ethical implications. These implications fall into two categories, more localized ethical matters raised by the procedures and purposes of various types of genetic engineering (as work involving manipulation of genes is often called), and larger ethical issues relating to the implications of genetic engineering for our understanding of humanity, and more generally for the status and nature of life in the universe. The former category includes those ethical issues that are directly raised by the fact that the whole of the human genome has now been mapped. Given that testing for genetic diseases is now possible, this raises a host of ethical questions: when and how much testing should we do, and who has control over, and who should have access to, the results? Should employers, schools, the government, or health insurance companies have access to the results of an individual's genetic test? Would it be ethical for pregnant mothers to get a genetic test on their babies, and to abort the baby if they are not satisfied with the results of the test? This also raises the possibility of genetic enhancement to produce desirable traits in children (e.g., intelligence, athleticism, good looks, an issue we will come back to in our discussion of cloning). Some of the larger ethical issues raised by the mapping of the genome include genetic determinism versus reason, free will, and personal experience in influencing human behavior (nature vs. nurture), the potential to radically alter the nature of a species, to create new species, possibly even to create life artificially, and the possible effects of genetic engineering on our overall understanding of what it means to be a human being (and, therefore, on the value of life).

The first point to make about these difficult questions is that they cannot be answered in the domain of science. As we noted in earlier chapters, science tries to identify empirical facts about the physical universe, through a variety of methods and techniques, and to formulate theories to explain how these facts came about, but this approach cannot enlighten us about the correct ethical response to a particular issue. This is because, to take the example of genetic engineering, learning how to manipulate DNA in human genes so that we can bring about a variety of new effects (e.g., cure disease, or code for blue eyes) does not tell us what the *moral* thing to do is. It does not follow that because we know how to do something today in science (or any discipline) that we did not know how to do yesterday, that the new practice is moral. It is important always to leave the science to the scientists, but this does not mean that we should leave ethics to the scientists, and this includes ethical judgments about the appropriateness of some forms of scientific research.

The second point is that scientists tend to commit this mistake frequently in our society, a mistake that Socrates identified long ago in Plato's *Apology*, when he pointed out that because the poets and craftsmen were good technically at writing poetry and at building things, respectively, they then made the mistake of thinking they were experts on morality, politics, and law as well. We might express this point by noting that scientists usually cannot resist making value judgments about the importance of their research; there is nothing wrong, of course, with having an ethical view with regard to the possible uses of one's research, but a problem arises when scientists invoke their authority as scientists to lend special weight to their ethical views, thereby unduly influencing the general public. The temptation to subtly appeal to one's scientific expertise in order to give extra weight to one's moral viewpoints is almost irresistible. But given the wide-ranging ethical questions raised by modern science, this is an error we must expose and get beyond if society is to make informed judgments about the way modern scientific research is to be utilized. The special expertise of scientists in their various fields does not give them any special expertise in the area of ethics. Scientists must also be on guard against advocating political and ethical beliefs that are founded on the *assumption* that all human behavior is genetically determined. According to geneticist, Richard Lewontin, this happens in various theories of biological, psychological, and cultural reductionism. Lewontin writes eloquently about how scientists routinely employ speculative science to advocate moral and political agendas while all the time trying to appear as if they are politically disinterested.[6]

The third important point is that in our pluralist society many of us will approach difficult ethical questions raised by new scientific research, like the mapping of the human genome, from *the point of view of our worldviews, or philosophies of life*. Our worldview will contain our beliefs about the nature of reality, the nature of the human person, as well as our ethical and political beliefs, and will therefore be a decisive influence on how we live and act, on how we raise our families, and on how we think society should be organized. But one of the disconcerting features of modern, pluralist, democratic societies is that there are often several worldviews competing in the public square, various religious ones as well as various secularist ones. This is one of the inevitable consequences of a living in a free society. What this means, from a practical point of view, is that we may not be able to reach any broad agreement about complex ethical matters, about, for example, who should have access to genetic information, or whether parents should be allowed to genetically enhance their children, or whether scientists should be allowed to produce embryos for research, or whether we should tamper with the nature of the human species.

This leads to our fourth point: *who gets to decide* which answer to these ethical questions shall prevail at the level of law in a democratic society? This is a difficult, complex question, but one we need to reflect on because *some answer* (and therefore *someone's* view) on each of these questions must eventually prevail at the level of law. Should the more difficult and controversial (and potentially culture-changing) ethical questions be decided democratically by a direct vote of the people, or by the government (acting supposedly on behalf of the people), or by the courts, or by some (elite) group? (By way of comparison, it can be helpful here to think about how the following issues *were* decided upon in various societies: divorce, abortion, the legalization of pornography, the creation of sperm banks, surrogate motherhood, *in vitro* fertilization, euthanasia, etc.).

The fifth point to emphasize is that even though we may disagree on many matters of principle at the level of worldviews (e.g., whether human life is or is not a fundamental value), there are many common values we can and do agree on, and so at least some ethical progress is possible. For example, we can (probably) all agree that genetic engineering procedures must take due regard to the safety of the patients involved, that the results of genetic testing should be kept confidential, that insurance companies and employers should not be allowed access to these records as a condition of service, that all parties involved should be honest, caring, and so forth. But this agreement will not solve all our problems because it does not extend to the issues of whether genetically enhancing a child is moral, whether aborting a fetus with a birth defect is moral, whether cloning oneself is moral.

This brings us to our last point, which concerns more directly religious and secularist responses to the questions originating out of the human genome project. Secularism has tended to be more permissive on theses types of ethical problems than most religions, sometimes even appearing to slip into moral relativism, the view that there are no objective moral values, that ethics is primarily a matter of personal (or sometimes cultural) taste. Although most secularists still believe in moral absolutes on issues relating to abortion, cloning, euthanasia, and surrogate motherhood, it is accurate to say that secularist views in general have tended toward the position of allowing these practices to be legal in society, adopting a "what's wrong with them" type of attitude rather than offering much by way of a positive defense of them. They are much impressed by the utilitarian argument that the potential for cures outweighs any harm that might result from some of these practices (e.g., creating embryos for research); and because they tend to take a quite absolutist position on human freedom, the secularist view is that little restriction should be placed on other practices, such as genetic enhancements and cloning, in a democratic society. Since secularists are committed to the worldview of secularism, they also reject views common in religious traditions that appeal to the arguments that life is a gift from God, that life is sacred and should not be tampered with, that genetic engineering interferes with God's design plan, and that human beings have a human nature (an essence) which should not be violated. Though in the matter of genetic engineering, even secularists are worried by what is sometimes called the "slippery slope argument," the argument that once a society legalizes some of these practices (e.g., genetic manipulation to cure disease), then by small incremental steps the floodgates gradually open (to allow, e.g., genetic manipulation for "designer" traits), making it difficult to regulate or control any future practices (the same thing occurred after the legalization of divorce, pornography, and abortion in many countries).

Religious responses to the human genome project and its possibilities have tended to be more conservative, though we must also stress that more liberal religious denominations have sometimes sided with the secularists on many of these matters. But most religious responses will stress the common values we mentioned above (hopefully values most worldviews can agree on), as well as emphasizing the need to protect individuals from the might (both financial and political) of large businesses who have a vested financial interest in much of this scientific research. The religious response will also emphasize the fact that each human being is a child of God, and has a basic dignity that should not be violated. Religious thinkers will be concerned about the exploitation of the individual person by large bureaucracies in our capitalist-driven, pleasure-seeking, entertainment-saturated culture, a culture that already reveals alarming tendencies in this area (e.g., cosmetic surgery, therapeutic abortions, and contractual marriages).

Theologians and religious leaders, therefore, will be generally critical of attempts to use genetic information to penalize people, or discriminate against them, or exploit them in some way, such as denying them a job or health insurance based on genetic testing. They will welcome the new knowledge (as most people will) if it is used to cure disease, develop new drugs, benefit agricultural programs and the environment, as long as adequate safety is maintained, something that is currently not the case (genetically modified food, for instance, is commonly available, usually without labeling, in our supermarkets, and with little attempt being made to test for harmful side effects). Religious thinkers, such as Gilbert Meilaender,[7] are particularly worried about the larger questions that the human genome project raises, those concerning the manipulation of human genes, and the genes of other species, a process that raises questions about the nature of humanity itself, questions to which we must now turn.

Stem cells and cloning

One of the areas where genetic engineering broadly understood is now a reality is the area of stem cell research and cloning. Let us consider stem cell research first. Stem cells are unspecialized cells that contain all of our genetic information, and that can renew themselves for long periods through cell division. (They are called "stem cells" because all of the other cells in our body stem from them.) They are significant because, under certain physiological or experimental conditions, stem cells can be induced or "turned on" to become cells with specialized functions such as heart muscle cells, or insulin-producing cells. These cells are described as "pluripotent," meaning that they have the ability to divide into more stem cells, and have the potential to become all cell types of the body (e.g., brain cells, pancreatic cells, etc.); some stem cells in the very early stages of life (the first few days) may even have the ability to develop into (in theory at least) a complete human being.[8]

There are two sources of stem cells, human tissue (adult stem cells), and human embryos (embryonic stem cells). Adult stem cells (so called because the cells have already matured) are present in all of the major organs of our bodies, and can also be found in umbilical cord blood, placenta, human fat tissue, among other places. Embryonic stem cells are obtained by destroying the embryo and harvesting its cells, a practice which is the source of most of the ethical controversy surrounding stem cells. Although research involving adult stem cells has led to noteworthy cures (e.g., bone marrow transplants), and has been going on for much longer than embryonic stem cell research, the latter has been the focus of recent scientific attention because researchers argue that the cells from embryos are more numerous, and more pluripotent than adult stem cells, and so have enormous research potential for leading to significant medical cures. As a result of these claims, embryonic stem cell research has attracted considerable funding, and media attention, and has also generated public controversy in various countries, especially the United States. The hope is that this research can be used to cure a variety of diseases like Parkinson's disease and Alzheimer's disease by developing various gene therapies using the stem cells.

One source of controversy regarding embryonic stem cells is that they can only be obtained from embryos. This problem leads us straight to the issue of cloning. In 1996, a British research team, led by Ian Wilmut, successfully produced a cloned sheep, called Dolly. The cloning process, known as somatic cell nuclear transfer, involved the following steps: (1) An egg cell was taken from the first sheep; (2) The cell's nucleus and DNA were removed; (3) A skin or other cell is taken from a second sheep (which contains that sheep's DNA); (4) This cell is then fused with the first sheep's egg cell by means of an electrical charge; (5) The egg cell then begins growing and developing into a blastocyst (an early stage embryo); (6) After six days, the embryo was then implanted into the womb of a third sheep; (7) Five months later, Dolly, the world's best-known sheep, was born! (In the whole process, 277 eggs were fused with donor cells, which led to only 29 viable embryos, which produced only one live lamb at birth, Dolly.) Dolly is a clone, or a replica, of the sheep whose skin cell provided the DNA, which means that Dolly's DNA and the donor sheep's DNA are genetically identical. Dolly's birth, and the success of the cloning technique, prompted much discussion about whether it would be ethical to use the same procedure to clone a human being. Dr. Wilmut, interviewed at the time, said it would not be. But in 2005, he was granted a license from the British Government to clone human embryos for research purposes.[9]

The reason for this change in attitude on behalf of many is that it was quickly recognized that cloned embryos would be a fruitful source of stem cells to assist the process of embryonic stem cell research. This led to a fusion of sorts of the two issues of cloning and stem cells, and also motivated the distinction between reproductive cloning and therapeutic cloning. Reproductive cloning is the process of producing a cloned human baby in the same way that Dolly was produced. Most people are opposed to this, including most scientists. But many support therapeutic cloning. This is where the embryo that is produced in step 5 above of the cloning procedure is destroyed after a few days, and the stem cells are then extracted from it and used in research. These are said to be the best stem cells because they can be developed into all tissue types. Stem cells obtained in this way could be used to help a man with heart disease, for instance, because he could be the provider of the initial DNA cell, which means that the cells taken from the embryo created with his DNA would be identical to his own, and would likely be more successful in the treatment of his heart disease, so the theory goes.

Although many find reproductive cloning repugnant, it is interesting to wonder if it will ever occur. As the *New York Times* reported eight months after Dolly was born, although people's initial reaction to human cloning was "never," for some this quickly became "why not?"[10] Some argue that reproductive cloning is only a further extension of practices that we already allow like surrogate motherhood and *in vitro* fertilization. But why would we want to clone human beings? There are several reasons that have been suggested, which include: to help infertile couples have children; to circumvent genetic diseases that run in families; to create an organ donor for a currently sick child; to create a replica of your dead child; or create a replica of yourself! Cloning may also be used to protect endangered species or to recreate extinct species (a scenario dramatized in the movie, *Jurassic Park*). In the area of agriculture, cloning is currently being experimented with to create more productive farm animals, and more productive crops.

There are other even more sinister possibilities that the process of human cloning would make technically possible. Some of these include: taking the material to produce a clone from embryos, thereby allowing embryos to become biological parents, and at the same time creating a cloned child with no living parents;[11] the possibility of cloning the dead, by somehow preserving the deceased's skin tissue!; cloning a person without their knowledge (especially for use in embryo research)!; the possibility of genetic engineering of the cloned material to produce designer traits in children (the path of eugenics, which would eventually put other vulnerable groups at risk as well, such as the elderly and those with disabilities);[12] the possibility of producing chimeras for experimental purposes, that is, fusing animal DNA with human genetic material, or *vice versa*, or implanting animal genetic material into human cells, or *vice versa*. It has also been suggested that cloning might make men superfluous (a disaster!) because it is obviously possible to produce a clone using an egg and a female DNA donor, if, say, all men were wiped out by a disease (another disaster!). It is also possible for a clone's grandmother and mother to be the same person, if an embryo created with DNA from a child was then implanted in the womb of the child's mother. A perfected technique of human cloning would move these troubling possibilities closer to reality.

This leads us to consider some of the ethical implications of stem cell research and cloning. We must first emphasize that, since these are relatively new areas of research, they have not yet been subject to detailed religious and ethical analysis, as other issues have; theologians and philosophers are still thinking their way through them, as are scientists and other intellectuals. But we can offer a few guidelines on the main ethical questions raised by this research. Since embryonic stem cell research involves the creation and destruction of embryos, thereby linking this issue to the issue of abortion, many oppose it because it involves destroying the embryo. If one is against abortion, one will likely be against this form of research. (Although this controversy may be dissolved if an ongoing research program aimed at transforming adult stem cells into embryonic stem cells is successful.) Scientists who support embryonic research have tried to sidestep this argument in two ways. The first is to appeal to a utilitarian argument, an argument that is sometimes invoked by scientists who are tempted to cut ethical corners. This argument has resulted in many scientific research organizations adopting "an end justifies the means" approach toward their research. The utilitarian approach is founded on the idea that if the end is regarded as sufficiently moral, such as curing Parkinson's disease, then even immoral means can be justified to secure this end, including the deliberate creation and destruction of embryos, the creation of hybrid animal/human embryos, speculative genetic engineering projects, etc.

The second approach is to obfuscate on the meaning of the term "cloning" by suggesting that therapeutic cloning is not the same type of cloning as reproductive cloning. Although this attempt at obfuscation is more common in the United States (where scientists frequently talk as if there is a difference in kind, and not just in degree, between a blastocyst and an embryo, a deception some also justify on utilitarian grounds), we need to be clear that the only difference between the two is that in therapeutic cloning the embryo is not implanted in a womb and brought to term. But in both forms of cloning the technique used is the same, and a human embryo is produced in both cases (one which would come to term if implanted in a womb, assuming all technical problems have been solved). When thinking about the ethics of this matter, one needs not only to consider the morality of abortion (a large issue that we cannot get into here), but also whether one would adopt the utilitarian position if one had an illness oneself, or a family member had an illness, that could possibly be cured by using stem cells derived from embryos (in the same way we might consider whether we would eat bread that had been made by slave labor, or drink coffee that had been made by exploited workers, if one could show that a greater good would result). A major, and many believe, fatal problem facing the utilitarian approach is that its advocates cannot say that any action is ever right or wrong in principle, but only right or wrong insofar as it adds to or detracts from the overall good. Therefore, it is a moral theory that can sanction just about any kind of immoral action, even killing or stealing, if it is believed that it will lead to a greater overall good.

This leads us to focus on the question of whether cloning is moral or immoral in itself (i.e., in principle), as distinct from it being moral or immoral in some of its practical consequences in society. The distinction between an action being wrong in principle, and being wrong in its practical effects, is helpful when thinking about ethical issues, especially ones that will have consequences for society. Although our society is fairly evenly split on the morality of therapeutic cloning because it involves the destruction of human embryos, almost everyone is against reproductive cloning. From the point of view of religious belief, cloning in general can be seen as wrong in itself because it is interfering with the natural way that human beings are created, the fusion of egg and sperm. It would in effect be tampering with God's creative process. Catholic theologians, in particular, would appeal to natural moral law, and argue that this law prohibits tampering with human reproduction. While many theologians across many different religions would agree that just because a thing occurs naturally, it does not follow automatically that it is good, and so it does not automatically follow that interfering with nature is bad, they feel that the process of cloning "crosses the line" (leading to us "playing God"), thereby violating the mystery of what it means to be human.[13]

A second reason to support the argument that cloning is wrong in itself is that a cloned human being would be biologically different from any other human being that ever lived because it would have the DNA of only one parent (the DNA donor). This crosses the line for many people from curing disease, and minimizing defects, to interfering with the essence of what it means to be human. A third reason for why cloning is wrong in itself is because it would likely create an identity problem for the clone, a problem that would have a serious effect on a person's well being. In addition to the fact that the clone would be an identical copy of another human being, he or she would also not have a mother and a father in the normal sense (because he or she would not have the DNA of both parents). Of course, from a religious point of view, a clone would still be a real human being and would have a soul, yet it would be biologically unique when compared to the rest of humankind. A fourth reason for why cloning (and genetic engineering) might be regarded as wrong in principle is that they would compromise the uniqueness of human beings because our very structure can now be manipulated and changed biologically. This would be a grave threat to human dignity, especially if it became common in society (we see the same thing on a smaller scale now with cosmetic and elective surgeries to correct perceived physical defects). It could also compromise our free will to some extent, if our lives are significantly mapped out for us by the decisions of others before we are born, rather than by our own decisions (though it must be noted that our reason and free will, as well as our environment, all play significant roles in our development, which limits the influence of our genetic and physical makeup on the kind of person we eventually turn out to be, and so "genes are not destiny"; recall our discussion of determinism in Chapter 5).

If one is coming from a secularist perspective, one may not be much impressed with these arguments, but the secularist needs to recognize that his secularist worldview is driving his ethical responses to questions raised by this research (e.g., the secularist might believe there is no "mystery" to human life, or reject natural law, and so why can't we manipulate human genes, if it is to promote a greater good, such as curing disease, or overcoming physical defects, or infertility?). If one approaches these matters from a religious perspective, then similarly this perspective will define one's responses. This shows us that ethical questions often come down to a debate between different worldviews (especially when we are debating matters of principle), and that the rationality of our worldview is therefore of crucial importance, as is how our worldview compares in this respect with other worldviews. Just as important—given our pluralist, democratic society—as having a rationally defensible position, is how these difficult ethical questions are to be settled at the political level, and who gets to have a say in settling them, as we pointed out earlier. (My own view is that these questions are so important that they should be settled democratically by a vote of the people, but this large topic is beyond the scope of this book.[14])

Many are also worried about the practical effects of cloning in society, aside from the question of whether it is right or wrong in principle. For instance, cloning is still a very dangerous procedure, and the side effects of the process for human beings are not yet known (many of the cloned animals have died young, including Dolly). This is a crucial point not just for the clone, but also for the clone's offspring. It could be that cloning could have a deleterious effect on the broader population over a few generations. Another practical problem is the "slippery slope" effect referred to above, now applied to cloning: we start off allowing therapeutic cloning; this then leads to reproductive cloning, which leads to designer babies, and so forth. These are general fears that many worry about because of the way sinful human beings behave when faced with various temptations: the lure of the fame and fortune that can be gained from pursuing this research; the desire for perfect children; the inability to face inconvenience, suffering, etc. The slippery slope argument must be handled with caution, and does not apply in all areas of life, but we have seen it play out in areas like abortion and divorce in the past, and so it is a legitimate worry that it will play out in the area of genetic engineering as well.

Conclusion: some lessons for scientists and religious believers

While we can at least have a fairly civilized debate in a modern, pluralist, democratic society about the practical effects of legalizing a certain practice, like cloning, and can also agree that abuses might occur and that they would be wrong, it is much harder for us to debate matters where we differ in principle. This is because disagreements in principle nearly always come back to disagreements at the level of our worldviews, as we have noted. It might be possible to have a rational discussion of an ethical issue like cloning by leaving our worldviews aside (both religious and secularist) as much as we can, and attempting to discuss the matter in a purely philosophical way by appeal to logic, rational argument, evidence, and human experience, as much as possible. While I as a philosopher advocate this approach as the best way forward, many in our contemporary culture have no confidence that it can succeed; many despair that the worldviews are becoming further and further apart, that people are becoming increasingly polarized in their views, and that they are more likely to see those they disagree with as not just wrong but as immoral, or irrational, or worse. As a result, we are often tempted to regard the attainment and use of raw political power as the only way to achieve our ethical goals for society. Of course, the issues at stake are serious for the future of modern culture. Indeed, what we have here is basically a set of different views about the nature of human beings, and questions about the nature of human beings always come back to our overall views about the universe, and the purpose of human life—whether there is a design plan behind it all—which only returns us to the contentious clash of worldviews once again.

While there is no easy solution to this "practical problem of pluralism," I would like to end our discussion by briefly considering some lessons for scientists and religious thinkers that would help move the discussion forward, that would improve both the practice and outlook of both disciplines, as well as the broader discussion in society, including the ethical discussion. First, science must be less narrow in its approach to its subject matter. Scientists (especially agenda-setting scientists) need to develop a greater appreciation for the philosophical, religious, and moral implications of their work. They need not necessarily formally address these implications themselves, but they should recognize them, be sensitive to them, and occasionally talk about them in and outside of their discipline (indeed they should make a point in some contexts of raising these questions instead of resolutely ignoring them or pretending that they don't exist, e.g., in educational contexts, or in documentaries on science subjects). Second, scientists need to be aware of the naturalistic/secularist bias that is a driving force behind much of their discipline, and take steps to get rid of it, just as they would not tolerate a religious bias.

Third, religious believers should not be afraid of science, but should welcome it as a further way to understand God's creation. Coupled with the willingness of scientists to occasionally address religious issues, this would have the effect of lessening tensions all around, of helping students in our schools to enjoy science, and of ensuring further public support of, and goodwill toward, science. Indeed, we must recognize that religions are not blameless in the tension that sometimes exists between the two areas, that both sides have contributed to the rise of the "conflict model" as a way of understanding science and religion. But just as religious believers should not be afraid of scientific research, so do scientists need to separate the facts of scientific theories (e.g., evolution), from speculation about these facts, and from their own worldviews more generally.

Fourth, this brings us to the training of scientists today. Those who work in science-related areas, broadly conceived, including biologists, chemists, physicists, astronomers, doctors, health care workers, psychologists, occupational therapists, and nurses (to name only a small few) are often trained exclusively in the skills needed for their job. They frequently have no background in the liberal arts, or in religion, philosophy or ethics. As a result, they sometimes fail to appreciate the human and moral side of their jobs, how their work affects the people they are dealing with as patients, clients, subjects, family members, citizens, as members of the public, and as human beings. It is sadly true that many scientists today, especially at large research institutions, have an excellent, but very narrow, training. This means that they are generally not competent to discuss many of the more ultimate questions raised by their disciplines, and often develop a negative and sometimes hostile attitude toward these questions, which they then pass on to their students. Unfortunately, this is a quite serious problem, and it will take a wholesale rethinking of the way we teach science and science-related subjects in order to correct it.

On the philosophical and religious side, there is still a great deal of ignorance about science, and this is not always the fault of scientists, or programs of scientific education, though if we are to be honest we must conclude that scientists bear a lot of responsibility for the dismal state of scientific knowledge among the public. But, as a final point, philosophers, theologians, ethicists, and religious believers, and other interested parties, need to become better educated in the latest scientific theories, and to reflect further on their philosophical, religious, and ethical implications for the larger questions confronting humankind. Undertaking such a task, as I hope one can see from this book, will take one upon a fascinating journey through many of the awe-inspiring mysteries of creation, leading to a deeper understanding that will further promote fertile and rewarding dialogue between religion and science.

Notes

Chapter 1

1. Ian Barbour was among the first to identify what became the standard models for thinking about the relationship between religion and science; see Ian Barbour, *Religion and Science: Historical and Contemporary Issues* (San Francisco, CA: Harper, 1997), ch. 4. See Mikael Stenmark's *How to Relate Science and Religion* (Grand Rapids, MI: Eerdmans, 2004), which proposes an interesting alterative to Barbour's view.
2. See J. W. Draper's, *History of the Conflict between Religion and Science* (New York: Cosimo Classics, 2005) (1874), and Andrew Dickson White's, *A History of the Warfare of Science with Theology* (New York: Prometheus, 1993) (1896), works hostile to religion that exaggerated and promoted the conflict thesis.
3. As an example, see Christian de Duve, *Life Evolving* (New York: Oxford U.P., 2002), p.285.
4. For more on Barth's views, see Geoffrey W. Bromiley, *Introduction to the Theology of Karl Barth* (Edinburgh: T. & T. Clark, 1979).
5. See Stephen J. Gould, *Rocks of Ages* (New York: Ballentine, 1999), p.6.
6. See Thomas Torrance, *Theological Science* (Oxford: Oxford U.P., 1969); Langdon Gilkey, *Creationism on Trial* (Minneapolis, MN: Winston Press, 1986); also his *Religion and the Scientific Future* (New York: Harper & Row, 1970).
7. Barbour describes the *dialogue* and the *integration* models as two different models, but I think they are best combined in the way described here; see Ian Barbour, *Religion and Science*, pp.90–105.
8. See Anthony Flew, *There is a God: How The World's Most Notorious Atheist Changed His Mind* (San Francisco, CA: Harper, 2007).

Chapter 2

1. See John Hedley Brooke, *Science and Religion: Some Historical Perspectives* (New York: Cambridge U.P., 1991), p.5. For other excellent historical overviews, see Richard Olson, *Science and Religion 1450-1900* (Baltimore, MD: Johns Hopkins, 2004); Ian Barbour, *Religion and Science*; Gary Ferngren (ed.), *Science & Religion: A Historical Introduction* (Baltimore, MD: Johns Hopkins, 2002).

2. See Edward Grant, *A History of Natural Philosophy: From the Ancient World to the Nineteenth Century* (New York: Cambridge U.P., 2007), p.44, pp.234–238, and also throughout the book for an unmatched account of the development of natural philosophy up to the nineteenth century.
3. See Aristotle, *Metaphysics*, Book I, p.10.
4. Ibid., Book IX.
5. See Aristotle, *On the Parts of Animals*.
6. See Aristotle, *Physics*, Book II, Part III.
7. Aristotle, *Nicomachean Ethics*, Book II.
8. Aristotle, *Metaphysics*, Book IV.
9. See Richard Blackwell, *Science, Religion and Authority* (Milwaukee: Marquette U.P., 1998); also St. Augustine, *On the Literal Meaning of Genesis*, trans. J. H. Taylor in J. Quasten (ed.), *Ancient Christian Writers* (New York: Newman Press, 1982), vols. 41–42.
10. See Grant, *A History of Natural Philosophy*, p.242ff.
11. See St. Thomas Aquinas, *Selected Writings*, ed. Ralph McInerny (New York: Penguin, 1998).
12. See *Aeterni Patris*, Encyclical of Pope Leo XII, issued August 4, 1879.
13. See St. Thomas Aquinas, *Selected Writings*, pp.115ff; also Ralph McInerny, *Aquinas and Analogy* (Washington, DC: Catholic University of America Press, 1998); also his *Aquinas* (Cambridge: Polity Press, 2004).
14. See St. Thomas Aquinas, *Selected Writings*, pp.354ff.
15. See Stanley L. Jaki, *Science and Creation* (Edinburgh: Scottish Academic Press, 1974); also Holmes Rolston, *Science and Religion: A Critical Survey* (Philadelphia, PA: Templeton Ed., 1987), p.39; also John Hedley Brooke, *Science and Religion*, ch.2.; also Reijer Hooykaas, *Religion and the Rise of Modern Science* (Edinburgh: Scottish Academic Press, 1973). For a recent Muslim perspective, see Seyyed Hossein Nasr, *Religion and the Order of Nature* (New York: Oxford U.P., 1996).
16. See Richard J. Blackwell, *Behind the Scenes at Galileo's Trial* (Notre Dame, IN: University of Notre Dame, 2006).
17. See Gale Christianson, *Isaac Newton* (New York: Oxford U.P., 2005).
18. See René Descartes, *Meditations* [1647] (London: Penguin, 1999).
19. Baron D'Holbach, *The System of Nature* [1770] (ch. XI), quoted from "We are completely determined," in Louis Pojman (ed.), *Philosophy: The Quest for Truth* (New York: Oxford U.P., 2008, seventh edn.), pp.384–385.
20. La Mettrie, *Man a Machine* [1748] (Indianapolis, IN: Hackett, 1994), p.59.
21. See John Hedley Brooke, *Science and Religion*, chs. 4 and 5, for more on mechanism and deism.
22. See Samuel Clarke, *Leibniz and Clarke Correspondence* [1717] (Indianapolis, IN: Hackett, 2000).
23. See Kerry Walters, *The American Deists* (Lawrence, KS: University Press of Kansas, 1992), and Thomas Paine, *The Age of Reason* (New York: Citadel, 1988) (1794)
24. See Ronald Numbers, *The Creationists* (Los Angeles, CA: University of California Press, 1992), and *Darwinism Comes to America* (Cambridge, MA: Harvard U.P., 1998).
25. See Paul C. Vitz, *Faith of the Fatherless: The Psychology of Atheism* (Dallas, TX: Spence, 1999).

Chapter 3

1. See Steven French, *Science: Key Concepts in Philosophy* (London: Continuum, 2007), ch. 1.
2. See Richard J. Blackwell, *Behind the Scenes at Galileo's Trial*, pp.66–70.
3. As an example, see John Polkinghorne, *The Faith of a Physicist* (Minneapolis, MN: Fortress, 1996), p.50; also his *Rochester Roundabout: The Story of High Energy Physics* (New York: Freeman/Longman, 1989), pp.158–176.
4. A good introduction is S. Block and E. Mares, *Realism and Anti-Realism* (Montreal: McGill U.P., 2007).
5. See Janet Kourany, *The Gender of Science* (New Jersey: Prentice Hall, 2001).
6. See W. V. Quine, *From a Logical Point of View* (Cambridge, MA: Harvard U.P., 1980) and *Ontological Relativity* (New York: Columbia U.P., 1977).
7. See the essays in Martin Curd and J. A. Cover (eds.), *Philosophy of Science* (New York: London, 1998), Parts 2, 9.
8. See ibid.
9. See Alan Hirschfeld, *The Electric Life of Michael Faraday* (New York: Walker, 2006), pp.161–173.
10. I am indebted to Steven French, *Science: Key Concepts in Philosophy*, p.95, for most of this list.
11. See Alan Guth, *The Inflationary Universe* (Cambridge, MA: Perseus, 1997), and Lee Smolin, *The Life of the Cosmos* (New York: Oxford U.P., 1999).
12. See Pierre Duhem, *The Aim and Structure of Physical Theory* (Princeton, NJ: Princeton U.P., 1954).
13. See Karl Popper, *Conjectures and Refutations* (London: Routledge & Kegan Paul, 1963).
14. For some representative works, see Richard Dawkins, *The God Delusion* (New York: Houghton Mifflin, 2006); also *The Blind Watchmaker* (New York: Norton, 1987); Carl Sagan, *Cosmos* (New York: Random House, 2002); John Searle, *Minds, Brains and Science* (Cambridge, MA: Harvard U.P., 1984); Francis Crick, *The Astonishing Hypothesis* (New York: Touchstone, 1995); Steven Weinberg, *Dreams of a Final Theory* (New York: Pantheon, 1992); Thomas Nagel, *The Last Word* (New York: Oxford U.P., 1997); Paul Kurtz, *Living Without Religion* (New York: Prometheus, 1994); Edward Wilson, *Consilience* (New York: Vintage, 1999); Peter Atkins, *The Creation* (New York: W. H. Freeman, 1981).
15. See Lynn Margulis and Dorian Sagan, *What is Life?* (Berkeley, CA: University of California Press, 2000).
16. Simon Conway Morris, *Life's Solution* (New York: Cambridge U.P., 2003), p.44; see pp.44–68 for a full discussion; also see Christian de Duve, *Life Evolving*, chs. 4–8.
17. See Francis Crick, *Life Itself* (New York: Simon and Schuster, 1982).
18. See Richard Dawkins, *The God Delusion*, p.272.
19. See Carl Sagan, *Cosmos*; and his *Billions and Billions* (New York: Ballantine, 1997) for his views on a variety of topics including religion and science, abortion, and the environment.
20. Carl Sagan, *Cosmos*, p.4.
21. Ibid., ch.8.

22. As quoted in *The Washington Times*, "DNA pioneers lash out at religion," March 24, 2003; see also Francis Crick, *What Mad Pursuit* (New York: Basic Books, 1988), p.11, p.17.
23. Francis Crick, *The Astonishing Hypothesis*, p.3.
24. Ibid., p.256.
25. See Owen Gingerich, *God's Universe* (Cambridge, MA: Harvard, 2006); Paul Davis, *God and the New Physics* (New York: Simon and Schuster, 1983); Francis Collins, *The Language of God* ((New York: Free Press, 2006); and Simon Conway Morris, *Life's Solution*.
26. Richard Lewontin, "Billions and Billions of Demons," *New York Review of Books*, January 9, 1997.

Chapter 4

1. See Charles Darwin, *The Origin of Species* (London: Penguin, 1982 edn.); for a life of Darwin, see John Bowlby, *Charles Darwin: A New Life* (New York: Norton, 1990).
2. For more on the history of evolution, see John Hedley Brooke, *Science and Religion*, ch. 7.
3. For good general introductions to the theory of evolution, see Brian and Deborah Charlesworth, *Evolution: A Very Short Introduction* (New York: Oxford U.P., 2003); Carl Zimmer, *Evolution* (New York: HarperCollins, 2001); and Ernst Mayr, *What Evolution Is* (New York: Basic Books, 2002).
4. See John Bowlby, *Charles Darwin: A New Life*, p.220.
5. See Stephen J. Gould, *Wonderful Life* (New York: Norton, 1990); and Simon Conway Morris, *The Crucible of Creation* (New York: Oxford U.P., 2000) for contrasting accounts of this period.
6. I am indebted to Kenneth Miller, *Finding Darwin's God* (San Francisco, CA: Harper, 1999), p.38, for this summary of evolutionary history.
7. See ibid., pp.94–99.
8. See Stephen J. Gould, *The Panda's Thumb* (New York: Norton, 1990), pp.181ff.
9. See Charles Darwin, *The Origin of Species*, p.217, p.219, pp.220–221.
10. For an overview of the problems in natural selection, see Holmes Rolston, *Science and Religion*, pp.95–100.
11. For more on the modern synthesis, see Peter Bowler, *Evolution: The History of an Idea* (Los Angeles, CA: University of California Press, 1989), pp.307–332.
12. Francis Collins, *The Language of God*, p.136.
13. Ibid., pp.136–137.
14. For specific examples of critical questions about various aspects of the theory, See John Polkinghorne, *The Faith of a Physicist*, p.17; Thomas Nagel, *The View from Nowhere* (Oxford, New York: Oxford U.P., 1986), pp.78–82; Holmes Rolston, *Science and Religion*, pp.94–100; Steven Stanley, *Macroevolution* (San Francisco, CA: Freeman, 1979), pp.192–193; Francis Crick, *What Mad Pursuit*, pp.30–31. See also the excellent symposium on "Creation/Evolution and Faith," involving Alvin Plantinga, Howard Van Till, and Ernan McMullin, in Robert Pennock (ed.), *Intelligent Design Creationism and Its Critics* (Cambridge, MA: MIT Press, 2001), pp.113–236.

15. For some examples, see Brian and Deborah Charlesworth, *Evolution: A Very Short Introduction*, p.113, and (on the evolution of the eye), pp.115–117; Richard Dawkins, *The Blind Watchmaker*, pp.77–109, for many fictional examples, including on the eye; also, p.136, p.240; and Christian de Duve, *Life Evolving*, p.200.
16. See Richard Dawkins and Jerry Coyne, "One side can be wrong," *The Guardian*, September, 2005.
17. For a critical discussion of various creationist views, see J. P. Moreland and John Mark Reynolds (eds.), *Three Views on Creation and Evolution* (Grand Rapids, MI: Zondervan, 1999); and Richard F. Carlson, *Science and Christianity: Four Views* (Downers Grove, IL: InterVarsity, 2000).
18. See Rudolf Bultmann, *New Testament and Mythology* (Minneapolis, MN: Fortress, 1984).
19. See Howard van Till, *The Fourth Day* (Grand Rapids, MI: Eerdmans, 1986); John Haught, *God After Darwin* (Colorado: Westview, 2000); John Polkinghorne, *The Faith of a Physicist*; Kenneth Miller, *Finding Darwin's God*.
20. See Philip Clayton, *God and Contemporary Science* (Grand Rapids, MI: Eerdmans, 1997), p.11.
21. See Edward O. Wilson, *Sociobiology: The New Synthesis* (Cambridge, MA: Harvard U.P, 1975); and *On Human Nature* (Cambridge, MA: Harvard U.P., 2004); see also Richard D. Alexander, *The Biology of Moral Systems* (New York: Aldine, 1987); see R. C. Lewontin, S. Rose, and L. J. Kamin, *Not in Our Genes: Biology, Ideology and Human Nature* (London: Penguin, 1990), for a critique of this view, and Larry Arnhart, *Darwinian Natural Right* (New York: State University of New York Press, 1998), for an alternative perspective.
22. Michael Ruse and Edward Wilson, "The Evolution of Ethics," in J. Huchingson (ed.), *Religion and the Natural Sciences* (Fort Worth, TX: Harcourt, 1993), p.310.
23. See Stephen Gould, *Wonderful Life*, pp.45–52.
24. See also Simon Conway Morris's, *Life's Solution*, which argues, appealing to the evidence from evolution (e.g., the eye has evolved independently six times) that life on earth is unlikely to be the product of chance; also Christian de Duve, *Life Evolving*, especially ch.12. There are discussions of chance and evolution from a variety of perspectives, in George Gaylord Simpson, *This View of Life* (Fort Worth, TX: Harcourt, 1966); Jacques Monad, *Chance and Necessity* (New York: Fontana, 1988); and Keith Ward, *God, Chance and Necessity* (Oxford: Oneworld, 1996).
25. An example of confusing chance with unpredictability can be found in Kenneth Miller, *Finding Darwin's God*, p.236.
26. See Nancey Murphy, *Bodies and Souls, or Spirited Bodies?* (New York: Cambridge U.P., 2006).
27. See Richard Dawkins, *The Blind Watchmaker*, pp.43–45.
28. Ibid., p.6.
29. See John Haught, *Responses to 101 Questions on God and Evolution* (New York: Paulist Press, 2001), pp.47–68.

Chapter 5

1. G. G. Simpson, *The Meaning of Evolution* (New Haven, CT: Yale U.P., 1949), p.344.
2. Paul Churchland, *Matter and Consciousness* (Cambridge, MA: MIT Press, 1988), p.21.

3. See René Descartes, *Meditations*, especially Meditation II and VI.
4. See Charles Taliaferro, "The give and take of biological naturalism: John Searle and the case for dualism," *Philosophia Christi*, vol. 7 (2), 2005, pp.447–462.
5. For further study, see Eric Matthews, *Mind: Key Concepts in Philosophy* (London: Continuum, 2005); E. J. Lowe, *An Introduction to the Philosophy of Mind* (Cambridge: Cambridge U.P., 2000); D. N. Robinson, *Consciousness and Mental Life* (New York: Columbia U.P., 2007); Charles Taliaferro, *Consciousness and the Mind of God* (New York: Cambridge U.P., 1994).
6. David Hume, *A Treatise of Human Nature*, Book I, Part IV, Section VI.
7. See Derek Parfit, *Reasons and Persons* (Oxford: Oxford U.P., 1986).
8. See the debate in S. Shoemaker and R. Swinburne, *Personal Identity* (New York: Blackwell, 1991).
9. See Robert Adams, "Flavors, Colors and God," in R. D. Geivett and Brendan Sweetman (eds.), *Contemporary Perspectives on Religious Epistemology* (New York: Oxford U.P., 1992), pp.225–240.
10. See Thomas Nagel, "What it is like to be a Bat," in John Heil (ed.), *Philosophy of Mind: A Guide and Anthology* (New York: Oxford, 2004), pp.528–538.
11. For an excellent discussion, see Robert Kane, *A Contemporary Introduction to Free Will* (New York: Oxford, 2005).
12. Holmes Rolston, *Science and Religion: A Critical Survey*, p.251.
13. See John M. Fischer and Mark Ravizza, *Responsibility and Control: A Theory of Moral Responsibility* (New York: Cambridge, 1999).
14. See B. F. Skinner, *Beyond Freedom and Dignity* (Indianapolis, IN: Hackett, 2002), and *Walden Two* (Indianapolis, IN: Hackett, 2005).
15. St. Thomas Aquinas, *Summa Theologiae*, Part II, II, Q.179, trans. Timothy McDermott (London: Hafner, 1964); see also Thomas Aquinas, *Selected Writings*, pp.410–428.
16. See Aristotle, *De Anima* (On The Soul).
17. For an excellent collection of readings on the question of immortality, see Paul Edwards (ed.), *Immortality* (Amherst, NY: Prometheus, 1997).
18. See Huston Smith, *The World's Religions* (San Francisco, CA: Harper, 1991), ch.2.
19. See René Descartes, *Discourse on Method* (New York: Penguin, 1980), pp.73–74.
20. See Alan Turing, "Computer Machinery and Intelligence," *Mind* 59 (1950), pp.433–460.
21. See John Searle, "Minds, brains and programs," in Louis Pojman (ed.), *Philosophy: The Quest for Truth* (New York: Oxford U.P., 2008, seventh edn.), pp.327–333; see also Searle, *Minds, Brains and Science* (Cambridge, MA: Harvard U.P., 1984), ch.2.

Chapter 6

1. See William Paley, *Natural Theology* (1802) (Whitefield, MT: Kessinger Facimile Edition, 2003).
2. Ibid., p.7.
3. Ibid., p.30.
4. See Richard Dawkins, *The Blind Watchmaker*, p.5.
5. As an example see Christian de Duve, *Life Evolving*, pp.200–201 on love and altruism.

6. See Paul Davies, *The Mind of God* (New York: Simon and Schuster, 1992), ch.3.
7. See Richard Swinburne, "The argument from design," in R. D. Geivett and Brendan Sweetman (eds.), *Contemporary Perspectives on Religious Epistemology* (New York: Oxford U.P., 1992), pp.201–211.
8. Ibid., p.205.
9. St. Thomas Aquinas, *Summa Theologiae*, Part Ia, II, 3, trans. Timothy McDermott (London: Hafner, 1964).
10. It is an interesting fact that many science reference works do not include an entry on the general topic of "laws of physics," or "laws of science."
11. Richard Dawkins, *The Blind Watchmaker*, p.43.
12. Dallas Willard, "The three-stage argument for the existence of God," in R. D. Geivett and Brendan Sweetman (eds.), *Contemporary Perspectives on Religious Epistemology*, p.218.
13. Ibid. Francis Crick also sometimes speaks too loosely about the laws of science, as this remark illustrates: "The laws of physics, it is believed, are the same everywhere in the universe. This is unlikely to be true of biology. We have no idea how similar extraterrestrial biology (if it exists) is to our own...." (*What Mad Pursuit*, p.138.) Crick here seems to be confusing the underlying laws with the specific mechanisms that might apply in a particular case of change.
14. Charles Taliaferro, *Contemporary Philosophy of Religion* (New York: Blackwell, 1998), p.365.
15. Dallas Willard, "The Three-Stage Argument," p.217.
16. See John Polkinghorne, *Science and Theology* (Minneapolis, MN: Fortress, 1998), pp.36–39; also John Barrow and Frank Tipler, *The Anthropic Cosmological Principle* (New York: Oxford, 1988); Paul Davies, *The Mind of God*, pp.213–215.
17. See Stephen Hawking, *A Brief History of Time* (New York: Bantam, 1988), pp.121ff.
18. For a fascinating account, see John D. Barrow and Frank J. Tipler, *The Anthropic Cosmological Principle* (Oxford: Clarendon Press, 1988).
19. See Stephen Hawking, *A Brief History of Time*, p.121, p.125.
20. See W. L. Craig: "The teleological argument and the anthropic principle," in W. L. Craig and M. McLeod (eds.), *The Logic of Rational Theism: Exploratory Essays* (Lewiston, NY: Mellen, 1990), p.128.
21. Freeman Dyson, *Disturbing the Universe* (New York: Harper, 1979), p.250.
22. Michael Martin, *Atheism: A Philosophical Justification* (Philadelphia, PA: Temple, 1990), p.133; see also Lee Smolin, *The Life of the Cosmos*.
23. See Stephen Hawking, *A Brief History of Time*, pp.124–125.
24. J. J. C. Smart and J. J. Haldane, *Atheism & Theism* (Oxford: Blackwell, 1996), p.18.
25. See Michael Behe, *Darwin's Black Box: The Biochemical Challenge to Evolution* (New York: Free Press, 2006) and *The Edge of Evolution* (New York: Free Press, 2008); William Dembski, *The Design Inference* (New York: Cambridge, 2006) and *No Free Lunch: Why Specified Complexity Cannot be Purchased without Intelligence* (Lanham, MD: Rowman and Littlefield, 2007).
26. Michael Behe, *Darwin's Black Box*, pp.70–72.
27. Kenneth Miller, "The Flagellum unspun," in W. A. Dembski and M. Ruse (eds.), *Debating Design: From Darwin to DNA* (New York: Cambridge U.P., 2004), pp.85–86.
28. James Arieti and Patrick Wilson, *The Scientific and the Divine* (New York: Rowman & Littlefield, 2003), p.257 (second emphasis mine, except for word "different").

29. See Phillip Johnson, *Evolution on Trial* (Downer's Grove, IL: InterVarsity Press, 1993); for a critique of Johnson, see Kenneth Miller, *Finding Darwin's God*; see also the exchanges between Johnson and his critics in Robert Pennock (ed.), *Intelligent Design Creationism and Its Critics* (Cambridge, MA: MIT Press, 2001).

Chapter 7

1. One of the most accessible books on modern scientific theories, including the big bang, is Stephen Hawking's, *A Brief History of Time,* to which I am indebted here. Another excellent resource is: Peter Coles, *Cosmology: A Very Short Introduction* (New York: Oxford U.P., 2001).
2. See Peter Coles, *Cosmology*, p.42.
3. See Stephen Hawking, *A Brief History of Time*, p.46.
4. See Peter Coles, *Cosmology*, p.36.
5. Ibid., pp.57–59.
6. For the Bonaventure/St. Thomas debate, see Cyril Vollert et al. (eds.), *St. Thomas Aquinas, Siger of Brabant, St. Bonaventure: On the Eternity of the World* (Milwaukee, WI: Marquette University Press, 1964).
7. See William L. Craig, *The Kalām Cosmological Argument* (Eugene, OR: Wipf and Stock, 1979); also his essay "Philosophical and scientific pointers to *Creatio ex Nihilo*," in R. D. Geivett and Brendan Sweetman (eds.), *Contemporary Perspectives on Religious Epistemology*, pp.185–200.
8. See also Paul Davies, *God and the New Physics*, pp.10–12, 199–201.
9. Dallas Willard, "The three-stage argument for the existence of God," in R. D. Geivett and Brendan Sweetman (eds.), *Contemporary Perspectives on Religious Epistemology*, p.216.
10. See Richard Dawkins, *The Blind Watchmaker*, p.316, and *The God Delusion*, p.77.
11. See Paul Draper, "A critique of the Kalam cosmological argument," in Louis Pojman (ed.), *Philosophy of Religion: An Anthology* (Belmont, CA: Wadsworth, 2003), pp.42–47.
12. See Russell's famous debate with Frederick Copleston on the existence of God, in Bertrand Russell, *Why I Am Not a Christian* (London: Allen & Unwin, 1957), pp.133–153.
13. See James Trefil (ed.), *Encyclopedia of Science and Technology* (New York: Routledge, 2001).
14. For a good discussion of quantum theory and some of its possible implications, see John Polkinghorne, *Science and Theology: An Introduction* (Minneapolis, MN: Fortress, 1998), pp.25–26.
15. For more on this debate, see Werner Heisenberg, *Physics and Philosophy* (New York: Prometheus, 1999).
16. See Stephen M. Barr, *Modern Physics and Ancient Faith* (Notre Dame, IN: University of Notre Dame Press, 2001), pp.227–244.
17. Ibid., p.268.
18. Francis Crick, *Of Molecules and Men*, (New York: Prometheus, 2004), p.14; see also Steven Weinberg, *Dreams of a Final Theory*.
19. See John Polkinghorne, *The Faith of a Physicist*; Francis Collins, *The Language of God*; Alister McGrath, *Science and Religion: An Introduction* (Oxford: Blackwell, 1999); Richard Swinburne, *The Existence of God* (New York: Oxford U.P., 2004).

20. See Anthony Flew, *There is a God*, p.89.
21. For an excellent discussion of the issues raised in this paragraph, see Philip Clayton, *God and Contemporary Science*, ch.7.
22. See Brian Davies, *An Introduction to the Philosophy of Religion* (New York; Oxford, 2004), pp.181–207; 222–231.
23. See St. Augustine, *City of God*, xii, sections 6–7; John Hick, *Evil and the God of Love* (New York: Harper and Row, 1966); C. S. Lewis, *The Problem of Pain* (New York: Macmillan, 1962).
24. See Charles Hartshorne, *Omnipotence and Other Theological Mistakes* (New York: State University of New York Press, 1983); see also John B. Cobb and David Ray Griffin, *Process Theology: An Introductory Exposition* (Philadelphia, PA: Westminster Press, 1976).
25. See Ian Barbour, *When Science Meets Religion* (San Francisco, CA: Harper, 2000), pp.34–36; 174–180.
26. Ibid., p.117
27. See John Haught, *God After Darwin*.
28. See Arthur Peacocke, *Theology for a Scientific Age* (Minneapolis, MN: Fortress, 1993); Nancey Murphy, Robert Russell and Arthur Peacocke (eds.), *Chaos and Complexity: Scientific Perspectives on Divine Action* (Berkeley, CA: CTNS, 1995); Philip Clayton, *God and Contemporary Science*; Howard van Till, *The Fourth Day*.

Chapter 8

1. See Francis Collins, *The Language of God*; another scientist to be admired in this area is Simon Conway Morris in his *Life's Solution*.
2. For an overview of the nature of DNA, see the exciting account in Francis Crick, *What Mad Pursuit*; see also national genome project websites: www.genome.gov/25520880, and www.ornl.gov/sci/techresources/Human_Genome/project/about.shtml
3. See www.genome.gov/25520880
4. See the fascinating account in Francis Collins, *The Language of God*, ch. 5.
5. Ibid., p.122.
6. See Richard Lewontin, *Biology as Ideology* (San Francisco, CA: HarperCollins, 1992); also R. Lewontin, S. Rose and J. Kamin, *Not in Our Genes: Biology, Ideology and Human Nature* (London: Penguin, 1984).
7. For Meilaender's view, and a variety of theological responses to ethical issues raised by cloning and genetic engineering, see Ronald Cole-Turner (ed.), *Beyond Cloning: Religion and the Remaking of Humanity* (Philadelphia, PA: Trinity Press, 2001).
8. For a clear, nontechnical account, see John F. Morris, "Stem cells, cloning and the human person," in John F. Morris (ed.), *Medicine, Health Care and Ethics: Catholic Voices* (Washington, DC: Catholic University of America Press, 2007), pp.252–299.
9. See "Scientist reports first cloning ever of adult mammal," *New York Times*, February 23, 1997, and "Britain grants 'Dolly' scientist cloning license," *New York Times*, February 9, 2005.

10. See "On cloning humans, 'never' turns swiftly into 'why not?'", *New York Times*, December 2, 1997.
11. For more on these various scenarios, and their ethical implications, see Leon Kass (Chairman), *Human Cloning and Human Dignity: The Report of the President's Council on Bioethics* (New York: Public Affairs, 2002).
12. Several thinkers have supported the idea of "genetic supermarkets," including Colin Gavaghan, *Defending the Genetic Supermarket* (London: UCL Press, 2006).
13. This view is defended by Donald M. Bruce and by Gilbert Meilaender in their essays in Ronald Cole-Turner (ed.), *Beyond Cloning: Religion and the Remaking of Humanity*.
14. See my *Why Politics Needs Religion: The Place of Religious Arguments in the Public Square* (Downer's Grove, IL: InterVarsity Press, 2006).

Guide to Further Reading

Alexander, Richard, *The Biology of Moral Systems* (New York: Aldine, 1987).
Aquinas, Thomas, *Selected Writings*, ed. Ralph McInerny (New York: Penguin, 1998).
—*Summa Theologiae,* trans. Timothy McDermott (London: Hafner, 1964).
Arieti, James and Patrick Wilson, *The Scientific and the Divine* (New York: Rowman & Littlefield, 2003).
Arnhart, Larry, *Darwinian Natural Right* (New York: State University of New York Press, 1998).
Artigas, Mariano, *The Mind of the Universe* (Philadelphia, PA: Templeton, 2000).
Atkins, Peter, *The Creation* (New York: W. H. Freeman, 1981).
Augustine, St., *On Genesis,* ed. B. Ramsey (New York: New City Press, 2004).
—*On the Literal Meaning of Genesis*, trans. J. H. Taylor in J. Quasten (ed.), *Ancient Christian Writers*, vols. 41–42 (New York: Newman Press, 1982).
—*City of God* (London: Penguin, 2003).
Barbour, Ian, *When Science Meets Religion* (San Francisco, CA: Harper, 2000).
—*Religion and Science: Historical and Contemporary Issues* (San Francisco, CA: Harper, 1997).
Barnes, Jonathan (ed.), *The Complete Works of Aristotle* (2 Vols) (Princeton, NJ.: Princeton, 1971).
Barr, Stephen M., *Modern Physics and Ancient Faith* (Notre Dame, IN: University of Notre Dame Press, 2001).
Barrow, John and Frank Tipler, *The Anthropic Cosmological Principle* (New York: Oxford, 1988).
Behe, Michael, *The Edge of Evolution* (New York: Free Press, 2008).
—*Darwin's Black Box: The Biochemical Challenge to Evolution* (New York: Free Press, 2006).
Blackwell, Richard, *Behind the Scenes at Galileo's Trial* (Notre Dame, IN: University of Notre Dame, 2006).
—*Science, Religion and Authority* (Milwaukee, WI: Marquette U.P., 1998).
Block, Stuart and Edwin Mares, *Realism and Anti-Realism* (Montreal: McGill U.P., 2007).
Bowlby, John, *Charles Darwin: A New Life* (New York: Norton, 1990).
Bowler, Peter, *Evolution: The History of an Idea* (Los Angeles, CA: University of California Press, 1989).
Bromiley, Geoffery, *Introduction to the Theology of Karl Barth* (Edinburgh: T & T Clark, 1979).
Brooke, John H., *Science and Religion: Some Historical Perspectives* (New York: Cambridge U.P., 1991).
Bultmann, Rudolf, *New Testament and Mythology* (Minneapolis, MN: Fortress, 1984).
Carlson, Richard, *Science and Christianity: Four Views* (Downers Grove, IL: InterVarsity, 2000).

Charlesworth, Brian, and Deborah Charlesworth, *Evolution: A Very Short Introduction* (New York: Oxford U.P., 2003).
Christianson, Gale, *Isaac Newton* (New York: Oxford U.P., 2005).
Churchland, Paul, *Matter and Consciousness* (Cambridge, MA: MIT Press, 1988).
Clarke, Samuel, *Leibniz and Clarke Correspondence* [1717] (Indianapolis, IN: Hackett, 2000).
Clayton, Philip, *God and Contemporary Science* (Grand Rapids, MI: Eerdman's, 1997).
Cobb, John B. and David Ray Griffin, *Process Theology: An Introductory Exposition* (Philadelphia, PA: Westminster Press, 1976).
Coles, Peter, *Cosmology: A Very Short Introduction* (New York: Oxford U.P., 2001).
Cole-Turner, Ronald (ed.), *Beyond Cloning: Religion and the Remaking of Humanity* (Philadelphia, PA: Trinity Press, 2001).
Collins, Francis, *The Language of God* (New York: Free Press, 2006).
Craig W. L., "The teleological argument and the anthropic principle," in W. L. Craig and M. McLeod (eds.), *The Logic of Rational Theism: Exploratory Essays* (Lewiston, NY: Mellen, 1990), pp.127–153.
—*The Kalām Cosmological Argument* (Eugene, OR: Wipf and Stock, 1979).
Crick, Francis, *The Astonishing Hypothesis* (New York: Touchstone, 1995).
—*What Mad Pursuit* (New York: Basic Books, 1988).
—*Of Molecules and Men* (New York: Prometheus, 2004).
—*Life Itself* (New York: Simon and Schuster, 1982).
Curd, Martin and J. A. Cover (eds.), *Philosophy of Science* (New York: London, 1998).
Darwin, Charles, *The Origin of Species* (London: Penguin, 1982 edn.).
Davies, Brian, *An Introduction to the Philosophy of Religion* (New York: Oxford U.P., 2004).
Davies, Paul, *The Mind of God* (New York: Simon and Schuster, 1992).
—*God and the New Physics* (New York: Simon and Schuster, 1983).
Davis, Joel, *Mapping the Code* (New York: Wiley, 1990).
Dawkins, Richard, *The God Delusion* (New York: Houghton Mifflin, 2006).
—*The Blind Watchmaker* (New York: Norton, 1987).
de Duve, Christian, *Life Evolving* (New York: Oxford U.P., 2002).
Dembski, William, *No Free Lunch: Why Specified Complexity Cannot be Purchased without Intelligence* (Lanham, MD: Rowman and Littlefield, 2007).
—*The Design Inference* (New York: Cambridge, 2006).
—*The Design Revolution* (Downer's Grove, IL: InterVarsity, 2004).
Dembski, W. and M. Ruse (eds.), *Debating Design: From Darwin to DNA* (New York: Cambridge U.P., 2004).
Dennett, Daniel, *Darwin's Dangerous Idea* (New York: Simon & Schuster, 1995).
Denton, Michael, *Nature's Destiny* (New York: Free Press, 1998).
Descartes, René, *Meditations* [1647] (London: Penguin, 1999).
—*Discourse on Method* (New York: Penguin, 1980).
Draper, J. W., *History of the Conflict between Religion and Science* (New York: Cosimo Classics, 2005) (1874).

Draper, Paul, "A critique of the Kalam cosmological argument," in Louis Pojman (ed.), *Philosophy of Religion: An Anthology* (Belmont, CA: Wadsworth, 2003), pp.42–47.

Drees, William, *Religion, Science and Naturalism* (New York: Cambridge, 1991).

Duhem, Pierre, *The Aim and Structure of Physical Theory* (Princeton, NJ: Princeton U.P., 1954).

Dyson, Freeman, *Disturbing the Universe* (New York: Harper, 1979).

Edwards, Paul (ed.), *Immortality* (Amherst, NY: Prometheus, 1997).

Ferngren, Gary (ed.), *Science & Religion: A Historical Introduction* (Baltimore, MD: Johns Hopkins, 2003).

Fischer, John and Mark Ravizza, S. J., *Responsibility and Control: A Theory of Moral Responsibility* (New York: Cambridge, 1999).

Flew, Anthony, *There is a God: How the World's Most Notorious Atheist Changed His Mind* (San Francisco, CA: Harper, 2007).

French, Steven, *Science: Key Concepts in Philosophy* (London: Continuum, 2007).

Gavaghan, Colin, *Defending the Genetic Supermarket* (London: UCL Press, 2006).

Geivett, R. Douglas and Brendan Sweetman (eds.), *Contemporary Perspectives on Religious Epistemology* (New York: Oxford U.P., 1992).

Giberson, Karl, *Saving Darwin: How to Be a Christian and Believe in Evolution* (New York: Harper, 2008).

Gilkey, Langdon, *Creationism on Trial* (Minneapolis, MN: Winston Press, 1986).

—*Religion and the Scientific Future* (New York: Harper & Row, 1970).

Gingerich, Owen, *God's Universe* (Cambridge, MA: Harvard, 2006).

Gould, Stephen J., *Rocks of Ages* (New York: Ballentine, 1999).

—*The Panda's Thumb* (New York: Norton, 1990).

—*Wonderful Life* (New York: Norton, 1990).

Grant, Edward, *A History of Natural Philosophy: From the Ancient World to the Nineteenth Century* (New York: Cambridge U.P., 2007).

Green, Joel and Stuart Palmer (eds.), *In Search of the Soul* (Downer's Grove, IL: InterVarsity, 2005).

Gribbin, John, *The Scientists: A History of Science Told through the Lives of Its Greatest Inventors* (New York: Random House, 2002).

Guth, Alan, *The Inflationary Universe* (Cambridge, MA: Perseus, 1997).

Hartshorne, Charles, *Omnipotence and Other Theological Mistakes* (New York: State University of New York Press, 1983).

Haught, John, *Responses to 101 Questions on God and Evolution* (New York: Paulist Press, 2001).

—*God After Darwin* (Colorado: Westview, 2000).

Hawking, Stephen, *A Brief History of Time* (New York: Bantam, 1988).

Heisenberg, Werner, *Physics and Philosophy* (New York: Prometheus, 1999).

Hick, John, *Evil and the God of Love* (New York: Harper and Row, 1966).

Hirschfeld, Alan, *The Electric Life of Michael Faraday* (New York: Walker, 2006).

Hooykaas, Reijer, *Religion and the Rise of Modern Science* (Edinburgh: Scottish Academic Press, 1973).

Hume, David, *A Treatise of Human Nature* (New York: Barnes and Noble, 2005).

Hunter, Cornelius, *Darwin's God: Evolution and the Problem of Evil* (Grand Rapids, MI: Brazos, 2002).

Jaki, Stanley, *Science and Creation* (Edinburgh: Scottish Academic Press, 1974).
Johnson, Phillip, *Evolution on Trial* (Downer's Grove, IL: InterVarsity Press, 1993).
Kane, Robert, *A Contemporary Introduction to Free Will* (New York: Oxford U. P., 2005).
Kass, Leon (ed.), *Human Cloning and Human Dignity: The Report of the President's Council on Bioethics* (New York: Public Affairs, 2002).
Kourany, Janet, *The Gender of Science* (New Jersey: Prentice Hall, 2001).
Kuhn, Thomas, *The Structure of Scientific Revolutions* (Chicago, IL: University of Chicago, 1970).
Kurtz, Paul, *Living Without Religion* (New York: Prometheus, 1994).
La Mettrie, Julien, *Man a Machine* [1748] (Indianapolis, IN: Hackett, 1994).
Laudan, Larry, *Science and Values* (Berkeley, CA: University of California Press, 1984).
Lewis, C. S., *The Problem of Pain* (New York: Macmillan, 1962).
Lewontin, Richard, *Biology as Ideology* (San Francisco, CA: HarperCollins, 1992).
Lewontin, R., S. Rose and J. Kamin, *Not in Our Genes: Biology, Ideology and Human Nature* (London: Penguin, 1984).
Lowe, E. J., *An Introduction to the Philosophy of Mind* (Cambridge: Cambridge U.P., 2000).
Manson, Neil (ed.), *God and Design: The Teleological Argument and Modern Science* (New York: Routledge, 2003).
Margulis, Lynn and Dorian Sagan, *What is Life?* (Berkeley, CA: University of California Press, 2000).
Martin, Michael, *Atheism: A Philosophical Justification* (Philadelphia, PA: Temple, 1990).
Matthews, Eric, *Mind: Key Concepts in Philosophy* (London: Continuum, 2005).
Matthews, Michael (ed.), *The Scientific Background to Modern Philosophy: Selected Readings* (Indianapolis, IN: Hackett, 1989).
Mayr, Ernst, *What Evolution Is* (New York: Basic Books, 2002).
McGrath, Alister, *Science and Religion: An Introduction* (Oxford: Blackwell, 1999).
McInerny, Ralph, *Aquinas* (Cambridge: Polity Press, 2004).
—*Aquinas and Analogy* (Washington, DC: Catholic University of America Press, 1998).
McMullin, Ernan (ed.), *Evolution and Creation* (Notre Dame: University of Notre Dame Press, 1985).
Midgley, Mary, *Evolution as a Religion* (London: Routledge, 2002).
Miller, Kenneth, *Finding Darwin's God* (San Francisco, CA: Harper, 1999).
Moltmann, Jurgen, *Science and Wisdom* (Canterbury: SCM Press, 2003).
Monad, Jacques, *Chance and Necessity* (New York: Fontana, 1988).
Moreland. J. P. and John Mark Reynolds (eds.), *Three Views on Creation and Evolution* (Grand Rapids, MI: Zondervan, 1999).
Morris, John F. (ed.), *Medicine, Health Care and Ethics: Catholic Voices* (Washington, DC: Catholic University of America Press, 2007).
Morris, Simon Conway, *Life's Solution* (New York: Cambridge U.P., 2003).
—*The Crucible of Creation* (New York: Oxford U.P., 2000).
Murphy, Nancey, *Bodies and Souls, or Spirited Bodies?* (New York: Cambridge U.P., 2006).
Murphy, Nancey, Robert Russell and Arthur Peacocke (eds.), *Chaos and Complexity: Scientific Perspectives on Divine Action* (Berkeley, CA: CTNS, 1995).
Nagel, Thomas, *The View from Nowhere* (Oxford, New York: Oxford U.P., 1986).

—*The Last Word* (New York: Oxford U.P., 1997).

—"What it is like to be a Bat," in John Heil (ed.), *Philosophy of Mind: A Guide and Anthology* (New York: Oxford U.P., 2004), pp.528–538.

Nasr, Seyyed Hossein, *Religion and the Order of Nature* (New York: Oxford U.P., 1996).

Numbers, Ronald, *Darwinism Comes to America* (Cambridge, MA: Harvard U.P., 1998).

—*The Creationists* (Los Angeles, CA: University of California Press, 1992).

O'Marchu, Diarmuid, *Quantum Theology: Spiritual Implications of the New Physics* (New York: Crossroad, 1997).

Olson, Richard, *Science and Religion 1450–1900* (Baltimore, MD: Johns Hopkins, 2004).

Paine, Thomas, *The Age of Reason* (New York: Citadel, 1988) (1794).

Paley, William, *Natural Theology* (1802) (Whitefield, MT: Kessinger Facimile Edition, 2003).

Pannenberg, Wolfhart, *Theology and the Philosophy of Science* (Philadelphia, PA: Westminster, 1976).

Parfit, Derek, *Reasons and Persons* (Oxford: Oxford U.P., 1986).

Peacocke, Arthur, *Theology for a Scientific Age* (Minneapolis, MN: Fortress, 1993).

Pennock, Robert (ed.), *Intelligent Design Creationism and Its Critics* (Cambridge, MA: MIT Press, 2001).

Peters, Ted and Martinez Hewlett, *Can You Believe in God and Evolution?* (Nashville, TN: Abingdon, 2003).

Pinker, Steven, *The Blank Slate: The Modern Denial of Human Nature* (New York: Viking, 2002).

Pojman, Louis (ed.), *Philosophy: The Quest for Truth* (New York: Oxford U.P., 2008, seventh edn.).

Polkinghore, John, *Science and Theology: An Introduction* (Minneapolis, MN: Fortress, 1998).

—*The Faith of a Physicist* (Minneapolis, MN: Fortress, 1996).

—*Rochester Roundabout: The Story of High Energy Physics* (New York: Freeman/Longman, 1989).

Popper, Karl, *Conjectures and Refutations* (London: Routledge & Kegan Paul, 1963).

Quine, W. V., *From a Logical Point of View* (Cambridge, MA: Harvard U.P., 1980).

—*Ontological Relativity* (New York: Columbia U.P., 1977).

Rahner, Karl, "Natural Science and Reasonable Faith," in *Theological Investigations*, vol. 21, trans. Hugh Riley (New York: Crossroad, 1988), pp.16–55.

Ratzsch, Del, *Science and its Limits* (Downer's Grove, IL: InterVarsity, 2000).

Robinson, D. N., *Consciousness and Mental Life* (New York: Columbia U.P., 2007).

Rolston, Holmes, *Science and Religion: A Critical Survey* (Philadelphia, PA: Templeton Ed., 1987).

Ruse, Michael, *Can a Darwinian be a Christian?* (New York: Cambridge, 2001).

Ruse, Michael and Edward Wilson, "The Evolution of Ethics," in J. Huchingson (ed.), *Religion and the Natural Sciences* (Fort Worth, TX: Harcourt, 1993), pp.308–312.

Russell, Bertrand, *Why I Am Not a Christian* (London: Allen & Unwin, 1957).

Sagan, Carl, *Cosmos* (New York: Random House, 2002).

—*Billions and Billions* (New York: Ballantine, 1997).

Searle, John, *Minds, Brains and Science* (Cambridge, MA: Harvard U.P., 1984).

—"Minds, brains and programs," in Louis Pojman (ed.), *Philosophy: The Quest for Truth*, (New York: Oxford U.P., 2008, seventh edn.), pp.327–333.

Shea, William R. and Mariano Artigas, *Galileo in Rome: The Rise and Fall of a Troublesome Genius* (New York: Oxford U.P., 2003).
Shoemaker, Sydney and Richard Swinburne, *Personal Identity* (New York: Blackwell, 1991).
Simpson, George, *This View of Life* (Fort Worth, TX: Harcourt, 1966).
—*The Meaning of Evolution* (New Haven, CT: Yale U.P., 1949).
Skinner, B. F., *Walden Two* (Indianapolis, IN: Hackett, 2005).
—*Beyond Freedom and Dignity* (Indianapolis, IN: Hackett, 2002).
Smart, J. J. and J. J. Haldane, *Atheism & Theism* (Oxford: Blackwell, 1996).
Smith, Huston, *The World's Religions* (San Francisco, CA: Harper, 1991).
Smolin, Lee, *The Life of the Cosmos* (New York: Oxford U.P., 1999).
Stanley, Steven, *Macroevolution* (San Francisco, CA: Freeman, 1979).
Stenmark, Mikael, *How to Relate Science and Religion* (Grand Rapids, MI: Eerdmans, 2004).
Sweetman, Brendan, *Religion: Key Concepts in Philosophy* (London: Continuum, 2007).
—*Why Politics Needs Religion: The Place of Religious Arguments in the Public Square* (Downer's Grove, IL: InterVarsity Press, 2006).
Swinburne, Richard, *The Existence of God* (New York: Oxford U.P., 2004).
Swinburne, Richard, "The argument from design," in R. D. Geivett and Brendan Sweetman (eds.), *Contemporary Perspectives on Religious Epistemology* (New York: Oxford U.P., 1992), pp.201–211.
Taliaferro, Charles, *Contemporary Philosophy of Religion* (New York: Blackwell, 1998).
—*Consciousness and the Mind of God* (New York: Cambridge U.P., 1994).
—"The give and take of biological naturalism: John Searle and the case for dualism," *Philosophia Christi*, vol. 7 (2), 2005, pp.447–462.
Teilhard de Chardin, Pierre, *The Phenomenon of Man* (New York: HarperCollins, 1959).
Torrance, Thomas, *Theological Science* (Oxford U.P., 1969).
Tracy, Thomas F., *The God Who Acts* (Philadelphia, PA: Pennsylvania State University, 1994).
Trefil, James, (ed.), *Encyclopedia of Science and Technology* (New York: Routledge, 2001).
Turing, Alan, "Computer Machinery and Intelligence," *Mind* 59 (1950), pp.433–460.
Van Till, Howard, *The Fourth Day* (Grand Rapids, MI: Eerdmans, 1986).
Vitz, Paul C., *Faith of the Fatherless: The Psychology of Atheism* (Dallas, TX: Spence, 1999).
Vollert Cyril, Lottie H. Kendzierski, Paul M. Byrne (eds.), *St. Thomas Aquinas, Siger of Brabant, St. Bonaventure: On the Eternity of the World* (Milwaukee, WI: Marquette University Press, 1964).
Walters, Kerry, *The American Deists* (Lawrence, KS: University Press of Kansas, 1992).
Ward, Keith, *God, Chance and Necessity* (Oxford: Oneworld, 1996).
Weinberg, Steven, *Dreams of a Final Theory* (New York: Pantheon, 1992).
Wells, Jonathan, *Icons of Evolution* (Washington, DC: Regnery, 2000).
Wertheim, Margaret, *Pythagoras' Trousers: God, Physics, and the Gender Wars* (New York: Norton, 1997).
White, Andrew Dickson, *A History of the Warfare of Science with Theology* (New York: Prometheus, 1993) (1896).
Wilson, Edward O., *On Human Nature* (Cambridge, MA: Harvard U.P., 2004).

—*Consilience* (New York: Vintage, 1999).

—*Sociobiology: The New Synthesis* (Cambridge, MA: Harvard U.P, 1975).

Zimmer, Carl, *Evolution* (New York: HarperCollins, 2001).

Życiński, Josef, *God and Evolution: Fundamental Questions of Christian Evolutionism*, trans. Kenneth W. Kemp and Zuzanna Maślanka (Washington, DC: Catholic University of America Press, 2006).

Index

abiogenesis 77, 143
abortion 199, 200, 203, 204, 205, 206
actuality 28–9
Adams, Robert 126
aeronautics 61
Al-Farabi 36
Al-Ghazali 36
Al-Kindi 36
Ambulocetus 96
amino acids 77, 195
analogy 37
Anixamander 27
Anselm, St. 34
anthropic argument 143, 158–63
anti-realism 67–9, 126
Aquinas, St. Thomas 22, 32, 33, 34, 35–40, 41, 42, 52, 120, 121, 134, 155, 175, 178–9, 185
Archaeopteryx 96
archeology 167
Arieti, James 168
Aristotle 22, 26–33, 35, 36, 38, 49, 64, 68, 86, 122, 134, 135, 148, 149, 151, 189
Arsenal FC 158
artificial intelligence 136–41
astronomy 2, 159, 171
astrophysics 2, 159, 171
atheism 8, 19, 52, 57, 75, 78, 101, 164
atomic theory 49, 110, 113, 183, 185
Augustine, St. 22, 33, 34–5, 41, 45, 46, 55, 106, 122, 135, 188
Averroes 36
Avicenna 36

Bacon, Francis 26
Bacon, Roger 8

bacterial flagellum 165, 168
Barbour, Ian 19, 188–9, 190, 210
Barr, Stephen 184
Barrow, John 159
Barth, Karl 15, 18
Behe, Michael 18, 165–6, 168–9
Bellarmine, Cardinal 45
Bible 6, 7, 12, 15, 20, 23, 41, 42, 54, 76, 86, 104–6
  see also revelation
big bang theory 9, 17, 18, 21, 23, 104, 113, 160–2, 172–4, 175
biochemistry 8
biology 7, 88, 111, 154, 184
Blackwell, Richard 34, 44, 45
body/mind problem 49–50, 121–7, 184
  see also consciousness; mind
Bonaventure, St. 174–5, 178
Boyle, Robert 4
Brahe, Tycho 44
Buddhism 135
Bultmann, Rudolf 106
Burgess Shale 92

Calvin, John 41, 43
Cambrian explosion 92
Carter, Brandon 159
catastrophism 87
Catholicism 7, 36, 40, 45
causation 27, 29–30
  Aristotle on 29–32
  primary and secondary 187
  see also laws of physics, chance, determinism
chance 54, 76, 91, 107–15, 120, 130, 143, 150, 154, 155, 158, 180, 189

change 27, 28, 156
chaos theory 72
chemistry 7, 61, 153, 184
Chinese room example 140–1
Christianity 6, 22, 32, 36
  and the rise of science 39–40
chromosomes 195
Churchland, Paul 120
Clarke, Samuel 52
Clayton, Philip 190
Clement, St. 33
cloning 3, 201–6
  reproductive 202, 204
  therapeutic 202, 204
Collins, Francis 19, 80, 100, 185, 192, 193, 195, 196
common descent 90, 91, 95, 97, 100, 166, 196
comparative anatomy 88
compatibilism 131
computers 61, 137–40
conflict model 11–14, 34, 45, 55, 78, 81, 193, 208
conscience 188
consciousness 2, 3, 23, 49, 50, 54, 55, 56, 79, 80, 113–14, 121–7, 134, 135, 139
  see also body/mind problem; mind
constructive empiricism 69–70
Contact (movie) 142, 144, 167
contingency and necessity *see* necessity and contingency
Copenhagen interpretation 183
Copernicus 44
cosmic evolution 79, 115, 180
cosmological argument 37, 113, 174–80
cosmology 72, 159, 192
Cosmos (TV series) 8
Craig, William 19, 160, 175–6, 179, 185
Cranmer, Thomas 41
creation, as a miracle 187
creationism 12, 101–2, 105, 163
creationism and evolution *see* evolution and creationism
Crick, Francis 22, 75, 76, 77, 79–80, 81, 120, 130, 151, 184, 185, 192, 194, 216
Cuvier, George 86–7

D'Holbach, Baron 22, 50

Darwin, Charles 22, 53–5, 85–97, 115, 119, 120, 150
Davies, Brian 187
Davies, Paul 19, 80, 152, 159, 185
Dawkins, Richard 19, 22, 60, 75–8, 81, 99, 103, 106, 107, 108, 110, 113, 115, 120, 150, 151, 155–6, 178, 192
de Duve, Christian 103, 143, 210
De revolutionibus 44
deism 22, 52, 180, 187
Dembski, William 165
democracy 129
Democritus 27
Derrida, Jacques 67
Descartes, René 49, 79, 121–4, 135, 138, 187
descent with modification *see* common descent
design 30, 76, 107–9, 115–17, 177
  arguments from 146–70, 177
determinism 50, 110–14, 129–34, 180, 182–4, 197, 206
dialogue model 18–20, 34, 180, 190
Diderot, Denis 51, 120
differences in kind vs. degree 38, 55, 99, 116, 120
dinosaurs 93
Dionysius 35
DNA 2, 99–101, 194–6, 202, 205
Dolly (sheep) 206
Draper, Paul 179
dualism 50, 121, 129, 135, 138
Duhem, Pierre 72
Dyson, Freeman 161

Eastern Religion 7, 40, 135
Einstein, Albert 66, 173, 181–3, 185
electricity 65, 70, 71, 85
electromagnetism 84
electronics 61, 182
electrons 70, 160, 182
emergentism 115
empirical evidence 21, 64, 67
energy 5, 7, 76, 79, 116, 124, 139, 151, 152, 155, 156, 182, 187
Enlightenment 9, 42, 43, 49
epiphenomenalism 124
essence 28, 29, 151
ether 66, 71

ethics *see* morality
Eucharist 41
evil, problem of 188
evolution 2, 5, 10, 12, 14, 17, 19, 21, 23, 35, 39, 42, 48, 53–5, 70, 71–2, 73, 76, 82–117, 120, 130, 143, 146, 147, 151, 155, 164, 187, 190, 192, 213
   and the Bible 104–6
   and creationism 12, 16, 35, 104–6
   evidence for 93–104
   history of 85–9
   implications of 104–17
   and modern culture 82–5
extraterrestrial intelligence 2, 142–5
eye, development of 97–8, 102, 149, 151, 166, 214

faith 18, 39, 41
   and reason 6, 15, 33, 35, 42–3
falsifiability 73, 96
finches 90–1, 94, 102
Fischer, John 131
Flew, Anthony 19, 186
fossil record 86–8, 93, 94–6
Franklin, Rosalind 194
free will 3, 9, 21, 31, 38, 50, 55, 107, 113–15, 128–34, 137, 184, 188, 197, 205
Freud, Sigmund 22, 55–7, 119, 120, 132

Galapagos Islands 72, 86, 90, 91, 95
Galileo 4, 14, 20, 22, 26, 27, 30, 35, 44–7, 64–5, 68, 84
Geivett, R. D. 215, 216, 217
genes 2, 99–101, 107, 111, 195, 196, 197, 200, 206
Genesis, Book of 34–5, 42, 54, 76, 104, 116, 148
genetic engineering 197–209
genetics 2, 24, 76, 99–101, 192, 194–6
   morality of 196–200
genus 89, 91
geocentricism 44–5, 65
geology 88, 89
Gilkey, Langdon 16
Gingerich, Owen 80
God 5, 6, 10, 15, 18, 21, 35, 37–8, 39, 51, 52, 95, 101, 104, 116, 120, 144, 163, 174–80, 185–91

action in the world 185–9
arguments for the existence of 146–70, 174–80
Aristotle on 32
Aquinas on 37–8, 185
and evil 188
of the gaps 167–8, 170, 186, 188
Gould, Stephen 15–16, 75, 96, 103, 108, 112, 113
gravity 47, 74, 160, 173, 174, 181
Gray, Asa 55, 99
Gregory, St. 33
Guth, Alan 72

Hartshorne, Charles 189
Haught, John 19, 106, 117, 188, 189
Hawking, Stephen 160, 162, 173
Heidegger, Martin 67
Heisenberg, Werner 182–4, 185
heliocentricism 44–5, 64–5
Heraclitus 27
Hick, John 188
Hinduism 135
Homo sapiens 2, 17, 53–4, 55, 92–3, 107–9, 120, 141
"how" questions 16–17, 47–8
Hubble telescope 62, 70, 174
Hubble, Edwin 172
human genome project 2, 194–6
human nature 31, 38, 114, 137, 188, 197, 207
human person 2, 23, 50, 120 42
Hume, David 125, 157–8
Hutton, James 86, 88
Huxley, Thomas 55, 89, 106

imago dei 40
immortality 79, 134–6
Incarnation 39
Independence model 14–15
inflationary universe 72
instrumentalism 72–3
Intelligent Design theory 12, 163–70
intentionality 125–6
irreducible complexities 165–6

Jaki, Stanley 39
Jesus 42, 106

John of Damascus 34
Johnson, Phillip 165, 169–70
Judaism 7

Kant, Immanuel 67, 122
Kelvin, Lord 55
Kepler, Johannes 4, 44, 153
Kuhn, Thomas 69

La Mettrie, Julian 22, 51, 120
Lamarck, Jean 86–7, 91
Laplace, Pierre 50, 120
Laudan, Larry 69
laws of physics 46, 50, 52, 73, 76, 88, 107, 110, 114, 116, 119, 130, 152–8, 169, 171, 174, 180, 182, 186, 216
Lewis, C. S. 188
Lewontin, Richard 81, 198
life, origin of 116, 143
  see also anthropic argument
light year 142, 172
Linnaeus, Carl 86
Locke, John 52, 122
Luther, Martin 15, 40
Lyell, Charles 86, 88, 99

macroevolution 54, 91–3, 96, 97, 98
magnetism 71
Malthus, Thomas 90
Margulis, Lynn 76
Martin, Michael 162
Marxism 73
materialism 22, 50, 80, 114, 124, 126–7, 184
mathematics 8, 27, 46, 49, 153, 185
matter 5, 7, 76, 79, 116, 124, 139, 151, 152, 155, 156, 187
  and form 27, 28
  prime 29
McGrath, Alister 19, 185
Meilaender, Gilbert 200
Mendel, Gregor 99
metaphysical naturalism 145, 165, 170, 193
metaphysics 27
methodological naturalism 145, 165, 170
Michelson-Morley experiment 181
microbiology 8, 147
microevolution 91, 98
Miescher, Friedrich 194

Milky Way 129, 172
Miller, Kenneth 95, 106, 167–8, 169
Miller, Stanley 77
mind 79–80, 99, 113–15
  see also consciousness
mind/brain identity 124
miracles 106, 186, 187, 190
models in religion and science 11–20
modern synthesis 100
moral relativism 4, 199
morality 1, 2, 9, 16, 62, 83, 120, 129, 189, 192–209
Morris, Simon 77, 80
multiple universes 161
Murphy, Nancey 115, 190
mutations 99, 111, 165, 196

Nagel, Thomas 127
natural law 8, 205, 206
natural philosophy 27, 39
natural selection 53, 72, 90, 91, 92, 97–9, 103, 147, 150, 165, 166, 168, 169
natural theology 146, 171, 185
naturalism 10, 19, 48, 51, 56, 60, 74–81, 106, 116, 120, 127, 131, 144, 145, 192
  see also metaphysical; methodological
nature 27, 30, 36, 46, 50, 110, 112, 113, 120, 149
Nature, Book of 20
Neanderthal man 93
necessity and contingency 32, 37, 107–9, 111, 178
negative theology 37
neurology 2, 192
Newton, Isaac 4, 20, 22, 40, 44, 46–9, 52, 73, 19, 152, 173, 180, 181, 193
nominalism 28
nuclear forces 160, 174

objective knowledge 27, 49, 59, 63–71
  see also truth
observations claims 63, 65, 67, 69, 71
Ohm, Georg 65
Ohm's law 65, 110, 153

Paley, William 147–52, 164
Pannenberg, Wolfhart 190
Parmenides 27

particle physics 8
Peacocke, Arthur 190
Penzias, Arno 173
personal identity 124–5, 134, 135
philosophy 15, 18, 20–1, 33, 36, 39, 42–3, 48, 83, 119, 170
philosophy of religion 20, 146
phlogiston 71
photosynthesis 84
physics 7, 61, 153, 180, 184
Planck, Max 183, 185
Plato 33, 35, 122, 134, 135, 172, 197
Plotinus 35, 135
politics 1, 5, 10, 68, 75
Polkinghorne, John 106, 159, 185
Pope, The 41, 45
Popper, Karl 73
potentiality 28–9
prayer 14, 187, 188, 189
Pre-Socratics 27, 147
Principia Mathematica 47
process theism 188–9
proteins 77, 195
Protestantism 7, 15, 40
pseudoscience 73
psychoanalysis 56, 73
Ptolemy 44
punishment, theories of 114, 120, 129
Pythagoras 8, 27

qualia 126
quantum mechanics 72, 113, 182–3, 190
Quine, W. V. 69

randomness *see* chance
Ravizza, Mark 131
realism 66–7
reason 2, 31, 38, 42–3, 49, 52, 55, 99, 188, 197
reductionism 57, 122–3, 132, 185, 198
Reformation 22, 39, 40–4
Reid, Thomas 122
reincarnation 135
relativism 68, 69, 74, 182
relativity, theory of 66, 73, 173, 181, 183
religion 12, 20, 48, 57, 62, 77, 83, 192
  definition of 5–6
  natural 52

religious pluralism 43
religious worldview 1, 3, 33, 60, 108, 134, 199–200, 205
resurrection 106
revelation 6, 15, 36, 38, 41, 45, 52, 188
  see also Bible
Rolston, Holmes 130
Rousseau, J. J. 52
Ruse, Michael 107
Russell, Bertrand 179

Sagan, Carl 22, 60, 75, 76, 78–9, 108, 115, 120, 142, 184, 192
salvation 1, 42, 43, 135–6
Scheiner, Christoph 64, 68
Schrodinger, Erwin 185
science 3, 12, 27, 31, 36, 39, 42, 59–63, 74–81, 83, 119, 164, 167, 170
  definition of 7–8
scientific faith argument 127
scientific method 46–7
scientific theories 63–4, 71–4, 83
scientism 75
scientists 8, 84, 40, 193, 197, 207
Searle, John 75, 140
secularism 4–5, 9–11, 13, 19, 33, 75, 78, 199, 206
sense experience 63
sensus divinitatis 43
simplicity, principle of 74
Simpson, G. G. 121
Skinner, B. F. 133
Smart, J. J. C. 162
sociobiology 187
Socrates 197
sola scriptura 42
somatic cell nuclear transfer 201
soul 3, 5, 51, 135–6, 205
space 62, 148, 174, 180–1
species 89–91, 107
  transitional 96–7
Spencer, Herbert 54
steady state theory 174
stem cells 2, 201–6
Stenmark, Mikael 210
string theory 72
substance 27–8, 49
survival of the fittest 54, 90, 150

Sweetman, Brendan 215, 216, 217, 219
Swinburne, Richard 19, 152–8, 185

Taliaferro, Charles 157
technology 61–2
teleology 28, 29–31, 48, 107, 151
testability 74
theism 19, 22, 52, 145
  process 188–9
  traditional 37, 187
theistic evolution 116
theology 4, 6, 12, 15, 16, 20, 21, 31, 33, 36, 49, 106, 119, 186
theory of everything 184
thermodynamics, second law of 175–6
time 174, 175, 180
Tipler, Frank 159
Torrance, Thomas 16
Tracy, Thomas 186
tree of life 92, 93, 96, 100, 104
Trinity 39
truth 19, 34, 36, 46
  see also objective knowledge
Turing, Alan 139

ultimate questions 2, 20, 31, 59, 77, 79, 116, 144, 170, 174, 177, 193, 208

uncertainty principle 182
universals 28
universe 36, 79, 115–17, 147, 172–4
  as machine 47, 49, 52, 119
Urey, Harold 77
Urey-Miller experiment 77, 195

van Till, Howard 106, 190
virtue 31, 38, 188
Voltaire 52

Wallace, Alfred 99
Ward, Keith 19, 185
watch analogy 148
Watson, James 194, 195
Weinberg, Steven 75, 184
Whitehead, Alfred 188
"why" questions 16–17, 47–8
Wilkins, Maurice 194
Willard, Dallas 155–6, 157, 177
Wilmut, Ian 201, 202
Wilson, E. O. 75, 107, 108, 192
Wilson, Patrick 168
Wilson, Robert 173
worldviews 1, 20, 84, 198

Zwingli, Ulrich 41